The Man Who Ran Away

The Man Who Ran Away

and Other Stories of Trinidad

in the 1920s and 1930s

by

Alfred H. Mendes

Edited and with an introduction
by

Michèle Levy

University of the West Indies Press
Jamaica • Barbados • Trinidad and Tobago

University of the West Indies Press
1A Aqueduct Flats   Mona
Kingston 7   Jamaica
www.uwipress.com

10 09 08 07 06   5 4 3 2 1

CATALOGUING IN PUBLICATION DATA

Mendes, Alfred H. (Alfred Hubert), 1897–1991
The man who ran away and other stories of Trinidad
in the 1920s and 1930s / by Alfred H. Mendes;
edited and with an introduction by Michèle Levy
p. cm.

ISBN: 976-640-173-X

1. Short stories, Trinidadian. I. Levy, Michèle. II. Title.

PR9279.9.M57M3 2006   823.914

Book and cover design by Robert Harris.
roberth@cwjamaica.com

Set in Adobe Caslon 10.5/14 x 24

Printed in the United States of America

For Ellen, my wife,
for her patience and tolerance
– Alfred H. Mendes, 1983

and

For Noel,
with the editor's love
– Michèle Levy, 2005

Contents

Editor's Note

Five of the twelve stories anthologized here have appeared else-where. "Sé-sé" was published in the *Quarterly Magazine,* edited by Austin M. Nolte (Third Quarter, 1932), under the pseudonym "Hubert Alfred". "Boodhoo" was originally published in the *Beacon,* edited by Albert Gomes (March, April, May 1932). It also appeared in the reprint of the *Beacon* (Millwood, NY: Kraus Reprint, 1977) and was included in *From Trinidad: An Anthology of Early West Indian Writing,* edited by Reinhard W. Sander (London: Hodder and Stoughton; New York: Holmes and Meier, 1978). "Colour" also appeared in the *Beacon* (June, August, September, October, November 1933), and in the Kraus reprint. "The Man Who Ran Away" was published in the *West Indian Review,* edited by Esther Chapman (July 1936). "Béti", the most recent of the stories to have been published, appeared under the title "An Ironic Sales Story" in the *Trinidad Singer Magazine* (nos. 3 and 9, 1966), which Mendes edited at the time.

Of the seven unpublished stories, the title page of "Not a Love Story" car-ries the Long Island address of Mendes's brother Frank, where Mendes lived, off and on, from November 1933 until his marriage in 1938. It may, however, have been written earlier. In a letter in the *Trinidad Guardian* (11 May 1930), responding to a critique of *Trinidad* 1, no. 2, by Dr W.V. Tothill, Mendes notes: "A friend of mine recently pointed out to me that there is not a single story in this issue of *Trinidad* based on the theme of love." The title of this story is sufficiently singular to make a connection with his friend's observation plausible, in which case, Mendes may have written this story shortly after April 1930, when *Trinidad* 1, no. 2, was issued.

References in an unpublished story, "In a Restaurant", to "Shango", and to a book of poems which the persona (and Mendes) was expecting to be reviewed (probably *The Poet's Quest* [1927]), allow for a tentative dating of 1928–29. "Three Rebels" carries the stamp of Mendes's New York agent, John Trounstine, which places it in the period 1933–40. Like "Not a Love Story", it may have been written before Mendes left Trinidad in 1933.

There are no manuscript details available to give a more precise dating to "Neighbours", "One Day for John Small", "Malvina's Nennen" and "Laura's Return".

A glossary of Eastern Caribbean terms has been provided (pp. 186–89). For further details, see Richard Allsopp, ed., *Dictionary of Caribbean English Usage* (Kingston: University of the West Indies Press, 2003) and John Mendes, *Cote ce, cote la: Trinidad and Tobago Dictionary* (Arima, Trinidad: John Mendes, 1986). A list of Alfred Mendes's major publications appears at the end of this collection.

Introduction

The Portuguese Creole writer Alfred Hubert Mendes was born in Port of Spain, Trinidad in 1897, and died in Barbados in 1991. He was educated in Trinidad at the Queen's Royal College until 1912, when at the age of fifteen he was sent to school in England. In 1915, his father brought him home to Trinidad after the outbreak of the Great War of 1914–18. Once there, however, Mendes defied his father's attempts to keep him safe. He enlisted with the Merchants and Planters Contingents of Trinidad, and departed for the arena of battle in Flanders, where he saw action as a rifleman. He returned to Trinidad in 1919. In all, he spent roughly seven years in Europe. Aside from another seven years spent writing and working in New York City, from 1933 to 1940, Mendes made his home in the West Indies. The span of his long life covers Trinidad's emergence from British Crown Colony into fully independent nationhood, but his métier as writer belongs especially to the 1920s and 1930s. This was the period of his most prolific creative writing, when the novels and short stories for which he is best known were published. This was also the period which the University of the West Indies had in mind when it conferred the degree of Doctor of Letters on Alfred Mendes in 1972, for his role in the development of West Indian literature.

Between 1920 and 1940, Mendes published four slender volumes of poetry, and wrote nine novels, and a great many short stories, ninety-nine titles for which have so far come to light. Two of the novels, *Pitch Lake* and *Black Fauns*, were published in 1934 and 1935, respectively. To this period also belong the stories published in the *Beacon* between March 1931 and November 1933. Mendes published other short stories in local and foreign magazines, but many of these periodicals are now extremely difficult to track down, or have disappeared altogether. The seven unpublished novels, still in manuscript, were burned by Mendes in New York in 1940, during a period of severe depression and economic hardship, apparently in a symbolic rejection of his craft.

After his return to Trinidad in 1940 Mendes's writing moved into the less demanding phase of journalism. While working in the colonial civil service, he was arts critic for the *Trinidad Guardian*, and wrote, or republished, a handful of stories in its Sunday supplement. From 1966 until 1972, while working as personnel manager at Singer Sewing Machine Company, Mendes edited the in-house publication the *Trinidad Singer*, in which he published some stories of his own. His last major piece of writing was his autobiography, written in retirement in Barbados between 1975 and 1978, and published posthumously in 2002.

Mendes realized while still a schoolboy that what he most wanted to do in life was to write. This urge crystallized after his return to Trinidad in 1919 from the war in Europe, into the desire to write about his island home from the perspective of a native: one who had "tasted the cascadura", as he wrote in a retrospective of 1983. He threw himself into the cultural life of the colony: joining literary and debating societies; attending performances by local amateur dramatic groups and foreign touring companies; seeking out other aspiring writers, artists and musicians for intellectual discussion; and constantly writing. In the 1920s he was working in his wealthy father's provisions business. Out of this experience came stories such as "One Day for John Small", about the commission agents, cocoa growers, businessmen and merchants with whom he dealt on a daily basis. He wrote about members of his own ethnic group, the Portuguese, with whom he socialized regularly (*Pitch Lake* is set in the Portuguese community of Trinidad) and about the expatriate society which revolved around the colonial government.

Mendes was third-generation Portuguese Creole, the eldest of six children. Initially his family was not well off, and the Mendeses lived in a working-class area of Belmont. His father, a merchant, proved to be a highly successful businessman, and as their financial status improved, the Mendeses moved to middle-class sections of Port of Spain, eventually settling in a large house on Stanmore Avenue. This became the family home at different periods for Mendes, his four brothers and sister, and their respective families.

His father's wealth brought influence and social mobility for the family, but Mendes himself was never wealthy. His father wished Mendes to settle down after his return from Europe and work in the family businesses. Marriage in 1919 and the birth of a son compelled him to fall in with his father's plans. A second marriage a year after his first wife died of pneumonia in 1921, kept him employed until 1933, when he left Trinidad for New York City with the intention of making a name for himself as a writer. He did not go to university, and as a young man he had no professional training to fall back on. He worked at a variety of jobs in New York City, including assignments in the Writers' Project of the Roosevelt Works Progress Administration, where he met and socialized with leading American writers of the day. But until he joined the colonial civil service in Trinidad in 1946, he remained largely dependent on family businesses for his livelihood.

It is ironic that Mendes, driven by the need to provide for his family, should have ended up working for the colonial government, rising eventually to the position of general manager of Port Services department. Although born into a colonial society and to some extent shaped by it, he was anti-colonialist and fiercely critical of the hierarchical social structures of his native island. His war experiences had sharpened his compassion and broadened his outlook. Politically he was Marxist, at least in his youth, and intolerant of all forms of oppression. He was especially critical of the racism and snobbery which he observed in Port of Spain society, and of what he considered the undue influence of the Roman Catholic Church in its affairs.

Mendes's mother, who died in 1912, had been a Catholic, but his father was a staunch Presbyterian, and Mendes repeated the religious conflict in their marriage in his own second marriage to a devout Catholic. His second marriage was unhappy, and when the colonial government introduced divorce legislation in 1931, Mendes had a vested interest in seeing it passed. He threw himself into the public debate which raged until the act was passed in 1933; he deluged the press with letters and articles, sneaking out into Port of Spain's streets early in the morning to put up posters endorsing the legislation. His activism became such an irritant to the Catholic community that the colonial governor, Sir Claud Hollis, warned Mendes's father to get his son out of the country until the act was passed, or risk his being prosecuted for blasphemy.

Mendes went to Grenada, where he had relatives, and stayed until the act was passed in January 1933. During this period of his life, he had also tangled with the legal authorities as a result of one of his short stories. A young man named Septimus Louhar, whom Mendes admitted to using as a model for the protagonist of "Sweetman",[1] sued him successfully for libel in 1932.[2] Mendes was deeply affected by the case, and was afterwards very careful not to write anything potentially libellous, or at least not to offer it for publication. The threat of another court case would have been sufficient encouragement to him to take a holiday in Grenada. In any case, by this time the battle had virtually been won by the pro-divorce faction.

Mendes and his wife were not divorced until 1938, by which time he had been settled in New York for five years, and had met Ellen Perachini, who became his third wife and mother of his last two sons.

All of Mendes's fiction was to some extent autobiographical, and certain characters and situations in the stories are recognizable from descriptions in his autobiography and correspondence. It is probably not sensible to try to trace all of his stories back to real-life encounters, since allowance should certainly be made for artistic licence. While his writing can perhaps allow an insight into the writer himself, there is no doubt that Mendes's acute powers of observation and this propensity for transposing the experiences of his daily existence into his fiction, coupled with his prolific and varied output, make his an authentic voice in any attempt to understand and explicate Trinidad's society in the 1920s and early 1930s.

Influences and Development

Mendes's early writing shows the influence of Greek and Roman writers, Shakespeare, and the great European poets and novelists of the nineteenth century whose work he had devoured while at school. His poetry, written mainly in the formative 1920s, reflects this youthful taste and was subsequently rejected by Mendes as immature and derivative. His long poem, *The Poet's Quest,* certainly falls into the latter category with respect to its verse form. It

---

1. *Beacon* 1, no. 7 (1931).

2. Alfred Mendes, *The Autobiography of Alfred H. Mendes,* edited by Michèle Levy (Kingston: University of the West Indies Press, 2002), 78.

is written mainly in decasyllabic couplets. Its subject-matter is more interesting, however. Using the voyage of the poet as metaphor, it allegorizes an imag-
inative progression in the poet's career from old, European allegiances to those
of a new world (Trinidad), yet to be shaped. Despite the tired vehicle, there
is a freshness and vigour in the poem's movement which stems from the
enthusiasm and energy of the poet (and Mendes), and the excited sense that
he has reached – and recognized – a turning-point in his writing concerns.

Two major influences may be noted in Mendes's indigenizing of his craft.
The first, his experience of trench warfare and all its horrors during the Great
War, plays an extremely important part in his subsequent development. A
telling image from *The Poet's Quest* testifies to the lasting effect of his wartime
experiences:

> On legs
> Maimed from the crippling wounds of wasting war,
> Limped thrown-off morsels from the human store
> Of cannon-fodder;

And in the *Beacon* he wrote:

> I remember the months I spent in the
> trenches with lice playing hide-and-seek about
> my body in the midst of mud and the stench
>   of decomposed bodies.
>
> and I remember the futility
> and the wickedness
> and the beastliness of it all[3]

A prose account, "Over the Top", describes an actual engagement in which
Mendes took part.[4] He fought alongside soldiers of mainly working-class
origins, for whom he developed profound respect and affection and, in the
extremes of combat, dependence. He himself fought bravely and in 1918 was
awarded the Military Medal for outstanding courage under enemy fire.
Understanding of the huge scale of human tragedy involved came later, along
with anger and contempt for the authorities responsible. Convictions of the
equality and brotherhood of mankind, stimulated by his experiences in the
trenches, were reinforced by the second influence, the great social upheaval in

---

3. *Beacon* (May 1933): 21.
4. *Beacon* (May 1931): 24–27.

Russia which culminated in the Bolshevist uprising in 1917. At the time, and certainly for the early part of his creative life, he perceived the Russian Revolution as a hugely liberating social and intellectual force.

Mendes brought his understanding of a need for world-wide change in attitudes and social structures back to Trinidad. As he experimented with his writing, searching for the appropriate medium to articulate his ideas, he began to read contemporary writers and to collect first editions of their works. These later formed part of an extensive library at his house in Richmond Street. The working-class English writer D.H. Lawrence in particular exerted a powerful influence on Mendes's ideas and writing; in this collection it is especially visible in "Boodhoo", with its frank treatment of race, class and sex. The influence of the modernist Irish writer James Joyce's *Ulysses* may be observed in the structure of "One Day for John Small", in which Small's odyssey through Port of Spain echoes that of Leopold Bloom through the streets of Dublin, beginning and ending, like Bloom's, in bed.

At least as important in his development as his voracious appetite for reading and absorbing, was Alfred Mendes's interaction with other writers and intellectuals. Early in the 1920s he met C.L.R. James, who was then a teacher at the Queen's Royal College. In later life, in interviews and in his autobiography, he spoke of James as the catalyst, both for his own career as a writer, and for the establishment of a serious literary movement in Trinidad.[5] Similarly, James stated in an interview with Daryl Cumber Dance: "There is no discussing that period without knowing the importance that Mendes had in it."[6] United by their love of books and music, and their passion for writing, the two men became close friends, meeting frequently to exchange books and ideas and theories of writing. They attracted other men and women with an interest in the arts, notably Ralph de Boissière, and soon a coterie developed which Mendes called "the Trinidad Group".[7] This group was later to be known to scholars as "the *Beacon* Group", after the magazine which published their articles and stories from 1931 until 1933.

Several magazines and journals were published in Trinidad during the 1920s and 1930s. Mendes, whose family worshipped at St Ann's Presbyterian

---

5. Mendes, *Autobiography,* 72.

6. Daryl Cumber Dance, *New World Adams: Conversations with Contemporary West Indian Writers* (Leeds: Peepal Tree Books, 1992), 111.

7. Mendes, *Autobiography,* 72.

Church, the "Portuguese Church", helped to edit its journal, the *Trinidad Presbyterian,* in the mid-1920s. Mendes also published stories, articles and poems of his own in the journal during this time. Other contemporary journals which published his work were the *Quarterly Magazine of the Richmond Street Literary and Debating Association*; the *Quarterly Magazine*; the *Royalian*; the *Trinidadian*; and the *Forum,* which was published in Barbados. Another member of the group, Jean de Boissière, cousin of Ralph, published "Callaloo" and "Picong". Together, Mendes and James edited *Trinidad* 1, no. 1 (December 1929) and *Trinidad* 1, no. 2 (April 1930).

The first issue of their joint effort broke new ground with stories that focused on the lives of the Trinidadian working-class. James's barrack-yard story "Triumph" occasioned widespread public protest, chiefly on grounds of lack of taste. The second issue, importantly, contained Mendes's manifesto "A Commentary", which used the public reaction to "Triumph" as a starting-point to sort out his own ideas about writing.

James did not entirely approve of Mendes's reading of the more experimental writers. In a letter of 1928, he adjured Mendes to

> [s]top choking your own ideas and visions of things with that incessant stream of modern novels. I do not think that anything else but confusion lies that way. Read the classic writers and any modern novelists or poets or historians who really appeal. But I am convinced that for a young writer this incessant tapping into the fashions of the day is bad.

Mendes, however, was in the process of sloughing off Victorian influences and striving to find his own narrative voice. James was interested in the Victorian writers as stylists, but Mendes associated them with prudishness and hypocrisy. He wrote in his "Commentary":

> This Victorianism, as exposed in the writings of most of the novelists of the period, insisted that maidens should be prim and proper, that the contours and lines of objects should be concealed by laces and embroideries, that philosophies should deny the realities of evil, that children should be spoon-fed with a thick soup of lies, and that the good life was conditioned by expurgated speech, going to church, and in nine cases out of ten smiling when you should frown and frowning when you should smile.[8]

8. Reinhard W. Sander, ed., *From Trinidad: An Anthology of Early West Indian Writing* (London: Hodder and Stoughton, 1978), 21.

When James's short story "La Divina Pastora" was published in England in 1927 in the *Saturday Review,* Mendes and his circle were encouraged to try for foreign outlets for their work, with some degree of success. But for the establishment of a Trinidad-centred literature, the most important journal of the time was the *Beacon.* Under the direction of its editor, Albert Gomes, the *Beacon* offered a much broader scope of interests in its contributions than had hitherto appeared, and took a more strongly political line while actively promoting fine writing. Between 1931 and 1932, it staged a short-story writing competition, with, for the editors, somewhat disappointing results.[9] The magazine enjoyed a wide, often scandalized readership at all levels, eventually folding through lack of funds at the same time that Mendes decamped for the United States to concentrate on his writing, and to try to turn it into a viable career.

The Stories

In an introduction to an unpublished collection of his stories assembled in 1983, Mendes defined the short story as "essentially the study of human behaviour in any restricted segment of time". He went on to discuss the aims of *Beacon* writers as follows: "As a group of West Indian writers, we were faced with the problem of writing West Indian stories, the singularities of which would have to be background, dialect, and a preponderance of black characters, and, of course, the mores and customs of the poor people."[10] However, the title which he chose for his collection, *A Pattern of People* (inspired perhaps by Sir Arthur Grimble's *A Pattern of Islands*), suggests that for him, the primary area of interest may have been Trinidad's melting-pot of races. The richest and most dense of the stories tend to reflect this multiracial tapestry rather than concentrating on a single social stratum or ethnic background. "Boodhoo", "Malvina's Nennen" and "The Man Who Ran Away" depict African, East Indian and Chinese Creoles, along with English and Spanish Creoles, and European expatriates.

Mendes took care to particularize the settings of his stories. The editor of the *Beacon* had advised entrants in its short story competition "to spend less

---

9. *Beacon* (January–February 1932): 1.

10. Alfred Mendes, introduction to "A Pattern of People" (unpublished manuscript, 1983; private collection).

time on florid descriptions of our hills, valleys and the moonlight on the Queen's Park Savannah. Those things are only incidental to a good story."[11] Mendes thought otherwise. In a review of an art exhibition for the *Trinidad Guardian* he wrote: "I am . . . convinced that before a people can claim the right to call themselves cultured they must first have absorbed into their creative expressions the texture and spirit of their immediate environment."[12] In retrospect he could have been describing his own fiction. The heat, light and stench of the barrack-yard in "The Man Who Ran Away" and "Sé-sé"; the bustling commercial quarter of Port of Spain in "One Day for John Small"; the trees cowering like crouching animals ready to spring in "Shango"; and *pace* the *Beacon*'s editor, the savannah grass like a sheet of water in the moonlight, in "Malvina's Nennen"; these images are so vivid as to be almost tangible. Perhaps the most significant use of background is to be found in "Boodhoo", with its starry nights, brilliant flora, and birdsong, in which the radiant tropical landscape is used to reflect the inner conflict and eventual dissolution of the protagonist Minnie Lawrence.

Two stories in this selection, "The Man Who Ran Away" and "Sé-sé", have barrack-yard settings. The barrack-yard story was developed by *Beacon* writers as a credible medium for exploring the lives of the working-class poor. Mendes and C.L.R. James were its chief exponents, and a fellow writer, James Cummings, who lived in a barrack-yard, wrote a searing description of his surroundings.[13]

The barrack-yard was peculiar to Trinidad. It was a tenement in which poor people lived in a series of wooden rooms like horse-boxes, according to Cummings, with a communal area for washing and cooking through which ran a canal or gutter. The inhabitants were usually African Trinidadians, especially women, but poverty could impel other races to find accommodation there. The barrack-yard in "The Man Who Ran Away" is inhabited by the black Mrs Augustus, the Chinese Mrs Kai Chin and her mixed-race daughter, and the mixed-race prostitute Maria.

Mendes wrote one novel, *Black Fauns,* and two other short stories about life in the barrack-yard: "Afternoon in Trinidad" and "Lulu Gets Married" (*Pablo's Fandango*). An early novella, *The Barrackyarders* (c.1925–26), has unfor-

11. *Beacon* (January–February 1932): 1.
12. *Trinidad Guardian,* 9 November 1947, 11.
13. *Beacon* (October 1931): 21–22.

tunately not yet turned up. The convention of locating the centre of interest within the barrack-yard as a self-sufficient micro-world had been established in James's "Triumph", the first story in this sub-genre to be published. "The Man Who Ran Away" is unusual in that the point of view is located primarily (though ironically) in the perspective of the outsider, the repressed and timid landlord, rather than with the feisty tenants who close ranks to cheat him out of his rent.

Mendes's understanding of the barrack-yard way of life came out of personal experience. In Rhonda Cobham's introduction to *Black Fauns* he describes spending about six months visiting and occasionally sleeping over in a barrack-yard near his home, as preparation for writing the novel.[14] He was at this period violently anti-Catholic, at odds with his Catholic wife, and actively involved in the public debate over proposed divorce legislation in Trinidad (see above). The satirical depiction of unquestioning piety in this story and in the slighter, humorous "Sé-sé" undoubtedly stems from this personal prejudice.

In striving to establish a significant identity for the African Trinidadian working class, Mendes may seem to present-day readers to have gone overboard in his descriptions of distinctive racial features. This must be understood in the context of the 1920s and 1930s, when Mendes and his friends were breaking new ground in their choice of literary subjects, and searching for appropriate ways to present them. His evident sympathy and respect for his barrack-yarders' struggles to carve out a life for themselves, and his perception of their worthiness as subjects for his fiction, are what finally count. As with the many other characters who people his stories, he celebrates their humanity, warts and all.

Mendes claimed that he was not fluent in Creole (unlike his father, whom Mendes mischievously placed in "One Day for John Small" as one of the cocoa growers approached by the broker Small). Unquestionably, though, he did have a sharp ear for its idiom and cadences, and an outstanding flair for dialogue. In the two barrack-yard stories and "One Day for John Small", which recounts the activities of a working-class hustler during a single day in Port of Spain, the Creole exchanges help to define the characters and give life to their situations.

---

14. Rhonda Cobham, introduction to Alfred Mendes, *Black Fauns* (London and Port of Spain: New Beacon Books, 1984), xi.

The story of Small, a charmer with limited personal ambition but bound-less hopes for his son Harry, whom he intends to finance through school and university, and thereafter into a professional career, points to a familiar theme in West Indian writing: the desire for social advancement through education. The short "Neighbours" also examines social aspirations through the sensitive issue of housing.

"Neighbours" is told in the first person by the Portuguese Creole husband who, like Mendes, has friends among the black and mixed-race intellectuals of Port of Spain, and a wife who barely tolerates them (Mendes's second wife was not sympathetic towards his writing). The story involves a social-climbing neighbour of mixed race, her brown-skinned husband, and her black cook, with whom the husband has had a hitherto undisclosed affair. Mrs Carlton's social ambitions tumble into the dust when she comes to grips with the cook over a trifling sum of money, and the cook, goaded to fury, screams out her secret for all to hear.

The biting irony with which class, colour and social aspirations are examined here does not spare the narrator's wife. The narrator himself barely escapes through his ignorance of the true state of affairs. His ill-timed attempt to scale the garden wall and part the combatants is a leavening touch of humour in an otherwise bleak tale of hypocrisy and pretension.

"Not a Love Story" re-enacts the colonizing process. It tells of the engagement of a cultured Chinese Trinidadian girl to an English professor, and the consternation which this mixed-race alliance causes in the tight little circle of expatriates clustered around the agricultural college at St Augustine. With Grace Lee Hong, Mendes has departed from his usual working-class Chinese characters: small shopkeepers such as Lee Sing in "One Day for John Small" and the impoverished Mrs Kai Chin in "The Man Who Ran Away", who are wily and tough enough to negotiate a space for themselves among their economic peers. Grace is a member of the middle class. Her father is an influential figure in the colonial community, and she is accustomed to moving in the best circles. She is considerably better mannered, and probably better educated, than the expatriate wife who humiliates her. As with the Portuguese Creole Nora in "Bert and Betty Briggs – English" (*Pablo's Fandango*), the social structure of the colony allows for Trinidadians in their own country to be marginalized by foreigners.

The short "Shango" and much longer "Three Rebels" contain overtly auto-biographical material. In "Shango", written, like "Neighbours", in the first person, the three main characters appear to have been based on Mendes himself (although this time he makes himself English), C.L.R. James, and their friend Frank V.S. Evans. The three young men have attended a performance by a visiting English theatre company and are engaged in somewhat pretentious criticism of the actors over a late-night drink, when they are reminded of a further engagement for the night, at a very different kind of theatre: a Shango ceremony. The collision of worlds and the effect of the ritual dance on the narrator and especially on "Frederick", the James persona, form the heart as well as the climax of the story.

James himself in later life remembered writing about the Shango, but he was never afterwards able to locate the manuscript. He wrote to Reinhard Sander about a story that "dealt with an educated black man who was a Christian by birth and upbringing. But he went to see some African dancing up on Laventille Hill. He was swept away by the dancing and plunged into it".[15] While Mendes's version may have resulted from a discussion about the topic with James, it is more probable that he and his friends did actually attend a Shango ceremony and have an experience comparable to the one he describes here. Mendes's sons recall that their father often attended Shango ceremonies, and was made very welcome by the participants.

"Three Rebels" describes an unusual *ménage à trois,* at least for the time of writing, and the bizarre prank which they devise to alleviate boredom one steamily hot night in Port of Spain. The characters of the rebels appear to have been based on friends of Mendes: Toni on Jean "Toni" de Boissière, a fellow *Beacon* writer; Arthur on the artist Hugh Stollmeyer; and Helen Lee Choy on the painter and journalist Ivy Achoy. Undoubtedly, there is a desire to shock in Mendes's depiction of in-your-face Bohemia: the relationship between Toni and Arthur would have deeply disturbed the average middle-class Trinidadian of the time. The story also examines the isolation of the artist in an environment that is basically hostile to creative endeavour, a position with which Mendes himself, whose father disapproved of his writing ambitions, would have been only too familiar.

"Béti", the most recent of the stories, may seem at first glance to be the odd one out in a collection chosen from the fiction of the 1920s and 1930s. It is likely, however, that the first section of the story, which deals with Béti and

---

15. Reinhard W. Sander, "The Trinidad Awakening: West Indian Literature of the 1930s" (PhD diss., University of Texas at Austin, 1979), 212–13n7.

Ram's childhood on a coconut estate in Cedros, dates from that early period. This section may have originally formed part of a novel, *Béti*, which Mendes destroyed in New York, and of which he had been especially fond. It should be of considerable interest to anyone assessing the corpus of Mendes's writing.

Mendes was particularly interested in the lives of the East Indian community in Trinidad, perhaps as a result of a liaison with a young Indian woman after the failure of his second marriage. In addition to "Boodhoo", which is set on an estate with East Indian labourers and includes a story within a story about an unfaithful Indian wife and her jealous husband, he wrote a story set entirely in an East Indian agricultural community, "And Then the Hurricane Came" (*Pablo's Fandango*), and a short story, "Ramjit Das".[16] Apart from "Ramjit Das", which tells of a young bridegroom who rejects the traditional marriage arranged for him by his parents and elopes with the girl of his choice, the common factor in these stories is the triangle of relationships, with the women always beautiful and seductive. The ending of "And Then the Hurricane Came" is violent and tragic, and the sense in "Béti" is that the outcome of the meeting between Béti and the Singer sales representative Peter Farley could easily have been the same. There is a brooding quality about this story, at variance with Béti's sunny, wayward childhood, which underlines the horror in Ram's. The story also hints that given the appropriate circumstances, the violent death of Ram's mother at his father's hands could be re-enacted in their own marriage.

"Boodhoo", "Malvina's Nennen" and "Laura's Return" are stories of middle-class Trinidadian life, involving mixed-race relationships. In "Boodhoo" and "Malvina's Nennen" these relationships cross class boundaries. Of "Malvina's Nennen" Mendes wrote, "The first part is a modification of the barrack-yard, the second part takes the reader to the white and wealthy upper-class, and finally the two classes are brought together for the dénouement."[17] In all three stories, sexual betrayal becomes the metaphor for everything that is wrong in colonial society: the sickness and hypocrisy which Mendes describes in his "Commentary" as the product of Victorian cover-ups. In addition, in "Malvina's Nennen" Mendes exposes the morally questionable method by which Thomas Marsden has achieved his life's ambition of knighthood by the

---

16. *Trinidad Guardian Weekly*, 15 June 1947.

17. Mendes, introduction.

British government: funding contingents of young Trinidadian men to fight for Britain in the Great War. Mendes had enlisted with the Merchants and Planters Contingents in the spirit of adventure, and in quest of new experiences to fuel his writing. He may also have been rebelling against his father's attempts to determine his future. This story suggests that, ten or eleven years after his return from the slaughter he had encountered in France and Belgium, his perspective on the entire exercise (like that of Thomas Marsden after his soul-searching) was coloured by anger and disillusionment.

In "Boodhoo" and "Laura's Return", as in *The Poet's Quest*, Mendes employs the voyage out to Trinidad made by Minnie and Laura as a metaphor for a spiritual and emotional journey, ending in figurative shipwreck for both young women. Mendes's classical education reasserts itself in "Boodhoo", where the complexity of relationships is deepened by structural patterning which recalls an ancient Mediterranean myth: that of the Cretan princess Phaedra, her marriage to Theseus, King of Athens, and her disastrous passion for her stepson Hippolytus. His debt to D.H. Lawrence in this story, noted above, extends even to "Memsahib's" tryst with her servant in the moonlit wood, recalling Lady Chatterley's assignation with her gamekeeper, Mellors.

The longest of the stories, "Colour", is set in Grenada, where Mendes had relatives, and which he described in his autobiography as "the Eden, the paradise of my earliest years".[18] The island's pristine beauty is lovingly evoked. Against the glowing background unfolds a slow, thoughtful examination of a mixed marriage; the pretences which it imposes on the "brown" husband and his "white" American wife; and the emotional and psychological repercussions which their visit produces in his family circle. Mendes spends considerable time in describing not only the physical landscape of Grenada, but also the tranquil, timeless way of life there: church on Sunday, followed by band concerts in the afternoon; picnics at Grand Anse Beach; and the feverish excitement generated in the sleepy little community by the glittering ball at Government House.

It is a measure of Mendes's skill in delineating character that the three women most prominent in "Colour", Cora, Milly and Freida, though totally different from each other, are entirely credible. Milly, plain, gentle and pious, has no desire ever to leave home. Her sister Cora is pretty, forceful and intelligent, and has a "past". Though deeply rooted like her sister, she is stifled

---

18. Mendes, *Autobiography*, 20.

intellectually by small-island life and longs for escape. (Significantly, this story was serialized in the *Beacon* in the months preceding Mendes's departure for New York in 1933.) Their American sister-in-law Freida is stunningly attractive, modern and "liberated", but torn between love for her husband and the racial prejudice with which she has grown up. During the course of Freida's visit, the women evolve into a kind of understanding and acceptance of each other's differences, not always happily. The sordid little shock at the story's climax invites condemnation, not wholly of Freida, but rather of the learned attitudes which are ultimately responsible for it. The fact, too, that Freida's brother-in-law Jack is antagonistic towards "white" people helps to provide balance in Mendes's subtle exploration of racial attitudes.

In later years, Mendes was to recognize that the short story was the most successful medium for the articulation of his ideas. While in retirement in Barbados, he was able to look back on the early period of his writing and assess the contribution he had made:

> we lived and worked from the very commencement of the incredibly rapid changes taking place in the social order. Indeed, we were in . . . a way participants in the making of these changes . . .
>
> Those who followed in our footsteps: Naipaul, Lamming, Selvon and the Jamaicans, exposed as they were to later economic, political and social upheavals, could draw upon these sources for the enrichment of their work.[19]

In a radio programme in 1974 Anson Gonzalez confirmed the importance of Mendes and C.L.R. James in the development of West Indian writing:

> James' and Mendes' places in the field of creative writing are assured, not only because their concern with the working classes as subjects of literature has formed the cornerstone of Trinidadian and West Indian creative writing, but also because their efforts, in their youth, must have been made at great personal sacrifice. The artist or writer has traditionally, especially in the West Indies, been looked upon as an outcast or at best looked at with amused disfavour.[20]

Many of Mendes's themes are familiar in West Indian writing. Chosen for their variety, his stories cover the struggles of women to exist in the barrack-

---

19. Mendes, introduction.

20. Anson Gonzales, *Trinidad and Tobago Literature and History on Air* (Port of Spain: National Cultural Council of Trinidad and Tobago, 1974), 7.

yard and in domestic service; the uneasy coexistence of the Creole middle-class with the colonial hierarchy; the problems faced by the artist in a society largely indifferent to the creative life; the importance of education as a means to social mobility; and the divided self: the islander torn between love of home and the need for greater freedoms; and they convey a sense of vital and other lives being lived within, and in spite of, the social structuring of the time: the self-defining communities of barrack-yarders, East Indian labourers, and Shango dancers. There is even a degree of sympathy for the colonizer. "Boodhoo" and "Laura's Return" examine the psychic disintegration of European women who migrate from the known old world to the unknown new, with its alien values and culture, with an almost feminine sensitivity to their predicament.

Whatever their situation or preoccupation, Mendes's characters spring to life as typically human, with strengths and weaknesses peculiarly their own. To read their stories is to understand something of what it must have been like to live in a small, island colony during the *interbellum,* when the need for a revolution in social attitudes and practices coexisted with traditions and continuities wherein lay the moral strengths and identity of its people.

The Man Who Ran Away

Juan Quintero, a tall, ascetic-looking man, inherited from his wife a row of barrack-rooms in the poorer and more disreputable quarter of Port of Spain. His wife had died one year before, and Juan was still grieving for her. They had lived together for fifteen years, and during all that long time never a harsh word had passed between them. Juan had wished, time and again, that his wife would bear him a child, and particularly a boy, but she died childless and the priest said to him: "It is the Lord's will," and that comforted him.

For the whole course of his married life, Juan had been faithful to his wife. He regarded with horror those men who, though married, went around with other women. Brought up in a strictly Catholic home, he had, strangely enough, lived a chaste life as a young man and could now boast that his wife was the only woman he had ever had. His friends, when they heard him utter that boast, said to themselves and to each other afterwards that there was no wonder Juan was so pale and namby-pamby-looking.

While his wife was alive, every month-end saw Juan going from room to room of the barracks to collect the rent. He detested these monthly visits because at such times he heard the most filthy language, and more often than not experienced difficulty in extracting the rent from the tenants. Also, once or twice he had found himself entertaining lewd thoughts about a particularly attractive woman who occupied one of the rooms. Juan knew her to be a prostitute, and had on several occasions considered it advisable to give her notice to quit, but because she paid her rent regularly and was always polite and cordial to him, he decided that he would leave her where she was. As he went to confession after each visit and received absolution, his conscience was at ease and he felt safe.

When his wife died, Juan was so upset and so engrossed in his grief that he found it impossible to take any active part in the affairs of life, and handed over the collection of his rents to an agent. As time went on, however, and his grief became less and less absorbing, he regretted more and more having to pay ten per cent to the agent. He even, one night, eleven months after his wife's death, sat up and calculated what he had lost by the fact of his not having himself continued to collect his rents. In spite of the grief still lodged in his breast, his mind was sufficiently unoccupied to be appalled by the sum staring at him from the paper. The next morning he wrote to the agent, dispensing with his services.

It was a Monday morning in December when, for the first time since his wife's death, Juan found himself in the disreputable quarter of Port of Spain where his barrack-rooms were located. It was a bright, sunny morning, but Juan's heart was heavy with grief because the old occupation of collecting rents brought back memories of his wife to him. He remembered how always on his return home after such an arduous and unpleasant task, she would greet him with loving words and affectionate kisses. Who was there to greet him on his return this morning? He thought of the empty house and his eyes grew dim with tears, and he was about, once again, to think of God as being unjust in His dealings with him, when he recalled what the priest had told him about God sending this affliction to him as a trial of his faith, and he grew calm and reconciled. He feared that if he flew in the face of God, his chances of inheriting the kingdom of heaven would be jeopardized.

Juan, tall and thin and dressed in a black suit with a black felt hat on his head, walked on and gave himself over to pious thoughts. As he passed a church, he raised his hat and made the sign of the cross. He walked on steadily, looking neither to right nor left, so engrossed was he with pious memories of his wife. That she was a plain-looking woman had seldom disturbed him. Indeed, as he looked around and saw the temptations to which the pretty wives of his friends were exposed, he considered himself a lucky man that his wife was plain-looking: she, he knew, would receive no unholy invitation from any man. But there were moments, few and far between, when Juan had wished that his wife was pretty and handsome in order that he might feel other men looking at her and desiring her. That would have given him a certain pride in himself, a sense of his own good taste. But these moments were short and always left him feeling guilty and tainted.

His dream of the night before, in which his wife had reappeared to him like Milton's Alcestis from the grave, set his mind running backward. He remembered those rare occasions when his wife, her partial nakedness concealed by the night, came to him with a gesture and throaty sigh of complete surrender. The mere memory of these occasions now sent his heart in a wild scamper and conjured up before him a vision of bare thighs and luscious breasts. The sunlight poured down on his black hat and he found himself blaming the sun for sending this warm current through his blood. Taking out his handkerchief, he coughed into it, a phlegmatic cough that racked his weak chest and gave him a momentary sensation of giddiness. He walked on with his habitual stoop, now glancing to right and left through the corner of his eyes and noticing for the first time the crowds of people passing back and forth. Suddenly he felt strange in the midst of so many people: it was such a long time since he had been out in the street at such an hour. He hurried on as if he were being pursued, and the noises of passing cars and jabbering pedestrians all around frightened and perplexed him. His was a temperament, he decided, that needed the seclusion of his house if he must be at peace: never again would he come out in the open to be exposed like this, ashamed and intimidated.

Now why had he dreamed in such a way of his wife the night before? But just as this thought came to him, he was walking towards the gate which led into the yard where his barrack-rooms were. As he came abreast of the gate his courage failed him and he nearly turned back. This had never before happened to him. Without knowing how, he found himself standing at the end of the passage-way, gazing into the yard. He saw the familiar heap of stones in the middle of the yard on which the tenants bleached their clothes. He saw the wire-lines on which the tenants hung their washing to dry. The old familiar stench of stagnant water and stale urine came to him and he coughed his phlegmatic cough once again. Then, remembering that the purpose of his visit was to receive, if possible, his rents, he slouched in with as firm a step as he could manage. Timidly he knocked at the first door. There was no answer. He knocked again; and with this second knocking a dog leapt out from a neighbouring room, dashed up to his heels and began yapping for all it was worth. Juan was terribly frightened and wanted to run, but could not. His legs shook beneath him and again he felt a sudden giddiness come over him. He thought he was going to faint, and he thought the dog had already bitten him. He was almost sure that he felt a pain in the calf of his leg. But the next moment a woman appeared in the frame of the door through which the dog had leapt and, in a quiet, sibilant voice, summoned the dog to her. He recognized the woman as the prostitute he used to see whenever, in the days gone by, he had visited the place for his wife's rents. She was in *déshabille*. She did not appear to recognize him, for without saying a word, she went into her room with the dog in her arms and shut the door after her. In the meantime, the door at which Juan had knocked opened. Juan gave a little cough and said:

"Good morning, Madam. I've come to collect the rent."

"De rent?" the woman said, her black acreage of face hollowed with resentment and anger. "Whey's Mr Benoit?"

Juan coughed again, this time into his handkerchief in order that he might have a little time before answering. At last he murmured:

"Mr Benoit is no longer with me, Madam."

"Who's you?" the woman demanded.

"I'm Mr Quintero. I'm the owner of these rooms. I'm . . ."

"Enh enh, you'se Mr Quintero. Come in, *bourgeois*, come in. I didn't know it was you," and her acreage of face was valleyed suddenly by smiles.

Juan entered. He remembered the room quite well, but what a transformation it had undergone since he had last seen it! It was spick and span, the floor was cleanly scrubbed, the curtains were clean and starched, everything was in its place, the antimacassars looked bright, the cat in the corner looked clean and content, the photographs hanging on the partitions seemed to have life in them: what a transformation since he had last seen it!

"Sit dong, *bourgeois*, sit dong," Mrs Augustus said.

Juan sat in a stiff-backed chair.

"Not dere, *bourgeois*, not dere," Mrs Augustus said. "Look a nice rocker."

Juan shifted to the rocker.

"I glad you come yourself," Mrs Augustus said, herself sitting in the stiff-backed chair Juan had vacated. "I glad to see you because I got a complain' to mek."

This statement disturbed Juan, because he thought Mrs Augustus was going to ask him to make some alteration or addition or repairs to her room.

4

He did not like spending money unnecessarily, for he regarded the spending of money for the comfort of his tenants as unnecessary expenditure. Juan was a typical Trinidad landlord. He kept silent, his eyes fixed in a weak stare on a spot a little to the left of Mrs Augustus's face: he could never look people in the eyes.

"Is about dat prostitute, dat whore," Mrs Augustus said, her voice raucous with venom. Her whole fat person overflowed the seat of the chair, and quivered. Juan, with a meek and mild expression on his ascetic face, winced inwardly at the use of such words. He was afraid to speak.

"You has to gie she notice to quit, Mr Quintero, she scandalizing de whole neighbourhood. Everybody know whey she is: a street whore." Juan winced again. "No respec'able body goin' live in dese rooms if she stayin' dere. Look last night: a scandal, Mr Quintero, a blasted scandal. De woman get on in de worse way. She get drunk, she have men dere, she curse dem. She curse all a' we, at de top of her voice. Mr Quintero, she's a blackguard, an' if she stay, I move and all you oder tenants." Mrs Augustus breathed stertorously while her fat person quivered and overflowed the chair.

Juan, not prepared for this outburst, didn't know what to say. He sat limp in his rocker, fearing the woman's wrath. He couldn't reconcile the neat and tidy aspect of the room with her present mood. He took one tentative little rock, but the sudden movement made him too aware of his plight, so he steadied the chair and sat still. He sat still for a long time, waiting for Mrs Augustus to say something. But Mrs Augustus said nothing, only breathed stertorously and quivered in her chair. So he mumbled at last:

"That's too bad."

"Too bad, you says Mr Quintero? Dat's all you says, Mr Quintero? Enh, enh! Too bad, too bad? It ain' plenty worse dan dat, *bourgeois*? Look, I tell you somet'ing. You come here tonight. Look, *bourgeois*, you come to my room, here, an' sit dong quiet widout dat son of a bitch knowin' you here. You sit dong quiet here an' hear fo' you'self how she scandalize de place. Look, she does mek us feel shame, me an' Mrs Kai Chin, de Chinese lady, and all de neighbourhood. Mrs Kai Chin got a daughter, Mr Quintero, a big daughter expose to all dis bad example dat whore does show she. You goin' leave de woman dere when all you tenants tellin' you to kick she out? You goin' leave she dere, I axe you Mr Quintero? You like ef you has a daughter for she to hear all dat cussing and drunkenness and carryin' on? You like dat, enh, enh?"

Juan sat still, listening to Mrs Augustus's tirade and still wondering what attitude he should adopt towards her. He had no desire to antagonize any one of his tenants, least of all Mrs Augustus, who appeared to keep his place so clean and well. It was difficult to get clean and careful tenants, he reflected. At the same time, whereas Mrs Augustus was a newcomer, the woman about whom she complained had been his tenant for the past three years and had always paid the rent regularly. It was also difficult, he reflected, indeed, more difficult and more important, to get tenants who were prompt with their rent-payments than tenants who kept rooms in a clean state. He didn't mean to commit himself at all, so he answered:

"I will see about it Mrs Augustus."

"Buh you got to see 'bout it now, *bourgeois*, now," Mrs Augustus said. "Look, I get someone, a decent respec'able soul to take de room as soon as she leave."

"All right, Mrs Augustus," Juan said, "I will see about it." Then he fell silent, playing with his fingers and waiting for his rent. After what had passed between them, he did not know how to ask just at this moment for the rent. Instead, he sat playing with his fingers with an abstracted look on his face and hoping against hope that Mrs Augustus would not put him to the necessity of asking for the rent. Mrs Augustus's eyes, sunk into two little graves of black flesh, gazed sullenly on him. Her voluminous skirt bulged around her like a balloon, and her head, banded with a huge multicoloured bandanna, was cocked on one side as if it were too huge and heavy for her neck to keep it straight up on her shoulders.

Juan pulled out his handkerchief and coughed. He was becoming more and more timid. He didn't like black people: he preferred East Indians and Chinese and mulattos. Try as he might to think otherwise (was he not a Christian and Roman Catholic at that?) their black pigmentation and ugliness were signs to him that they had been made by the devil, and if not by him, then by a god other than the one who had made white people.

"I will see about it, Mrs Augustus," Juan said in order to ward off the panic that was fast taking possession of him. Saying which, he rose, bade Mrs Augustus goodbye in a polite manner, and walked out of the room without asking for his rent. He felt like kicking himself when he once more found himself in the yard. His main desire now was to fly from the place, to get home as quickly as possible and discover there the peace and quiet that had deserted him since he had left an hour ago. He would communicate with his agent as soon as possible and arrange for the collecting of his rents as of old.

He stood in the yard and looked about him, gathering his wits. The sun poured streams of hot light onto the heap of bleaching stones and onto the breadfruit tree that grew in a corner of the yard. Not a fowl was in sight. Mrs Augustus's door was shut and for this privacy in which to pull himself together, he thanked his God by muttering, mechanically, an *ave*. Very slowly he came to himself. Very slowly it dawned on him that he had failed in the purpose of his visit, a thing that had never before happened to him. His long solitude, the long period of his grief, he decided, had unfitted him for the daily affairs of life. This thought upset him terribly and he straightened up his frail body to its full height as a gesture of defiance to it; and while he stood thus, a conflict of emotions in his breast, he recalled his fleeting vision of the prostitute in *déshabille*. His blood was roused into a quick flow and the tips of his fingers and the tips of his toes went cold. Then his heart gave a great bound and he determined, there and then, to show fight against his inclinations by deliberately walking across the yard and deliberately knocking on Mrs Kai Chin's door. A moment later he was in the room saying to Mrs Kai Chin in a clear, articulate tone:

"I've come for the rent, Madam."

Mrs Kai Chin was a very small, very yellow, oldish woman. The slit in her eyes, the two nostrils where a nose-bridge should have been, the long dark, dead hair falling in a plait down to her waist, told him at a glance that she was pure Chinese.

"De lent?" she said. "Sit dong, Mr Quintelo. Is a long time I no see you."

But Juan said no, he could not sit because he had little or no time to spare. And as if to reassure himself of the genuineness of his new resolution, he said in the same clear articulate tone:

"What is this I have been hearing about your neighbour, Mrs Kai Chin?"

And he sat. Mrs Kai Chin sat too. Juan's heavy, brooding eyes slowly took in the slovenliness of the room. Dust was everywhere, dust and cobwebs. Cobwebs straddled the corners of the ceiling and he saw spiders glued to the centre of each beautifully woven web. He hated spiders. He was afraid of them as women are reputed to be afraid of cockroaches and mice. The mere sight of them, so sinister in their stillness, turned his belly sick. He coughed, a nervous, artificial cough, that was more a grunt of dismay than anything else.

"You mean Miss Malia?" Mrs Kai Chin said.

At last he remembered the woman's name: Maria; but could think no more of it, for at that moment Mrs Kai Chin's daughter came from behind the screen where their bed was concealed. He was amazed to see how the child had grown in a year: tall, sinuous and brown, for her father, long since gone about his business, had been a coloured man.

"You remember my daughter, Mr Quintelo?" Mrs Kai Chin said.

For answer, Juan continued to stare at the girl in a queer, uncanny sort of way. Philomen, for that was her name, lowered her large slumberous eyes and murmured:

"Good morning."

"You leady fo' school, chil'?" Mrs Kai Chin said.

"Yes, Ma."

"All ligh'. An don' be too late as you was yesterday, you hear Philomen?"

"Yes, Ma," and Philomen walked out of the room, her tall, sinuous body swinging sensuously.

"She's grown a nice girl," Juan said at length.

"An' dat's my trouble," Mrs Kai Chin said. "I have to watch she like a cat. You know how it is wit' young, pletty girls like Philomen, Mr Quintelo? You know how it is? We have all de trouble to bling dem up, an' phoo! dey off wit' some fellow who ain' got a cent much less a tollar. Is vely, vely, hard!"

"Indeed," said Juan.

"Now if only some coot man'd come along, some mallied man whose wife is dead an' who have a little money, like you, fo' example, Mr Quintelo ..."

Juan's heavy, brooding eyes had a sudden glint in them which showed that he grasped Mrs Kai Chin's meaning. But without warning, his dead wife, who had come to him in a dream the night before, loomed suddenly large in his memory and obliterated his awareness of the world, bringing him face to face with all the holy angels and saints of God. Within his heart he uttered another *ave* and felt utterly bowed down with humiliation and uncleanness. When once again he saw the little woman before him, he said:

"What is this I have been hearing about your neighbour, Mrs Kai Chin?"

"You mean Miss Malia?" Mrs Kai Chin said again. "Don' listen to what Mrs Augustus tell you about her, Mr Quintelo. Las' night dey had a low because Mrs Augustus's man was in Miss Malia's loom. Mrs Augustus only jealous of Miss Malia, Mr Quintelo, only jealous. Dey's both de same t'ing an' we all got to live," and Mrs Kai Chin turned up her narrow slit-eyes and sighed.

Juan felt a great sense of relief surging over him, for what if Mrs Kai Chin too had insisted on his asking Maria to leave? At least, that was the way he put the problem to himself. Actually, he was glad that he wouldn't have to ask her to leave; first, because, for some reason which he could not himself analyse, he wanted her to stay on in his room; and secondly, because she paid her rent promptly. And now he found himself liking Mrs Kai Chin in spite of the cobwebs and spiders. He liked her because she was Philomen's mother, and he liked her also because of her attitude towards her neighbour. He sat back in his chair and no longer thought of his cough and his weak chest and his dead wife. He sat back in his chair and felt better than he had felt in many a long day. The world seemed suddenly to have put on bright colours for him and his spirit that had for so long been under a spell, as it were, first the spell of his living, amorous wife, and then the spell of his cold, hard grief, now began to thaw and warmth to flow through the veins of his body. Observing his black felt hat lying in his lap, he then and there decided that he would buy a new straw hat on his way home, a straw hat with a bright band, that he would put away once and for all the dark, sombre clothes he had been wearing since his wife's death: might these dark things not have helped deepen the gloom of his past year's life?

It occurred to him as he was bidding Mrs Kai Chin *au revoir* that she also had not paid him his rent; but Juan, his mood completely changed now, did not think it wise to ask Mrs Kai Chin for the money. Not receiving it now necessitated his early return. He would see *then* what Mrs Kai Chin would have further to say about Philomen. Cobwebs and spiders didn't, after all, matter so much when a pretty child could grow into lovely womanhood in the midst of them.

The dog barked loudly when he knocked on Miss Maria's door; but immediately he heard again the quiet, sibilant voice calling it to silence. And then the door opened and Maria stood looking down on him, blinking in the sunlight. She was still in *déshabille*. She was extraordinarily beautiful, Juan thought. Her brown skin was rich with sensuous life, so rich that Juan's desire was now to touch it, feel the warmth and the velvetness of it. Her hair, dark and wavy, was in disarray: she seemed to have just risen from bed. He could see her brown upstanding breasts under the thin muslin upper garment. Every now and again his eyes strayed to her breasts, for they excited him and filled his mind with lewd thoughts. And her knees were round and plump, with dimples, her legs shapely, and her hips curving down to the thighs in a rhythmic movement that stirred and roused. Something in him was elated. Nevertheless, he felt uncomfortable standing there like that in the burning sunlight. Pulling himself together, he said:

"Good morning. I'm Mr Quintero."

Maria did not show any surprise. In a very quiet voice she said:

"Well, I never. I didn't recognize you, Mr Quintero. Come in, come in."

Juan entered. The dog, with one eye open and the other closed, growled. Maria gave it a quiet, sibilant command, whereupon it fell silent. She moved very slowly, and yet with great charm, innocent and voluptuous at the same time. He took the nearest chair and sat quickly.

"Do you mind me like this?" she asked, quite nonchalantly. She spoke well and her voice was quiet and throaty.

He didn't answer; instead he looked away from her and at the room, but his eyes saw nothing. He was far too excited to see with his mind; and seeing without the mind is like hearing music without *listening* to it.

Suddenly she gave a low little snort of laughter. He was startled into looking at her. He could not understand what she had laughed at. He saw her sitting and leaning forward a little and her breasts were all exposed to his sight. Quickly he took his eyes away.

"I didn't know you when I saw you just now." she said. "You've changed."

"Changed?" he said.

"Yes. You've got thinner and you're pale. I heard of your wife's death. Of course that's why you're so pale and so thin."

He sat still. It disturbed him for a fleeting moment to hear this woman talking about his wife's death. For want of something to say, he sat quite still. All the movement and perturbation were inside of him in spite of his outward composure.

"You've come for the rent, I know." she said. "I haven't got it now."

"That's all right," he said quickly, on the spur of the moment, and glanced at her. She smiled, not with her eyes, only with her full, sensuous lips. Her eyes were languorous.

"You see, these are hard times, aren't they, Tommy?" she said, addressing the dog. The dog raised its head, looked at her dully, and then dropped it again.

"I know," he said. "These are hard times."

Again she gave a little snort of laughter and leaned slightly more forward to add:

"You must be lonely, Mr Quintero, without your wife." She said that in a very intimate voice, and it was all he could do to sit still, the nails of one hand firmly pressed into the flesh of the palm, for he was becoming more and

10

more excited. He tried hard in his terribly excited condition to invoke the aid of the Holy Mary, but could not. His last resource, the whole sum of his religious experience, was now beyond his reach; and strangely enough his excitement was topped with a peak of happiness.

"And yet, of course, your children must keep you company," she said and leaned back in her chair as if she resented the suggestion.

"I haven't any children." he said, thickly.

"Oh, that's too bad. A wife should always give her husband children. Don't you think?"

"Yes, of course, yes." Now he was actually angry that his wife had left him no children: that was something against her.

"Else, why a wife?" She added in her more intimate voice and leaned forward again.

"Yes, yes," he said, not knowing quite what he was saying.

"I pity you," she said, and he thought he detected in her voice a cynical note that roused him into self-defence.

"Pity me? Oh, you don't know me." But for all his resolution, he spoke in a bantering fashion.

"Perhaps I do, you naughty man. Perhaps I know you better that you know yourself."

Whereas Juan thought that he was becoming bolder and bolder, actually deep down inside of him, a little dark spark of fear lay silent and now began to grow and spread itself out. He tried to fight it back, to recoil from it, but like the slow, dark invasion of land by a blind mist, it rose and grew. He wanted to challenge the woman's insinuation, he felt a great burning desire for what he had so long been deprived of, he knew he wanted her, and yet he could not bring himself to the actual determination.

"You're afraid of your own shadow – darling," and once again she gave a little snort of laughter.

That stung him, but it was already too late. All his little artificial vaunting was closed over and swallowed up by this great fear – and then he knew that a panic was threatening to hold him in its strong, bony hands and shake him into action.

Maria rose from her chair. He, trembling in every limb and in every fibre of his spirit, rose too. With a quick, dexterous movement, the woman before him undid her shoulder-straps and her garment slid like a sheath from her.

Juan stood perfectly still for a moment. Then, quickly, he raised his arms to his face to shut out the living flesh of his temptation. With a little gasp and hatless, he ran out into the yard, nearly falling over in his haste. Suddenly the dog bounded up and was after him. He ran past the heap of bleaching stones; and in the unclean passage-way, leading out to the street, the dog sank its teeth into the calf of Juan's leg. Juan did not feel the pain, but continued running, hatless, through the streets. When he arrived at his house, he threw himself on his knees beside his bed and prayed for a long time.

Not a Love Story

And they nearly quarrelled over it, although it was only two months since they had been married. But Dr Stanton-Bellair was determined to have Grace Lee Hong to tea so, with a note of finality in his voice, he said to Doreen, his wife:

"It's no good talking any more about it. It isn't as if I want it, it isn't as if I like entertaining a Chinese girl, but it's got to be done. You know the position. I haven't to go into that again."

"I can't understand how any self-respecting Englishman can allow himself to become engaged to a Chinese girl," Doreen said. "Surely he can . . . well, he doesn't have to *marry* her. And it disrespects not only himself, but every other English person in the island. It's a form of selfishness, incredible selfishness, for it shows no consideration for other people's feelings. And above all, no consideration for you at all, for he knows that you, as his subordinate at the station, would have in any case to show her some sort of attention. It's just . . . just disgusting. You might have told me of this before bringing me out to . . . to such an indignity."

"Good Lord, Doreen, one would think that you would have refused to marry me if I had told you that Dr Strether, the head of our Station, was engaged to a Chinese girl."

"But not one of the other doctors has shown her any sort of attention."

"They haven't got to, they are single. But they're always pleasant to her whenever they meet her at Strether's bungalow. She might be Chinese, but she isn't a bad sort of girl, pleasant and quiet and sensitive. And quite refined."

"I'm tired of hearing you say that. I'm beginning to think that you approve of this . . . this business."

"But I tell you I don't. You know that. It's just so and we've got to make the best of it, Doreen."

"*I* have to make the best of it! *I!* Why should I? What'll the Burne-Joneses and the Laughtons and all our other friends think when they hear that we've had that . . . that girl here to tea? Here, if you please! Why, they'll think the less of us, that's all."

"No they won't. They'll understand," Dr Stanton-Bellair said lamely. "And Strether is no small fry. An authority on his subject, internationally known, always being quoted in the scientific magazines. And a good friend of H.G. Wells and J.B.S. Haldane and . . ."

"Oh shut up. I'm tired of hearing you say that too." There was a silence. "Well, if you insist . . ."

"I do," said the husband.

And the next morning Grace received a note from Mrs Stanton-Bellair inviting her to tea for the following afternoon. She was very surprised to get the invitation, for although she knew that Dr Stanton-Bellair liked her, she'd always felt that he liked her in a patronizing sort of way, simply because she was Dr Strether's fiancée. Of course, it went without saying that Mrs Stanton-Bellair did not like her. She'd met her only once and that was enough. The morning of her arrival in Trinidad, Grace had gone down to the jetty with Strether to welcome her to her new home, and there were also lots of professors there from the Imperial College of Tropical Agriculture with their wives, all friends of Dr Stanton-Bellair, and Mrs Stanton-Bellair had taken scarcely any notice of her, just a cold hand-shake which she couldn't very well avoid and a stiff "how d'ye do." So she was surprised to get this invitation. She stood with it in her hands for some moments, read and reread it, and at last went to her mother with it.

"That's very nice," old Mrs Lee Hong said, proud to think of her daughter as Dr Strether's fiancée and the friend of all these bigwig European professors and what not.

"I don't know if I should go," Grace said timidly.

The mother looked at her through two slits of eyes. "Don't be silly, child," she said. "You'll soon be Thomas's wife and it's nice to know that the doctor's friends want to be nice to you."

Grace had never told her mother anything of the snubs she had received from Thomas's "friends." Her mother had been in the habit of referring to these people as "the doctor's friends", but Grace had long since realized that Dr Strether could never have a friend amongst them. He wasn't their sort, their interests were not his, he went about living his life in his own iconoclastic fashion and they would doubtless long ago have dropped him were it not for the fact that he had a wide reputation as a scientist and was the friend of famous men. Grace furthermore knew that all the professors and bigwigs with their wives resented the idea of Dr Strether marrying her, but she did not mind because she was deeply in love with him, not because he was a great man, but simply for himself; and Dr Strether did not care what his *confrères* and others thought: he was doing what he was wanting to do and there was an end of it.

"Thomas will be surprised when he gets back from St Lucia to hear of this tea affair," Grace said.

"The doctor in St Lucia?" Mrs Lee Hong asked. "When did he go, enh?"

"He left the day before yesterday to visit the branch station there."

"But why didn't you tell me, child?" Grace did not reply.

"You're always hiding things from me. Why didn't you tell me, enh?" Grace remained silent and Mrs Lee Hong walked off, mumbling that she hoped "the silly girl" would go to the tea-party and enjoy herself.

All that morning Grace sat in her room and pondered the invitation, saying this minute that she would go and the next, her timidity getting the better of her, deciding not to go. She couldn't get out of her mind the cold greeting Mrs Stanton-Bellair had given her that morning on the jetty two months ago, and now it came back to her with double force and she couldn't see herself facing the woman again. At last she said to herself that she would go for Thomas's sake. I hope I won't meet anybody there, she thought.

That afternoon she went down to the beauty parlour and had her hair nicely fixed up. She didn't want to let Thomas down in the eyes of Mrs Stanton-Bellair, so she wanted to look as smart as possible, and that night she sat up for a long time discussing with her mother what frock she should wear.

It wasn't a matter of never-see-come-see with Grace, it wasn't as if she had had no genteel training. To the very contrary, her family was considered one of the "best" Chinese families in Port of Spain, they had all been westernized in habits through two generations of living in the island, and Grace's father was respected by everybody as being an upright, well-to-do business man; and wasn't he president of the Chinese club and consul for China? And Grace had done a lot of entertaining among her own people, so she knew what was what when it came to any sort of social activity. It was just simply that she felt out of place when in the midst of people who made it plain to her that she was not one of them, that she was outside their pale. And she had kept away. True enough, she had met one or two English people at Dr Strether's bungalow whom she liked. The Mollsons, for instance. When the Mollsons had first arrived in the island – Dr Mollson had come out to the Imperial College of Agriculture – Dr Strether had shown them a great deal of hospitality, and on all such occasions Grace had acted as hostess to them and they had been very nice to her. It was some time since she had seen them, but she felt that they were her friends and that she could always depend on them. They'd even got to calling each other by their Christian names. Mollson was Thomas's friend. Whenever they met, they talked about literature and world politics, especially about Soviet Russia, and music, and sometimes about genetics, their particular branch of scientific research.

The next afternoon Grace looked very pretty in her flowered frock and flowered hat to match, but her skin was so pale that Mrs Lee Hong said:

"Put a little rouge on your cheeks, my child."

"I don't like rouge, Ma. You know I've never used . . ."

"Don't be silly, girl. Put some on before you go. This is a special occasion."

Grace went into her room and put some rouge on her cheeks.

"How are you going up?" Mrs Lee Hong asked. The Stanton-Bellairs lived at St Augustine, a village twelve miles out of town. That was where the Cotton Research Station was, and also the Imperial College of Agriculture.

"By bus, of course," Grace said.

"Nothing of the kind, child. Your father has gone off to the country for the day with the car, so you must take a taxi."

"But why, Ma?"

"Don't be silly, child. How will it look with you arriving there by bus, enh?" and Mrs Lee Hong went to the phone and Grace overheard her saying: "And send me the nicest taxi you've got, please."

Grace felt very timid on the way up, and now that the moment was drawing near for her to face Mrs Stanton-Bellair once again, she didn't know how she would manage it. She kept searching her mind for things to say and kept thinking: I hope no one else is there.

Her hands were like ice when she greeted them.

It was a fine afternoon and the tea table was spread on the verandah at the back of the house. Grace didn't think anything about being entertained at the back of the house; she assumed that her hostess had been in the habit of entertaining her friends there because of the beautiful back lawn and the mountains burning with sunlight in the distance. A cool breeze blew through the verandah and the semps and keskidees were singing in the fruit trees that grew in a corner of the lawn. Everything was quiet and peaceful and green, and gradually Grace settled down comfortably, particularly after Mrs Stanton-Bellair was so kind as to insist on her taking off her hat. That made her feel more at home.

"Have you had news of Dr Strether?" the hostess asked.

"Oh no, there isn't time yet," Grace said.

"And when are you getting married, dear?"

"I . . . I really don't know. I think next year." Grace felt a bit embarrassed and decided that she was just being silly and childish.

"You'll be living in the bungalow, of course?" Mrs Stanton-Bellair asked with a sweet smile.

"Oh yes. At least, I think so."

"That'll be nice. It's lovely around here. When it's hot in town, it's delightfully cool here."

There was a silence broken only by the bird-songs and the breeze making a sibilant sound through the fruit trees.

"Don't you feel peculiar marrying a man not . . . well, not of your own race?" Mrs Stanton-Bellair asked in a kind voice.

"Oh no, I love him," Grace said simply. "I suppose that's all that matters, isn't it?"

"Quite, quite," Mrs Stanton-Bellair said, disarmed by Grace's naive expression and frank look.

"Dr Strether is a fine man," the host said, gazing out at the mountains.

Grace showed her gratitude by giving him one of her sweetest smiles.

"Have you many friends?" Mrs Stanton-Bellair asked.

"Lots," Grace said.

"Yes, he's a very fine fellow," the doctor said again, still gazing out at the mountains. "He's one of the finest geneticists in the British Empire, if not in the whole world. A very important man to science. *Very* important."

"Do you play tennis?" Mrs Stanton-Bellair asked before Grace had time to acknowledge her gratitude to her host.

"Nearly every day. Our club . . ."

"You have a club, eh?"

"I should like to tell you, Miss Lee Hong, that the Chinese as a community are very highly respected in the island," Dr Stanton-Bellair said, shifting his gaze from the mountains to the frail girl seated before him.

"Thank you, Doctor." Then to her hostess: "Yes, we have a club in town."

"Isn't your father the president of it and also consul for China, Miss Lee Hong?" the doctor asked.

Grace, for some unaccountable reason, felt shy and did not reply.

"Really! How interesting!" the doctor's wife said. "And I thought that the Chinese owned most of the retail shops in the island."

"So do the English in England," the doctor said. "Indeed, wasn't it Napoleon who called us a nation of shopkeepers?"

Mrs Stanton-Bellair gave her husband a quick, angry look, but said nothing. The doctor shifted his gaze back to the mountains, and after that the talk went along pleasantly between Grace and her hostess, the doctor every now and then adding something. Grace's timidity and shyness were leaving her more and more, she was actually warming towards Mrs Stanton-Bellair and was beginning to think that perhaps, after all, she had misjudged her in the past. Never again would she be so unkind as to judge anyone at a first meeting.

Then the front door bell rang.

Mrs Stanton-Bellair stirred uneasily in her chair.

"I wonder who that can be?" she said to her husband.

The coloured maid, all spick and span in blue dress, white apron and white cap, came in to announce Mrs Burne-Jones calling.

Mrs Stanton-Bellair looked quickly across the table at her husband. "Go out to her," she said, and her look said the rest.

The doctor rose quietly and went out of the room.

"Come, my dear," Mrs Stanton-Bellair said to Grace as soon as her husband was out of the room. "Perhaps you feel like a wash, eh?" and without waiting for a reply she took the girl by the arm and led her into the bathroom. "Make yourself at home," Mrs Stanton-Bellair said. "Here's a clean towel and there's the soap, my dear." She bolted the door silently from the outside as she left.

It was exactly as she had suspected; the doctor had brought Mrs Burne-Jones into the back verandah, and she said to herself that it was a very good thing she had thought of that before, in fact, just in time. The doctor kept looking at his wife as if he wanted to ask her a question, but she did not give him a chance; she kept up a flow of small talk with Mrs Burne-Jones.

"But my dear Doreen," Mrs Burne-Jones said after a while, seeing a third cup on the tea table, "why didn't you tell me that you had company to tea? I . . ."

"Not at all," Doreen said, casting a quick glance at her husband across the table. "That's the doctor's queer habit, my dear Mrs Burne-Jones. If he has three cups of tea, there must be three separate cups for him. Amusing, what?"

The ladies laughed and Mrs Burne-Jones said that that was a sure sign that the function of tea was never intended for men, and they laughed again. Dr Stanton-Bellair gazed out at the mountains without the trace of a smile on his face.

Mrs Burne-Jones rose soon after and said that she must be going as she had three other calls to make.

"It's so nice," she added, "to call on people whom you like, people whose company you enjoy. But ah, my dear, when they are people you don't like . . ." and she raised her eyes and shook her head.

"Whom are you calling on next?" Doreen asked banteringly,

"Please, please don't remind me of it!"

"Yes, our social behaviour is somewhat hypocritical," Dr Stanton-Bellair said acidly.

"Tut-tut!" and Mrs Burne-Jones, no doubt thinking the remark amusing, laughed.

As soon as the visitor had left, Mrs Stanton-Bellair hurried in to release her prisoner.

"You must think it unpardonably rude of me to have bolted you in like this," she said. "I don't know how I could have done such a thing. Force of habit, I daresay."

Grace said nothing. She didn't know what to say, she didn't know what to think. She felt utterly miserable and yet at the same time she experienced a sense of relief in not having had to meet Mrs Burne-Jones. She felt as if she would burst into tears at any minute and forced them back with all her little strength. She couldn't even listen to what her hostess was saying, she just sat there sipping her tea and dreading that she would make a fool of herself.

The doctor gazed out at the mountains with a hard expression in his eyes and the birds sang in the fruit trees.

"Won't you have another cup of tea?"

"No thanks," Grace said, the direct question rousing her.

"But you must, my dear! Do!"

"All right," Grace said.

And as she sipped her tea, she made up her mind to leave as soon as they rose from the table. But when the time arrived for her to leave she couldn't bring herself to it, as she thought it would be such discourteous treatment of her host and hostess, so she sat on listening to Mrs Stanton-Bellair talking at nineteen to the dozen. Her composure returned little by little and she even began to think that perhaps, after all, Mrs Stanton-Bellair was telling the truth when she said that force of habit had been responsible for bolting the bathroom door, when the front door bell rang again.

The sound startled Grace and she felt a little panicky. She felt like jumping up from her seat and running out of the bungalow and away from it as fast as her legs would carry her. Instead, she sat stiffly in her chair, every nerve taut, her fingers going cold and her heart beating for all it was worth.

The maid appeared and announced Mrs Mollson calling. The sound of the name Mollson acted on Grace's perturbation as an aspirin acts on a headache, for immediately she felt relieved, and was actually glad that she would be seeing her old friend again.

Mrs Stanton-Bellair did not move so the doctor rose, very slowly, trying to catch his wife's eye, and walked just as slowly out of the room.

"I can see you've got good taste," Mrs Stanton-Bellair said to Grace when they were alone. She rose from her chair. "Come with me, Miss Lee Hong, and have a look at this dress. See how you like it."

Grace followed her hostess through a corridor and into a large bed room and there Mrs Stanton-Bellair opened a wardrobe and took off from its hanger a dress which she spread out on the bed.

"Now the truth, my dear," she said. "Do you like it, or don't you? Dr Stanton-Bellair made me a present of it for my birthday."

Grace was about to reply, was about to say that although she did not think that she herself had good taste, yet anyone could see . . . when Mrs Stanton-

Bellair, excusing herself and murmuring that she would be back in a moment, went out of the room, closing the door after her.

Grace stood by the bed, staring at the closed door. Every limb of her body stiffened and her first impulse was to be very angry, but in a flash that passed away and a sense of inferiority, of utter helplessness took its place, and she felt alone in a very huge world. For the next ten minutes she didn't know what she did, feeling ever so small and miserable, and she wanted to cry, but tried her best not to.

When Mrs Stanton-Bellair returned to the room she found Grace sitting on the bed, staring blankly before her. As soon as Grace saw her, for some unaccountable reason hate suddenly flared up within her, hate for this fair, self-possessed English woman and everything around her.

"I'm so sorry, Miss Lee Hong . . ." but as soon as Mrs Stanton-Bellair saw the girl's face, so pathetic and pale, she stopped.

"Why, Miss Lee Hong, what's the matter? Why are you crying? Has anything hurt you, my dear?"

Grace stood up beside the bed and stared at the English woman for at least a minute without saying a word. She felt the blood leaving her head and rushing down to her feet, just as if she was going to faint. It was this queer sensation that made her walk out of the room, hurry past Dr Stanton-Bellair sitting in the back verandah and out the back door, through the passage way and into the street. Hatless and almost sobbing, she went down the street with short quick steps.

The doctor came running after her and calling out to her, but she broke into a run too, and the doctor, realizing how ridiculous it was for him, an English professor of physiology, to be seen running along the street in pursuit of a well-dressed Chinese girl, stopped and went back quickly to the bungalow.

Boodhoo

It was an afternoon in June and the rains had arrived a month before. Everywhere the island was green. The ladies at Mrs Lawrence's teaparty had no use for their fans, for a cool breeze blew in at the open windows of the bungalow. Mrs Lawrence remarked:

"It's a delightfully cool afternoon." All the other ladies acquiesced in their different ways: Mrs Hornby, fat and regal, nodded her head heavily; Mrs O'Halleran, in the act of sipping her tea, raised her eyebrows; Molly, Mrs O'Halleran's pretty daughter, murmured "yes" in chorus with the others.

The ladies gossiped desultorily of this and that, daintily munching light cakes and as daintily sipping their tea from exquisitely patterned china cups. Each was on her most important behaviour, for their hostess was a recent arrival in Trinidad.

"And how do you like the island?" Mrs Hornby asked.

"I don't quite know yet," Mrs Lawrence replied.

"Of course, it will take you some time to become acclimatized," ventured Mrs Lovelace, a delicate-looking creature with large eyes. "It took me a long time to accustom myself to the strange surroundings. The blacks and coolies I haven't even as yet got to know. They're a queer lot," and she turned up her pretty nose.

Mrs Hornby smiled voluminously. "My motto has always been, my dear

Mrs Lawrence, firmness. Be firm with them and they are like domesticated animals. No trouble at all . . ." She didn't add, however, that she changed her maids and cooks as often as there are months in the year. Mrs Lovelace knew that, but said nothing. To the accompaniment of clinking forks the talk continued.

Without the slightest warning, Mrs Hornby screamed and rose from the table, throwing one of the ornate china cups onto the floor. It smashed. The whole party rose, knocking their chairs over in the excitement, and a loud commotion followed.

"That wretched thing!" shouted Mrs Hornby, her ponderous arm raised with the index finger pointing in the direction of the partition facing her. "That wretched thing!" They all looked and saw a cockroach, waving its antennae excitedly. Mrs O'Halleran resumed her seat with a supercilious expression. "I'm not in the least afraid of roaches," she said. "They're harmless things." But Mrs Hornby would not sit until her hostess had called the maid to brush it away with a broom. The maid brushed it straight on the table, whereupon Mrs O'Halleran brought down her hand upon it violently. The roach popped with a sharp report, spilling its abdominal contents over a large area of the table cloth. Mrs O'Halleran was very disturbed. She offered profuse apologies, adding: "How silly of me not to have foreseen this!" Mrs Lawrence reassured her with quiet words and a smiling countenance.

The tea things were cleared away and the ladies were seated in the verandah, when Mrs Hornby remarked with a troubled look:

"I'm sorry I broke that cup. The natives here say it brings bad luck."

"Nonsense!" exclaimed Mrs O'Halleran. "And superstitious rot!"

"I don't know," Mrs Hornby said mysteriously.

"Exactly! And because you don't know you give it an unfavourable interpretation." But Mrs Hornby repeated "I don't know," and there the matter ended.

Mrs Lawrence offered cigarettes around and they were all smoking in a moment, except Mrs Lawrence. Someone asked:

"Aren't you smoking?"

"No. I have never smoked in my life. I don't like it."

"How do you know you don't like it if you've never tried it?" said Molly. Molly had just turned nineteen and Mrs Lawrence was about her age.

"I should say, I don't like to see women smoking." Realizing the *faux pas* she had committed, she hastened with: "Not that I see anything wrong with it."

"My dear Mrs Lawrence," Mrs Hornby said authoritatively, "you'll have to smoke if you stay in this island very long." Turning to the others: "You remember Eileen Smitherson?" she said. "She also thought she would never smoke," she explained to Mrs Lawrence. "She soon did it, however, and other things," she added, with the air of one who has a story to tell.

"Poor girl!" someone said. "I pity her. She was severely provoked."

"That's the lot of most of us in the tropics." It was Mrs O'Halleran speaking. "We are all provoked, but we don't all succumb to the provocation."

Mrs Lawrence did not understand, and said so.

"Her husband – our husbands," Mrs Hornby said sententiously.

"Your husbands?" Mrs Lawrence was yet more puzzled.

"Well, the tropics don't make ideal husbands of the men who have lived in their midst for any length of time. The climate, I suppose."

"Nonsense!" Mrs O'Halleran heatedly exclaimed. "All men have something evil in their natures."

"I agree," Mrs Hornby said, "but it takes the tropics to bring out the evil that is in them. In England it very seldom happens."

"England is a large country. This is a very small community. Evil doings can be lost in large countries, but they have nowhere to hide themselves in small islands like this." That was Mrs O'Halleran's final word on the matter.

The ladies stayed on until the darkness came down, when with a raucous sounding of horns, they drove away in their cars. Then the fireflies came out and sprinkled the environs of the bungalow with tiny dots of light, ceaselessly moving. It was all very strange to Minnie Lawrence, standing in the verandah of the bungalow. She heard the croaking of the frogs. It was a soothing, melancholy noise they made in the distance, but to her an ominous one. She had arrived in the island only a month before, and felt now as though she had been borne away on one of the magic carpets of the olden stories and dropped here in her sleep . . .

She heard a step on the gravel path that led from the street to the portico of the verandah. In the dusk she could see a vague form approaching.

"That you, Henry?" she called out. There was no answer, and she recognized Boodhoo, the half-caste boy. Boodhoo was a sort of factotum in the house, doing any odd job at any odd time. To her he was strange. Although he wore long trousers, she thought him young. He seemed to be a year or two

24

younger than she was. She could never tell whether she liked him or not. He seldom said anything in her presence, though on several occasions she had heard Henry talking with him in Hindoostani. She did not understand a word of the language. When she first saw him she was struck by his beauty. Turning to her husband, she had asked:

"Who is that young man?"

"That darkish boy, dear?"

"Yes."

"General man about the house. You'll find him very useful."

"But what is he?"

"Oh, Indian I suppose, with a drop of European blood. At least, I imagine so, for he's rather fair."

"European blood?" She was surprised and in a subtle way hurt.

"Well, yes," he replied, with a slight hesitation. Then she had asked:

"But does that often happen out here, Henry?"

"What dear?" he had asked, as though he had forgotten what they were talking about.

"Oh, that sort of thing," and she waved her hand to indicate Boodhoo.

"Well, yes," he replied, with a slight halt between the two words.

As she saw Boodhoo now walking past the bungalow to the back yard, she remembered what her guests had been talking about. A slight frown spread over her pretty face. It was unimaginable to her that white men, men of her blood, should be so filthy as to take to themselves these Indian women. And to have children by them! The thought nauseated her.

She heard another step coming up the gravel path. From the darkness emerged her husband's huge form. He ran up the short flight of steps and took her in his arms, bending forward to kiss her affectionately on the lips.

"I'm so glad you've come, Henry."

"Why, what's the matter, little girl? Your hands are cold."

"I don't know. A vague fear."

"What's frightened you?"

"Nothing at all."

He laughed her fear away. "The darkness eh, little girl? Why don't you put the light on?"

She didn't know why. He switched it on, the power supplied by a Delco plant housed a good way from the bungalow that its hum might not be disturbing.

"Hungry?" he asked, looking with pride at her splendid figure.

"Not very." And then she said pettishly: "You haven't even remembered to ask me about my tea, my first tea!"

"Phew!" he whistled through his teeth. "Clean forgot. And how did it come off, dear?" He held her at arms' length from him.

"Too late now. I shan't tell you."

He smoothed away her mock anger with kisses and she told him all.

"Glorious!" he said. "Glorious! You've made a hit, I'm sure, with those charming ladies."

"And they told me quite a lot of things about you." He looked down at her with a queer suddenness. She was smiling up at him. He smiled back.

"Nice things, dear?"

"Horrid things. At least, horrid innuendoes about all the European husbands in the island."

He laughed outright. "Nasty old ladies!" he said, shrugging his shoulders.

They both laughed. Then he went indoors to wash and change for dinner. She heard the splash of the water as he sluiced his face over the basin. She listened to his heavy steps as he moved about the room, whistling. Although he was twenty years older than she was, she often felt that he was as young as she. There was a delightful boyishness about him; and that, perhaps, added to his huge handsomeness, had persuaded her to accept his offer of marriage six months ago. She had never met him before that. He was home on furlough at the time. When he proposed she was quite frank with him, telling him that she did not care for him in that way, and even now it was difficult for her to analyse her feelings. Sometimes she thought she loved him; at other times an apathy came over her that distressed her considerably. And, too, she realized that her love of adventure had weighed heavily in favour of her marrying him. She could never settle herself down to a fixed state of things. She hankered after change. That had come naturally enough to her, for her father, as a bachelor, had travelled the world over until the fortune inherited from an Australian uncle had dwindled down to its last penny. When Henry came along, sunburnt, boisterous, she saw in him a means of escape. The prospect of going out to the West Indies enthralled her. He told her he was a planter, living in the country districts of one of the islands. That was still more inveigling, and she had been searching up records of Trinidad ever since she had met him. From them she learnt that it was cosmopolitan, very cosmopolitan. How fascinating to be in the midst of Chinese and Indians and Negroes, and crosses between them all! And where the cane and cocoa and coconuts grew! And where the despicable cold never strayed even for one day in the year!

In a few minutes he reappeared, fresh and smiling. "Ready, dear?" he asked. He took his pipe out, filled it, then lit it. Someone was walking noisily across the gravel path. "Who's that?" he shouted.

"I, sahib."

She looked up from the book she was reading. "Who?" she asked.

"Boodhoo."

She looked down again at the book. Abruptly she said:

"How long have you had him, Henry?"

He thought for a moment. "Several years, dear."

"Is he honest?"

"Why should you ask me that?"

"I don't know. But is he?"

"Perfectly."

"You see, I leave my things about rather carelessly."

"I've noticed that, dear. He won't touch them."

There was another silence. Then: "You must like the boy to have kept him so long, Henry?"

"Oh, I do, dear," he answered rather enthusiastically. "He's a good sort of fellow, very willing."

"Do you know his father?"

He did not reply immediately. "I think he's dead. I never knew him."

"And his mother?"

"Come, dear! You're making me jealous now!" he chaffed her. "He's a handsome boy, you know."

She blushed deeply. He could not notice it from where he sat.

The fireflies were gambolling in the night. There were a thousand stilly noises outside. A bird broke into a weird succession of contralto calls.

"What bird's that?" she asked.

"The natives call it the poor-me-one."

"What a queer name!"

"Isn't it, dear?" and he smiled at her.

"Perhaps it's calling for its mate," she suggested.

He glanced at her roguishly. "Naughty bird!" he remarked. They both laughed loudly. Soon after, they went to bed, and as he was tired he fell asleep immediately.

The following morning she busied herself about the house. Henry had already gone out into the fields. Every morning he left at sunrise. Minnie did not know that at crop season he would sometimes not return until late at night. At times he varied his hours, especially when grinding was in full swing. He would come in at six o'clock, bathe, have a quick dinner, and be out by seven, not to return till the early hours of the morning. She had seen very little of him for the month she had been on the estate. She wondered if this would continue throughout the year. Two days ago she had asked him.

"Yes, Min, I'm afraid it will. I'm a busy man. A very busy man."

She grew sulky. "Do you miss me a lot?" he asked, taking her in his arms.

She did not speak. She laid her head on his broad chest and shivered with a vague feeling of uneasiness. Though small, her figure, full, almost voluptuous, gave you the impression that she was full of life. Henry always arrived home in the evenings, dead-tired. He would fall asleep as soon as he rested his head on the pillow. He was so big and so childish, she thought. And yet, spiritually as well as physically, he was aloof from her. There was something in him which she could not understand; and that lack of understanding on her part had at odd moments told her that she did not love him. Before coming out to the island with him she had thought him very simple, a huge boy with open, boyish ideas; here, in these strange surroundings, she failed to understand him.

She moved about the bedroom, attending to diverse things. She was sadly amused when first she had seen the state of the room. Strands of cobweb straggled around the corners of the ceiling and partitions. There were several pictures of nude women hanging from the walls. Incongruously they fitted in with what little she knew of him then, and she taunted him about it one day. He smiled. She thought that he smiled only with his lips, for his blue eyes were expressionless.

"Shall I take them down, dear?" She didn't want them taken down; she only wanted to hear what he would say.

"Do as you like, Min. The house is yours, my poor gift to you. I put them up in my young days and forgot all about them."

"Your young days!" She noticed how he laughed to conceal his confusion. "You naughty boy!" she said. Then he laughed the laugh she knew so well.

She took all the pictures down, dusted them, and put them back exactly as they had been. She experienced great joy in making the house clean and habitable. Every evening now vases of coralita and exotic flowers greeted his tired eyes, and he showed his appreciation by telling her their names.

"That great bloom with the brown heart is the sunflower, dear."

"Oh, I know."

"Who told my little girl?"

"I asked Boodhoo one morning." He said nothing to that, but continued his instruction in names.

As the day wore on, the sky became overcast with a blanket of dull grey cloud, and the rain began to fall. It fell on the galvanized roof with a monotonous noise that depressed her. If only she had someone to talk to, she thought, for her household did not lend itself to communicativeness. There was Martha, her obese Barbadian cook, who was always in the kitchen, and the kitchen stood away from the bungalow. Occasionally she would hear her quarrelling with one of the Indian women skulking around the yard. It amused her to hear this bulky Negress vituperative with such exclamations as: "You nasty coolie woman!" She would shout such abuses out in a tone of voice that unmistakably said that the Indian woman was her inferior. Her maid was a mulattress. She called herself Constancia. One day she told Minnie that her great-grandfather was a Spaniard, not from Venezuela, but from Spain. She, too, was taciturn; in fact, sulky. And then there was Boodhoo. Towards him she felt entirely different. Martha and Constance (she preferred the abbreviated form of the name) simply did not matter. But Boodhoo, in an undefinable sort of way, mattered, for he interested her. His skin was of a coffee shade. His eyes were large and almond-shaped. Once or twice she caught them regarding her with a distressing intensity. She couldn't be sure at the time, but she thought she detected in their depths – they were deeply set – passion and longing. That had disturbed her. She blushed very easily and the colour mounted to her cheeks then. And since Henry had told her there was European blood in his veins her interest in him had increased. She had heard her father talk of such half-castes when she was a child. Little did she think then that she would one day be living in close proximity to one of them. Boodhoo occupied a room in the yard which she visited once, and found scrupulously clean. She did not know how she felt exactly about the pictures of nude women hanging from his walls. Perhaps Henry had given them to him.

For the balance of the day it rained. Towards afternoon the wind rose. It hurled itself with loud gusts of moaning against the bungalow. It whistled plaintively through the jalousies of the Demerara windows. She was sitting in the drawing-room, sewing. In one corner stood slantwise a piano. She was sorry now she had never learnt to play. Her mother had been too poor to give her that accomplishment, for her father had died when she was a girl of ten, leaving her mother and herself in want. The room was cosily furnished in a soothing colour-scheme of green. The bungalow faced the north. Through the glass-fronted doors she could just make out the outlines of the mountains shrouded in rain. She felt very lonely and very unhappy. Constancia had gone to town that day to see her people. Once a month Minnie was supposed to let her go, and this was the first time she had gone. She knew Boodhoo was on the back steps, squatted there, for she had seen him as she was coming into the drawing-room with her work. She heard thunder and it frightened her. Impulsively she called the half-caste boy.

"Yes, Memsahib?" His voice startled her. She looked up and saw him framed by the doorway. She was ashamed she had called him, and she could find nothing to say.

"Was that thunder, Boodhoo?"

"Yes, Memsahib." Another peal shook the bungalow, a long, low rumbling. She shivered. He was not looking at her, but on the green-carpeted floor.

"I'm afraid of thunder, Boodhoo." He let his eyes rest on her for a moment, but he did not speak. His silence was making her uncomfortable. She felt she must say something.

"Does it often rain like this?"

"This is the rainy season, Memsahib." He spoke English in the sing-song fashion of the Creole. He wore a rumpled pair of khaki trousers and a merino, and his hair was tousled about his head in a black, curly mass. A pair of multicoloured alpargatas adorned his small feet. She was not looking at him, but on the green-carpeted floor. Her work lay in her lap. The thunder continued its intermittent growling.

"Were you born here, Boodhoo?" He raised his head and looked at her. His gaze burned into her, and she flushed a deep red.

"Yes, Memsahib."

"On this estate?"

"I think so, Memsahib."

"Is your mother alive?"

"Yes, Memsahib."

She was glad she had called him for his presence was comforting.

"Where is she?"

"In Peñal."

"Peñal? Where is that?"

"Far from here. To the south," and he waved his arm as an indication of the direction.

"But why don't you live with her?"

"She's married, Memsahib."

"To your father?"

He did not answer. She repeated the question.

"No, Memsahib." His voice, she thought, was harsh.

"Where is your father?" She was enjoying this with a dark touch of curiosity.

Again Boodhoo did not answer. She repeated the question.

"I don't know, Memsahib."

She remembered what Henry had told her; what Mrs Hornby had said at tea the afternoon before. A long pause followed. She felt his gaze on her but dared not look up.

Then he did a strange thing. He advanced towards her quickly. Before she could realize what he was doing, he had placed his hand on her knee. She became petrified, for she saw a scorpion advancing up her muslin dress. His hand barred its way, and she made an attempt to move him but was helpless with her fear. The insect crawled on to his hand and he rose with it there. At any minute she expected to hear him scream out with the pain of its sting, but he walked very calmly to the door, shook the scorpion from his hand, and trod on it. It was some seconds before she spoke.

"Was that a scorpion, Boodhoo?"

"Yes, Memsahib. In the rainy season they come out."

"But aren't you afraid of them?"

He chuckled. "No, Memsahib. They can't sting me, but they can sting you."

"Why can't they sting you?"

"Because they can't, Memsahib. A Spanish man prayed over me once long ago." He had moved forward from the door and now stood over her, and each time she looked up she found his eyes on her. They seemed in her fancy like two pieces of red-hot coal. She was, however, growing accustomed to him.

"You probably saved my life, Boodhoo." She gave him one of her prettiest smiles.

"Yes, Memsahib."

A flash of lightning lit up the obscurity of the room. Minnie put her hands over her eyes. Lightning had always made her afraid; and now in the tropics, about which she had heard tales of such destructive storms – of thunder that hurled bolts to the earth; of winds that tore up everything in their wild stampede; of lightning that killed without any warning – she was more frightened than ever. A peal of thunder detonated and she thought it sounded in the room, just above her. She raised scared eyes to Boodhoo.

"You are afraid, Memsahib?" There was a shade of concern in his voice. His arms were folded across his chest.

"Yes, Boodhoo." She did not feel ashamed of the confession. Somehow or the other she could not regard him as a servant, a half-caste, now, for he was undisturbed in the midst of this elemental noise, a haven where she would find protection if she needed it.

"Thunder and lightning will do you nothing," he remarked.

"Do you think so, Boodhoo?" She had become like a child, helpless with her fear.

"I know so," he answered. "And I am here."

She raised her eyes to his. A wave of emotion swept over her.

"It is good of you to say that," she murmured.

For an instant they looked at each other. Then he bent down, fiercely put his arms around her and kissed her on the mouth. She lay passive in his embrace. The thunder bellowed again. She clung to him wildly.

Henry arrived at seven o'clock, dripping. She heard him whistling as he clattered across the dining room. He was a noisy fellow, and she liked him for his boisterousness, especially out here where everything was sinister in its sounds and silences. He came into the bedroom and found her lying across the bed. At first he thought she was asleep and abruptly ceased his whistling. Approaching the bed quietly, he leant over her and saw her eyes wide open. Then he switched the light on, lifted her from the bed, stood her on her feet and kissed her cold lips. With the quick perception of a man in love, he sensed something wrong.

"Why, what's it dear? You look pale and haggard."

"Headache." That was all she could say.

"Come, darling, we'll put that right in a minute," he said cheerily. "I thought it was much worse than that." He placed her affectionately on the bed and fussed around the room, whistling. Then he came to her.

"Take this," she heard him saying. "Five grains of aspirin, and in an hour you'll be your old self again." She swallowed the pill with a gulp of water.

That night Henry was more cheerful than ever, and all through their simple two-course dinner he chatted. He told her how there very nearly was a tragedy on the estate that day. Panalal – she knew Panalal? No, she didn't. Well, Panalal had long been suspecting his wife of infidelity. Her heart suddenly beat wildly. She dared not look at her husband. And Panalal had his suspicions verified today. Fortunately, the discovery was made in daylight, otherwise Mulemeah, Panalal's wife, would have been dead tonight, chopped with a cutlass. She shuddered. Oh yes, the Indians made no mistake about unfaithful wives! They were merciless when it came to that. It took six men to hold Panalal from his murder. Panalal was a hideous devil to see at that time – and he laughed.

"D'you know, there's humour in everything if only we would look for it," he was saying. "There was that man, in a towering rage, ready to commit the last word in human misdeeds. And for what? For a woman who is probably not worth her weight in brass! It's completely ludicrous!" His laugh was like a torment to her.

At last they rose. He was very solicitous over her indisposition, putting his arm around her waist and leading her to the verandah.

"And what did my little girl do all day, eh?" They were in darkness for Henry had not switched on the light. The weather had cleared somewhat, though the wind, like a drunken man, staggered against the bungalow every now and again with a groaning sound. A few stars twinkled. An army of frogs croaked. She was seated on his lap, nestling in the hollow of his arms.

"I was so afraid of the storm!"

"Storm?" He laughed outright.

She came to the matter on her mind. "You know, Henry, you shouldn't leave me all day like that. I hate to be alone. It frightens me, especially here where . . ." She paused.

"What is it, dear? Come, tell me," he urged.

"Oh, you know." His arms tightened around her.

"Aren't you happy, Min?"

"Oh yes, yes," she said quickly. "Perfectly. But here everything is strange, unfamiliar. What you told me at dinner, for instance. Supposing that had happened here?"

"But it can't, dear. The estate's barracks are nowhere near your little bungalow."

"I don't mean that exactly." She hesitated.

"Then what do you mean, Min?"

"Oh, you can't understand, Henry!" She rose pettishly and began to cry. He was on his feet in a moment, holding her to him.

"Haven't you grown to love me as yet, Min?" he asked tenderly.

"Oh yes, I have." At any other time she would have told the truth, but now the truth scared her. He was silent for a while, one hand patting her head. Then he asked, in a cold voice:

"Has anyone been telling you anything?"

"Oh no!" She thought she heard him sigh, but immediately he became bright. It was impossible to be serious with him for any length of time.

"Come, dear; let's sit. Your headache has disturbed you." He drew her gently to the chair. "You aren't accustomed to your new surroundings. It will take some time for you to become accustomed to them. And then everything will be all right." He chatted merrily along. But she was not listening to him so much as to the wind, like a drunken man, staggering against the bungalow with a groaning sound. She heard, too, the water dripping monotonously from the eaves to the concrete gutter below. Each drip was like a word of warning. That night she could not sleep.

A week passed by. The fresh colour had gone from Minnie's cheeks and they were hollow. Dark rings were gathering under her eyes, but if anything she was prettier, for her English face had taken on a new significance in its subtle change. Henry seemed not to notice anything wrong, for she tried to be bright when he was in the bungalow. He still left early in the morning, and sometimes did not come in to lunch, returning after nightfall. As usual, he came in with fatigue written on his face, went to bed and fell asleep immediately.

She had been trying to avoid Boodhoo; but how could she when he was always hovering about the bungalow: in the garden, on the steps, silent, enigmatical? She had not once looked his way for the week, but she felt his eyes on her every time she passed him. A cold shiver would run down her spine; her heart would hasten its beating; her eyes would grow dim.

It was Saturday and the mail had come. Boodhoo had gone down to the village a mile or so away and had fetched it for her. As he handed it to her, her eyes met his. All power of motion went from her for a moment. Then she took the mail, mechanically, and went indoors. She read her mother's letter and realized she had not understood a sentence, a word of it. She re-read it, attempting to concentrate on its meaning. Occasionally she would discover

34

her thoughts wandering, and would have to scan over again certain passages of it. She was surprised to find what little interest she was taking in it, and her mother had meant so much to her at one time! It surprised and pained her, for she loved her mother. Her other letters were left unopened on the wickerwork table before which she stood in the bedroom. They would have to wait, for now she was too upset to try to read them.

It was about three o'clock in the afternoon and the day was bright with a sultry heat. The heat was a portent of rain. A cicada was shrieking from a large mango tree that grew in the yard, shrieking for rain, as the natives say. The shrieks made her ears buzz and her head dizzy.

She had finished reading her mother's letter and was standing. She wore a long yellow gown, beneath which the handsome, tempting contours of her body showed. The features of her face expressed no feeling. No grief, no joy, no hope lurked in her dark eyes. So a river, when it is dried up in the dry season, expresses nothing.

Then she heard someone talking in a loud voice in the yard. It was a woman's voice and it sounded angry. She recognized it as neither Martha's nor Constancia's and the words were in a foreign language of which she understood nothing. Going through a door that led to a back room, she saw through the window a strange Indian woman in the yard. She was gesticulating wildly to the accompaniment of each wrathful ejaculation. Constancia and Martha were standing by, obviously interested in the commotion. She wondered who the woman was and whom she could be quarrelling with. She saw Boodhoo appear suddenly from his room. He shouted something at the woman which only seemed to make her more irate. Then Minnie realized that the woman's object of abuse (it could be nothing but abuse, judging from her tone and demeanour) was Boodhoo. He caught sight of Minnie standing at the window and walked back into his room. The woman followed him. An altercation ensued, in which Boodhoo's voice was calm, the woman's high-pitched.

"Stop that rowing!" Minnie cried out. The voices ceased and the woman came into the yard and stared at Minnie with a sullen curiosity, breathing heavily. Minnie called Boodhoo. He appeared at the doorway.

"Who is this woman?" she asked. He did not reply, but stood with his head bent.

"I his mother." the woman said loudly, insolently. Minnie looked at her and saw that she was small and pretty. She was wearing a flagrantly bright orhani and was barefooted.

"His mother! Then why are you making that noise?"

Before the woman could answer, Boodhoo ran up, caught her by the arm and began to pull her firmly from the yard. The woman said something shrilly in English, the words of which she did not catch. Minnie called to Boodhoo, for she did not like the way he was dragging his mother from the yard. He pretended not to hear; and before she could call him again they disappeared round the bend of the bungalow. Martha and Constancia returned to their work. Minnie went back to her room, and there, through some dropped jalousies, she saw Boodhoo remonstrating with his mother at the servants' gate, overspread with a bougainvillea vine in full bloom. They were talking in Hindoostani. A few minutes later the woman went away.

The incident had perturbed her and she determined to find out what had been the reason for it. She went to the back and summoned Boodhoo to her. He came to her with a calmness as though nothing had happened.

"Who was that woman?"

"My mother, Memsahib."

"Your mother? What was she doing here?"

He did not answer, but still on his face was that nonchalant air that told her nothing.

"What was she doing here, Boodhoo?" In trying to be stern her voice betrayed no particular mood.

He answered bitterly: "She came here to make trouble. I wouldn't let her, and she got vexed with me."

"What trouble?" There was an ominous silence. A cock crew in the yard, and another cock answered in the distance, and then another further away, until there was an antiphon of cock-a-doodle-doos in the sultry afternoon air. The keskidees were singing in the mango tree nearby.

"Memsahib, there is nothing to tell. You wouldn't understand."

Perhaps after all it was none of her business; and she thought there was a subdued resentment in Boodhoo's laconic answer. She dismissed him. They had avoided each other's glance for the minute or so of conversation.

Returning to her room, Minnie tried to read her other letters, but found it impossible to understand them. The one she opened was from an old school chum of hers, living in London. Here and there she caught references to a play, a dance, a visit to Brighton. Ordinarily, she would have been excited over the mere mention of these things. Now she was unresponsive, so she took up her sewing and went into the drawing-room with it. She preferred the drawing-room, for there were more windows to it, and hence more light in it. The mechanical action of sewing soothed her unstrung nerves.

Just when the rain began to fall – it was about seven o'clock and night had closed in an hour before – Henry arrived. She heard his horse neigh and went to the front to meet him. He was talking to Boodhoo in the vernacular, and though it was drizzling he was longer than usual. When he *did* come to her she missed the gaiety of his greeting, but gave no further thought to it.

"I'm ravenously hungry, Min," he called out to her from the bedroom, where he was getting cleaned up. She went in to him and found him almost naked.

"Why didn't you come to lunch?"

"Couldn't, dear."

"Did you have anything to eat?"

"Oh yes. One of the men on the estate shot a manicou in the morning."

"A manicou? What's that?"

He smiled at her. "A sort of large rat, dear."

"Rat?" She exclaimed, and shuddered.

He was amused by her repulsion from the word. "I said a *sort* of large rat, dear, not a large rat. It makes delicious eating. We roasted it over a wood-fire. I've brought in a portion of it for our dinner. You must tell me how you like it." Going up to her, the lather of his shaving-soap covering his chin with a white beard, his mood changed.

"Did you miss me, Min?"

"Yes."

"More than ever?"

"More than ever."

"I thought of you quite a lot, dear." He waited, as though expecting her to speak, but she did not speak. He put his arms around her and attempted to kiss her.

"Oo!" she cried, throwing her head back; "the soap!"

He forced her head to his and kissed her mouth, her eyes, her ears. Blotches of lather were left wherever he had kissed her.

"I told you not to do it!" she cried petulantly, and went to the mirror. She could not help laughing at the reflection of her face. He approached to hold her again, switching the light off as he did so. She eluded his grasp, but he ran after her. She flung herself on the bed and he held her there. She felt his hands cold, and in the darkness his eyes gleamed. She surrendered with a passionate embrace, and the wind rose in the bleak night to a melancholy soughing.

At dinner he was merry. She tasted the manicou, but its pungent smokiness was not to her liking.

"It's an acquired taste," he remarked.

After dinner they could not sit in the verandah as the wind was blowing from the north and lashing the rain fiercely on the marble floor. Henry changed into his pyjama suit and she put a gown on over her night-dress. Instead, they sat in the drawing-room with the windows closed. They had sat in silence for a while when she said:

"I've got something to tell you, Henry."

Henry was looking at her, and if she had seen his face at that moment, she would have noticed a change of expression creep over it, like the expression of one expecting danger and not knowing when it will come.

"Yes?" he said interrogatively, with a forced indifference.

"There was a woman in the yard today," she remarked tentatively.

"Oh! Do women never come into the yard?"

"An Indian woman."

"There are several belonging to the estate."

"She didn't belong to the estate."

He joined his fingers before him and they formed the miniature skeleton of a roof. The skeleton of the roof was trembling slightly, as though an earthquake was disturbing it.

"Well? And what did she want? Begging? These women are so fond of begging."

"Oh no. She kicked up a bit of a row. She said she was Boodhoo's mother." He grew ill at ease, shifting his position in the chair.

"I suppose all men must have mothers." It was the first time he had been cynical with her; and she observed, too, that he had dropped his customary terms of endearment. His words fell from his mouth with a staccato incisiveness.

"That's a silly remark, Henry."

"Oh, I'm sorry, Min. Only, I don't quite see the point of your telling me this."

His manner was intimidating. What if he had guessed something? What if Boodhoo, with his native simplicity, had told him? But no, she decided; no man would be as foolish as that, native or not. Assuming a conciliatory demeanour, she was on her guard immediately.

"Come, Henry, we won't quarrel over a coolie woman."

He winced, and then laughed with a wry distortion of his face. In his eyes there was no laughter.

"Would you like me to send Boodhoo away?"

A dull sensation of horror swept over her. "Oh, no, no!" she said, and then grew timid at her vehemence. "Why should you?" she asked, with an innocent modification of her voice.

"Well, I don't know. There would probably be no more women, *Indian*" – he pronounced the word deliberately – "women kicking up rows in the yard. Wouldn't that relieve you of anxiety?" Then he asked, abruptly: "What did she say?"

"Who?"

"The *Indian* woman" – again with the same deliberate pronunciation of the word "Indian".

"Nothing. Only that she was his mother." As an afterthought, she added: "She did shout out something as Boodhoo was dragging her from the yard. I didn't catch it, though."

His massive chest heaved with a deep breath as he settled himself more comfortably into the chair. The miniature skeleton of a roof broke in two.

"Dragging her from the yard?" There was an exultant note in the delivery of the sentence. "He shouldn't do that, and to his mother!"

"That's exactly what I thought and tried to prevent him, but he took no notice of me. He told me afterwards she was trying to make trouble." He was silent, his head bent over his chest, regarding her from upturned eyes. "What trouble could she have been wanting to make?" Again he was silent. "And she grew very angry with Boodhoo."

"I suppose because he wouldn't let her make the trouble."

"Yes. He said so. But what trouble could she have made?"

"Money, I daresay. I know he sends her money." They lapsed into silence, and soon they were chatting of other things, and soon they went to bed.

The following morning – it was Sunday – she rose early. Henry was already up, for she heard him splashing in the bath, singing lightly. He was singing a silly song, one of the latest American syncopated tunes that had taken the island by storm. The rain-clouds had gone the way that all rain-clouds must go after a time, and the sun showed itself on the bedroom floor in even rows of light, like a formation of soldiers seen from the air. It was being reflected through the jalousies. She was soon dressed in a white muslin frock. Very cool she seemed in it and very pretty. The night's rest had given her freshness.

She heard Henry coming. The bungalow shook as he lumbered across the dining-room. He was whistling, as usual.

"Up already, dear?" he greeted her.

"Are you sorry?" she smilingly teased him.

"To the contrary. Awfully glad. D'you know, Min, I can't imagine myself living with a lazy woman." The crude way in which he sometimes expressed himself irritated her. "Fancy having my coffee all alone in the morning! And fancy going out into the fields after kissing the lifeless lips of a sleeping wife!" (That was better.)

"Are you going out this morning?" she ventured, shyly regarding him.

"Yes, dear. On most Sunday mornings I go out." She looked disappointed. "I shall try to be early," he said, affectionately taking her in his arms. He, too, was soon dressed: riding khaki breeches, brown leggings, khaki shirt open at the neck and heavy brown boots.

He ate well with his coffee. She could scarcely eat at this early meal for she was unaccustomed to it. When he had finished he rose noisily, as noisily fetched his sombrero, bade her a tender goodbye, and went out. Looking after him as he swaggered off to his waiting horse, she thought him very handsome.

But this morning he did an unusual thing. He did not mount his horse immediately as he had probably been doing for years. He took the reins from Boodhoo and crooked his finger at him. Boodhoo followed his master as he walked his horse into the road, and Minnie, hastening to the verandah, was just in time to see them disappearing in earnest conversation. Boodhoo did not return until perhaps half-an-hour later. A suspicion entered her head and she called him.

"What was the sahib" – she used the word peculiarly – "saying to you this morning?"

"I am to go away, Memsahib." She caught her breath with a little gasp. They were standing in the shade of the pantry. Martha was in the kitchen. Constancia had gone into the vegetable garden to dig up some sweet potatoes. Minnie had sent her to that task a little before summoning Boodhoo, for she wanted to be alone with him. The Demerara window, though it stuck out, did not allow anyone to see them from the yard.

She went up to him impulsively. "Not that?" she asked.

He stood over her, rigid, gaunt, and his eyes were like two wells down which the sun seldom shines, mysterious, deep. She looked up at him pitifully. Her face held every sort of helplessness as she asked: "Are you going, Boodhoo?"

"The sahib has ordered it. I must go."

"When?"

"Tonight."

They both said nothing for a while. Her heart bumped uncomfortably against her breast and her fingers were ten icicles, and she had no feeling in them. Her cheeks were blanched.

"Do you want to go?"

"No." The monosyllable came from deep down in his chest, painfully.

"Then why go?"

For answer he put his arms about her, fiercely, rudely. She sobbed in his embrace, sobbed for the joy of it, sobbed with the despair of it. There was no tenderness in his touch, only a primitive harshness, and her nature responded.

"Will I never see you again?"

"Yes. One night I shall come. I shall come in the night. The night is dark and it is hard to see in it."

She understood, but a new fear invaded her heart.

"The sahib?" she asked.

"He will not know."

"How?"

"I shall come when he is out." He read the question on her lips. "I shall know when he is out."

"How will you know?"

"Ask no more questions. It's dangerous to ask any more questions."

Minnie heard a shuffling step. She moved hurriedly away from Boodhoo. Martha's ponderous body filled the doorway and overflowed into the pantry. A coarse, flat nose was embedded in her black face, like a stunted shrub in black soil. Her fat lips were nearly as wide as her face. There was a pleasant twinkle in her eyes, like a ray of light from a stormy sky.

"De fowl kill foo breakfas', Maam, is too skinny foo de master. De fowl had a pip, an' oi tol' Constance dat. But she say: "Kill it, Cookie." De master was vex' las' Sunday because de fowl was skinny. Mus' oi kill anoder one, Maam?"

"Yes, Martha." Martha turned with difficulty and shambled off.

When Minnie recovered herself, she found she was alone. Soon after there was a multitudinous cackling of fowls in the yard. The cackling tumult broke on her ears with a wakening effect. Then the noise subsided, and a solitary hen, with its premonition of death, gurgled with a final intensity, as though it would gurgle in ten short minutes for the months it was about to be robbed of.

Minnie went into her bedroom and sat to her sewing. Her thoughts whirled like a maelstrom about her head, so that the needle moved with an unwitting rapidity in her fingers. Thought after thought pressed down upon her, and then suddenly she remembered she had not asked Boodhoo why Henry had sent him away. Fear bloomed within her like a white flower, spreading its thorns into her brain, her heart, her soul.

She waited anxiously for Henry. At last she heard the distant clap-clop, clap-clop, clap-clop of his horse's hoofs. In a while he was by her side, laughing, kissing her on the lips, looking into her eyes. The white flower of fear withered, died. She could laugh back at him. She was happy, as happy as she had not been for months. Her sense of adventure was being stirred and her heart exulted. Henry noticed her exhilaration and was filled with a deep comfort, a boundless thankfulness.

One morning – it was about a fortnight after the incident of Boodhoo's mother – she was standing in her bedroom putting away her toilet table. It was extraordinary how the dust collected here, for the bungalow stood away from the main road and its ceaseless traffic. Every morning thin layers of dust dulled all the polished surfaces of the furniture, and every morning, with a cloth of chamois leather, she went from room to room. Her silver things too, mostly wedding presents that had helped so well in making her bungalow a home, she dusted. In glancing casually through the jalousies, her attention was arrested by a familiar figure skulking about the servants' gate. The bougainvillea vine, reaching arms of red bloom downwards as though it would grasp some friend to its bosom, hid the upper portion of the woman's body. The woman must have stood there for at least five minutes, and when she walked away she recognized her as Boodhoo's mother.

The same thing happened again a week later, in the afternoon. On this occasion she entered the yard and asked Martha for the mistress. Martha, with her wits about her, said that the madam had gone into town that day and would not be back before night. Then she went away.

Minnie wondered what she could be wanting with her, but her curiosity waned quickly each time, merging with a larger obsession – as two wisps of cloud on a sunny day will merge with a larger mass and be lost in it.

Two more weeks went by through a slushy succession of rainy days. Sometimes the sun shone and the keskidees sang in the guava tree. Minnie hungered, in a fever of anticipation, for that night that she knew held for her an untold fostering of bliss. She was waiting for it as a would-be mother awaits the birth of her baby, with the difference that whereas the would-be mother knows when her child is to be born, her own marvel was in the womb of uncertainty.

And then she knew.

"Sorry darling. I shan't be at home tonight." Each word fell like a harmless thunderbolt before her. She gasped, with her pretty lips parted.

"Not at home! What can you mean, Henry?" She could scarcely believe that she had heard aright.

"They are doing some work over at the factory tonight, dear, and I want to be there." He took a draught of coffee and then added: "If you knew these men, you would know what they are when they are left to themselves."

She mused for a moment. "What time will you be back?"

"I shall leave at eight and be back by daybreak. I want to rest this afternoon, so I shall stay in with you from lunch. Does that compensate, Min?"

"Quite." The understatement pleased him. How well he was getting to know her! An indifference towards any display of her deepest feelings: that was Minnie.

For the balance of the day Minnie could settle down to nothing. Henry slept in the afternoon like a top. She tried to sew, but could not. She tried to read. The words on the pages pirouetted, then they sang; then they played mischievous tricks with each other, like miniature marionettes. She heard the sweet whistle of a semp on the eaves of the bungalow. It seemed to be saying: hurrah! hurrah! hurrah! She listened to it with a rapt expression. Now and again a distant dog barked. That seemed to be saying something else altogether, but she would not listen to it. When Henry had gone to bed he had called her, suggesting that an afternoon rest would refresh her. She gave an excuse which she knew to be silly, and waited to hear him tell her that it was. He was silent, however, and soon she heard his stertorous breathing, and was glad to be alone with her dancing thoughts.

Everything was propitious. Dawn had flooded the island with a promise of fair weather. All day long the breezes were gaily flinging themselves athwart the green fields, whispering amorously as they glided through the branches of the trees that grew in the yard. White clouds, with jagged edges of silver, were borne frantically across the heavens, now like a group of children playing in a garden overgrown with forget-me-nots; now like a squadron of soldiers, with glittering swords, marching to victory; and as the day died down, leaving behind it a river of blood that flowed round the western horizon, the moon rose.

Henry woke at five, and she heard him calling her. When she entered the room he was lying on the bed. His cheeks were flushed and his eyes drooped drunkenly. Seeing him, a cold shiver passed through her body. Her head swam with sickening vertigo.

"Come, dear." She stood, irresolute.

"Had a good sleep?" she asked. He raised himself on his elbows.

"I'm calling you, Min." His voice was a little coarse. "If you don't come, I shall come for you." He was rising from the bed.

She scampered off from him like a hare from a hound, laughingly screaming: "No, no, no!"

That evening they dined in silence. Henry was morose.

He bade her good-bye with a little peck of a kiss. The clap-clop of his horse's hoofs came to her distinctly through the cool, clean air. She was alone. She had let Constancia go to town that day for her monthly holiday, telling her that she could stay away the night. Martha lived in the neighbouring village. Every night she went down to it to her little shanty which no man had ever made unhappy with his lordly ways. Martha prided herself on the fact that from the day her husband had died, some twenty years before in Barbados, she had had no use for men. "Men?" She would utter the word as though it scorched her lips. "Men? Lord bless mer!" and her fat shoulders would quiver like black jelly.

Minnie heard the clock striking the hour of eight. It struck slowly, as though loath to let time go his way. She stood and looked around her. She was wearing a short print dress. Her black hair, shingled (you would have thought she had some south European blood in her), was parted in the centre and smoothed down on either side. It shone beneath the electric light. Methodically, she switched off each light in the bungalow. The moonlight immediately took possession. Every object could be seen distinctly. There was no sound. Even the frogs had ceased their monotone. A cool breeze was passing through the bungalow. It stirred the curtains into a slow, rhythmic motion, backwards and forwards, like fantastic figures.

Minnie passed her hands across her forehead. It was clammy with a soft ooze of perspiration. Boom-boom-boom! Of course! That was her heart beating. It was good to be alive, and better still to be alive in this silent bungalow.

She sat down and tried to think, but no thought would come to her; and if any came, it would flit off like a fairy into the night. She rose and paced the floor. She walked on the carpet so her steps were muffled into a soft sound. Boom-boom-boom!

She went to the window and looked out. Three coconut trees reared their umbrellaed tops to the sky a little way off. Their long, slender leaves diddered, playing hide-and-seek with the moonlight. There were few stars. The moon, like a big, yellow-faced ogre, had chased them into hiding like scared children.

"Bang!" Her heart thumped a great boom. It was only the clock striking the half-hour.

She glanced round, instinctively. A patch of darkness at the door cast a shadow on the carpeted floor. The patch of darkness moved, took shape, advanced towards her and merged with her body.

"You have come, at last!"

"Sh, sh!" he cautioned her. "We must be careful." He was holding her to him so that her breasts ached against his chest.

"Why were you so long in coming?" Her arms, around his neck, were alabaster-white in the moonlight that streamed through the window.

"I had to make sure." He was breathing heavily. "I followed him along the road for at least a mile. I wanted to be sure that he had gone." He spoke in a hoarse whisper. "Then I ran back to you."

"Sit down. You're out of breath."

"No, not here."

"Where then?"

"We are going out." A tiny sound of alarm escaped her. "Don't be frightened. I know of a little wood at the back. We're going there."

"But why not stay here?"

"I heard" – he hesitated for the fraction of a second – "I heard the sahib say once that walls have ears. And besides, it wouldn't be right."

"What?" All her senses were dulled by the pain of her passion. He did not reply, but lifted her from her feet and held her like a feather in his arms and walked to the back of the bungalow. He opened the door. The click of the key in the lock knocked loudly on the darkness. He looked out. There was no stir in the yard. He lifted her again, roughly, and faltered down the steps with her. When he came to the narrow path at the back of the bungalow's outhouses he set her on her feet.

"I don't want to go there," Minnie murmured.

"You must." The laconic reply reassured her.

Together, never saying a word, they stealthily trod the soft path, clasping each other. They passed under the shade of spreading trees that thickened as they advanced until they came to the little wood that hid them from the sight of the passionate moon. The ground, with a layer of rotting leaves from which rose a dull, musky odour, was stippled with blots of light of all shapes. An owl, startled by their presence, hooted, and they listened to the heavy flap of its wings as it bore its passage through the opaque dusk. Then all was quiet. Only the breeze made a rustling sound as it threaded its way through the maze of leaves overhead. It was a lulling sound, as amorous as the cooing of innumerable doves. He sat on the broad root of an old immortelle tree and drew her down to him.

"Supposing he should come back whilst we are here?" A vestige of terror still lurked in her. He smoothed it away.

"He will not come back."

"Are you sure?"

"Yes."

In a few minutes they lay on the earth, with never a word passing between them. They lay and lingered, his hands coarsely and rudely groping about her body, until, with the ultimate embrace, their eternity fell around them in ruins. For a second they were still in each other's arms.

She rose quickly. A great shame, like a bird of prey, clawed at her spirit. Her dress was bundled up above her bare, tremulous knees. They gleamed in the chiaroscuro.

"Come," he said.

"No, no! Not again!" she cried hoarsely. An agonizing terror was seizing her. Precipitately she ran from him, ran through the dusky wood to the narrow path, along it like a clad bacchante until she came up to the bungalow, breathless. She waited and listened. Boom-boom-boom. That was the only sound, and it was her heart. As she entered, the clock struck ten. Then a great silence fell.

Two months later Minnie knew that something had happened to her . . . And that evening when Henry came home he found her stretched across the floor. He grew frightened, for she looked as though she were dead. Then he realized she had fainted, and guessed what the matter might be. Tenderly he carried her to the bed. A marvellous peace, edged with joy, suffused and permeated his spirit. When she revived and her great dark eyes were fixed on him, he bent low and kissed her on the mouth. Her lips were cold.

"Dear, dear little mother," he whispered into her ear.

She thought she was dreaming and put her hands out. Henry mistook the action for the hankering after a caress and gave it her with a deep compassion. She tried to scream at him, to tell him what a fool he was, but her tongue refused to shape the words. Instead, a little sound gurgled in her throat and she closed her eyes, falling into a dreamless slumber.

Two more months went by. The rains were still falling. The birds loved to sing in the dense green foliage of the trees around the bungalow, and they sang when it rained. Each note was a drop of rain turned into music. They sang when the sun shone. Their songs were sad in the rain. In the sunlight they were bright, blithe ditties.

At intervals she had observed Boodhoo loafing on the environs of the bungalow. He came only when Henry was out in the fields, but she could not look at him. The first time she had seen him after the incident of their flaring passion in the wood, a cold sweat had passed over her limbs. She felt she was going to faint. With a determined effort she controlled herself.

She was sitting in her bedroom. Constancia was busy about the room, dusting this and that. Since the discovery of her delicate condition, Henry had ordered her not to exert herself with any of the household duties. Of herself, she had no desire to do anything, for an inertia had taken possession of her with a relentless persistence. Only her brain was active. It had developed a new activity. For hours she would sit, thinking. Henry was kinder than ever, and she knew he was suffering with her, a suffering that was joy turned into suffering because of its depth.

Suddenly Constancia ceased her bustle. She went to the jalousies and looked through. Minnie asked her what she was looking at.

"The Indian woman, Madam."

"What Indian woman?"

"The woman who say she is Boodhoo's mother. The same one that make that noise in the yard some months ago. You remember, Madam?"

Yes, Minnie remembered.

"She's coming into the yard, Madam." Constancia was a little excited.

"Tell her I'm out, in town, anywhere."

Constancia was leaving the room, but Minnie called her back.

"If she wants me, show her in here."

"In here, Madam?" The maid's face showed surprise.

"Yes."

Outside, the sun was shining and the keskidees were asking their ceaseless questions in song: "Is love life? Is love life?"

Constancia re-entered the room. "She say she want to see you, Madam."

In a few seconds Constancia returned with the Indian woman. She wore the same bright orhani she was wearing the afternoon of some months back. She entered the room hesitatingly, with a wondering look in her eyes. Minnie noticed her impassive face, and saw now that she was older than she had at first thought. Her eyes were like Boodhoo's, large and almond shaped.

"Do you want me?" Minnie asked in a lifeless voice.

The woman nodded and glanced at Constancia awkwardly. Minnie made a sign to Constancia to leave the room, and the maid went out reluctantly. As soon as she had gone, the woman turned and closed the door. Then she asked:

"You know me?"

"No."

"You the sahib wife?"

"Yes." The woman chuckled and glanced quickly at Minnie's rounded figure.

"You make baby," and she chuckled again.

Minnie's lassitude was giving way to a timid anger. "Is that all you've come to tell me?" she asked, with more life in her voice.

A hard expression settled on the woman's face as she said: "No. Plenty more."

There was a short silence.

"You know Boodhoo?"

Yes, Minnie knew Boodhoo.

"He my son." Minnie knew that too.

"Where is the sahib?" the woman asked, lowering her voice.

"In the fields."

48

"Far?"

"Yes."

Then she said, slowly, impressively: "Boodhoo the sahib son."

Minnie did not flinch. Her face could not be paler than it was. Only the lids of her eyes quivered slightly, and her nostrils dilated, forming two pinched dimples on either side.

"Who is the mother?" she asked dully. The woman seemed not to notice the futility of the question.

"Me!" she cried, triumphantly.

A soft "Oh!" escaped Minnie's parched, pale lips. The grotesque realization was dawning on her. She gazed on the woman fixedly. The woman returned her gaze.

"You are lying," she said, with no verve in her voice. The woman chuckled.

Followed a throbbing silence. Minnie heard the woman speaking. Her words came to her like echoes from far away, growing nearer and nearer, like the thunder of an approaching storm.

"When the sahib first come, I work on the estate. I little girl then, perhaps fourteen. Us Indian never know how many year we have. Some of us born on the steamer coming from India. I born on this estate. The sahib see me, and every time he see me in the fields he look at me. I like him. He big man, nice face. I looked at him too. He meet me one night in the village, where I go buy something. He tell me follow him. I follow him. He walk a long time. I follow him all the time for I like him. He pass through this yard. That time this house not here. An old house here. This house build only two year now, when he tell me he go to his country, far away, to find wife. He take me that night behind this house, in a wood. He make love to me and tell me he love me. I go home that night crying, but happy. My mother glad, for the sahib make love to me that night. Then he put me in a house, a lonely house. He visit me when he want me. Boodhoo born one year afterwards. One more chil' come, a girl, but it dead. I cry very much, and the sahib cry too. Then he go to his country again, far away. I miss him very much, for I love him. When he come back, you come with him. He tell me he give me money. I no want money: I want him. But he still send money. Boodhoo bring it every month." The woman looked challengingly at Minnie and ended with: "I before you."

The keskidees in the trees outside were still asking their careless question in song: "Is love life?"

"Why have you told me this?" Minnie asked, after a long silence.

"I see you no know. Boodhoo tell me that too. The sahib make me unhappy. Why I no make the sahib unhappy too?" she asked, ingenuously.

"You are not making the sahib unhappy."

"You same thing."

Followed another throbbing silence. The Indian woman's gaze was fixed on Minnie. She was standing and looking down on her as a mistress looks down on her whipped dog. Minnie uttered no squeal. Her face gave no register of her feelings. It was blank, white, unutterably white and drawn.

"You may go," she said at last. The Indian woman went without another word. Minnie heard the crack of the hinge as the servants' gate was opened. Constancia appeared at the door.

"Your milk, Madam?" Minnie did not hear her. "Your milk, Madam?" She raised tired eyes.

"No, Constance. Leave me alone for a while."

When she was alone she tried to marshal her thoughts. They turned into imps, prodding her brain with red-hot brands, dancing about her head, laughing at her with hideous delight, screaming murderous maledictions at her – the phantasmagoria of a disordered mind. She rose and went to the mirror, stood before it and laughed at the strange apparition she saw before her. The apparition laughed silently at her. She grew serious. Behind the apparition, a revolver was hanging on the wall. It was so near. She stretched out her hand to reach it. Her hand touched the chilly glass and she hastily withdrew. When she looked round, the revolver was there, on the wall. She tried to take it down. It was too high up. She stood on the bed, slipped and fell with a heavy thud to the floor . . .

When she regained consciousness there was a sickly light in the room. Someone was sitting beside her. She turned her head but it ached so much she could only turn it a little way.

"You are awake, Madam?" It was Constancia.

"What has happened, Constance?"

"You fell, Madam." She remembered every detail in a flash.

"Where is Mr Lawrence?"

"He's in the village. He went for medicine. The doctor was here."

"Have you told him anything?"

"Like what, Madam?"

"About the Indian woman being here."

"No, Madam. In the excitement I forgot."

"Don't tell him anything."

"But Madam . . ."

"I say don't tell him anything. Do you understand?"

"Very well, Madam."

The few words exhausted her. Henry came in soon after. He came into the room on tiptoe, his massive body as silent as a mouse. Going to the bed, Constancia whispered something to him. His face lighted up. He bent over Minnie and she opened her eyes. He kissed her softly on the face. It was as though a moth had brushed her cheek in its cumbrous flight.

A month passed by and Minnie was up again. Doctor Rivers, the district medical officer, a coloured man, thought she had had a wonderful escape from abortion and probably death.

"She's a strong little woman, Mr Lawrence. Splendid physique," he remarked, as he paid his last visit.

Then the rains went away and the dry season set in. The countrysides of the island became dry and brown. The northern range of mountains could be seen from the bungalow like a mass of brown, interspersed with patches of yellow where the poui was in bloom. Here and there, spent bush fires were marked by curling columns of smoke that were being continually sublimed to light. The heat was severe on some days; on others a wind came sweeping down with a welcome relief.

And then one bright, hot afternoon Minnie was delivered of her baby. Henry was out in the fields and had to be sent for. He came galloping in, his face browner than ever.

"Is she all right?" he anxiously asked the strange nurse coming out from the room of labour.

"She has not delivered yet." The nurse wore a troubled look.

"Can I go in?"

"I think you'd better not, sir. She's easily excited."

All that afternoon there was a quiet bustle in the bungalow. Even Martha's aid was requisitioned. The nurse and Constance went to and fro. Then the doctor arrived. When he came out from the room, Henry hurried up to him with twitching fingers.

"Yes," he answered, "she's doing well." He paused before proceeding. "There's something, though, for which I can do nothing. Something worrying her. On the brain."

Thirty minutes passed. The clock struck five. Each knock was like a blow on Henry's heart. Outside, the haze lay over the fields like an etherealized sea, choppy with a rhythmic disturbance. Then Henry heard a little cry, and then another that was stronger. A few minutes later the door opened and the nurse appeared. She wore a frightened look. He rushed up to her. All she said was: "Don't go into the room, sir."

Henry gasped and his brown face assumed a yellow hue. His whole massive frame shook as he collapsed in a chair nearby. He uttered no word. Another cry sounded in the room, a long, shrill cry, the cry of a new-born babe. Then the doctor entered and laid his hand sympathetically on Henry's shoulder.

"Don't go into the room, Mr Lawrence; not just yet. Your wife has just died. She should have come through all right, but there was something wrong, mentally; upset her condition immensely. Always does, you know." Patting him on the shoulder, he went out and drove away in his car.

Ten minutes later Constancia entered, bearing a flannel bundle. Henry put his arms out for the baby, and looked down at the little thing with its blue eyes, pink skin and fair hair.

Outside the keskidees were questioning for the last time before seeking their night-roosts,

"Is love life? Is love life? Is love life?"

Malvina's Nennen

Over the island the moon spilled silver light. No cloud was in the sky, and the air was so still that not even the delicate leaves of the bamboo trees moved. In Port of Spain the huge expanse of savannah grass shone like a placid sheet of water. From way off came the croak of a solitary frog. To the north the mountains loomed up darkly, loomed up like a bank of dense cloud. Midnight had long gone by. Even the town's trolley cars were home in their barns.

Malvina walked quickly along the pitched path encircling the Savannah. Despite the reassuring light of the moon, she was timid. Time and again she had heard of young women, out at this still hour, being assaulted. Every now and again she glanced over her shoulder to make sure that no one was following her. Her heart beat pit-a-pat, the tips of her fingers went cold. Quickly she glanced over her shoulder again, sure that she had heard a sound. There was no one, but she hastened her step.

Should she take the short-cut across the Savannah? It would cut off nearly a mile of the distance. She had often done it – in daylight. Indeed, this was the first time she had found herself out in the loneliness of the early morning hours. She glanced at the houses flanking the other side of the road. They were all in darkness and the moonlight glimmered on their facades. Nothing moved, only herself. With sudden resolution, she swung to the right and into the Savannah, determined to beat down her rising fear.

The touch of the soft, yielding grass underfoot startled her. Now the sound of her footsteps was gone, the frog ceased its melancholy calling, and a heavy silence descended upon her world. Should she turn back and seek the soothing company of her footfalls on the hard path? She kept on.

"Holy Mother," she whispered, "protect me."

She stopped, suddenly, her heart in her throat. What was that? She listened intently, her legs shaking, a cold sweat breaking out on her. Again the cry reached her ears, and the impulse to run back to the path seized her. She couldn't move. The cry continued, then trailed off into a weak whimper. Intently she listened, gazing at the huge old saman tree silhouetted against the sky. The edge of its shadow upon the grass was almost at her feet.

At first she couldn't believe her ears. She peered into the dark, trying to see through the deep shadow under the tree. Gingerly she approached, her curiosity now subduing the immediate force of her fear. Again the cry pierced the stillness, and she moved with light, quick steps to the base of the saman. A dark object lay at her feet. Stooping, her exploring fingers touched a face.

"Mother of God!" she murmured. "It's a baby!"

She could see it now, lying in the bottom of a basket. And just as she was about to take it tenderly into her arms, the sound of a heavy footstep on the walk came to her. For a moment she was transfixed with fright. The baby uttered a plaintive note, and she glanced back. A huge black man was running towards her, a policeman. She sprang to her feet and made off as fast as her legs would carry her, but a rude grasp on her shoulder brought her to a halt.

"Deserting your baby, eh?" said Constable York, a little breathlessly. "An' you so young! What you young girls coming to these days is nobody's business. You not satisfy dat God give you a baby, but you must . . ."

"Oh God, Officer, it isn't my baby," Malvina faltered, fear clutching at her insides.

Constable York laughed, his teeth shining whitely against his black face. "I hear dat story before."

"I swear, Officer, I swear before my . . ."

"Leave that for the magistrate, young woman. This isn' de court house. Where does you live?"

"Wit' my nennen in Maraval."

"Your godmother, eh? An' your husband?"

"I haven' no husband."

"Hunh, I did suspect that. What's your name?"

"But Mister Policeman, I ain' do nothing, it isn' . . ."

"Answer my question. You not talkin' to de preacher now, you talkin' to a representative of de king! What's your name?"

"Malvina Mountjoy."

Peering at her, he saw that she was an attractive coloured girl. Her skin was brown, her face beautiful, her figure shapely. "A nice name, an' a nice girl too," he said. "You nigger people too, too foolish, an' you does lie more than Ananias," he added sternly. "I catch you in de very act of abandoning your little baby, your own flesh an' blood. I catch you red-handed, an' still you must lie. Young woman, there is times when to tell a lie is to convic' you right off, you don' know that?"

Malvina wrung her hands and her face was distorted with terror.

Constable York looked her over for a while, trying to make up his mind as to what he should do. The baby began to cry again.

"Come on," he said. "Pick up your bundle an' let's go."

"Where?" she asked fearfully.

"To de station."

"But . . . but I tell you it isn' my baby!"

The constable lost patience. "I don' want to hear dat again," he said acidly. "Save your breath for de inspector. An' tell him de truth, you hear?"

Taking her by the arm, he led her under the tree. Malvina's eyes filled with tears and she began to sob. The policeman looked at her in surprise. Always before, his prisoners had been tough customers and he had had to manhandle them. This was something new in his official experience and he didn't quite know what to do about it. Hesitantly he stood, the infant's screech filling the silence.

"So you don' want to take up what belong to you, eh?" he said at last. "All right. My mother did have seventeen children an' my wife have eight already, so I know how to hold a baby as if I was woman myself;" saying which, he stooped and took the little thing into his capacious arms.

"Follow me," he commanded, and they walked off.

The station was alive with movement and light. To Malvina, coming into it from the night, it seemed as if day had suddenly broken. She wiped her tears away, but terror was in her heart. Policemen were everywhere. Humbly she followed Constable York, wondering what would become of her, what her godmother was thinking of her absence, lamenting her reckless decision to cut across the Savannah. Holy Mary, she thought, protect me, and she made the sign of the cross.

At last she came into a spacious room lit by a shimmering glass chandelier suspended from the ceiling. Glancing up, she saw a raised platform, a desk on it, and behind the desk a white man in uniform. Rows of benches stood before the platform; on them sat a few people, all Negroes. One man was drunk; a woman had a red gash across her face; a lanky youth, marijuana in his eyes, slouched on another bench.

Constable York's turn came.

"Well?" drawled Lieutenant Lawson. He had just come on duty, straight from his club. His face was flushed with drink and he was obviously in an ugly mood.

York cleared his throat importantly as he stood with Malvina beside him. The women in the room giggled at the sight of the big policeman with a baby in his arms.

"Silence!" snapped Lieutenant Lawson.

The baby began to cry as the constable cleared his throat again.

"Sir," he said, raising his voice to be heard, "I just got to my beat at the top of Dundonald Street an' de Savannah when a cry descended upon my ears . . ."

"Descended?" Lieutenant Lawson asked with irritation.

"I heard a cry, sir. At dat time of the night, when everybody has gone to sleep an' . . ."

"Stick to the facts, Constable!"

"Yes, sir. I heard a cry an' then I perceive dis young person here. She alleges her name is Malvina Mountjoy, an' that she livin' with her nennen . . ."

"Nennen?"

"Dat's her godmother, sir."

"Go on."

"I did perceive her runnin' from under a tree in de Savannah. Pursuant to my duty, I pursued an' apprehended her in de act of abandonin' her own baby, sir."

The old story once again, thought Lieutenant Lawson, bored, sleepy and annoyed. Every time he was on duty they were brought in to him, these women with unwanted babies. He glared at the cowering Malvina.

"What were you doing out at this time of night?" he shot at her.

"I was home last night when a neighbour come in an' say there was a job for me at a lady house in Woodbrook, sir. I did want to wait for mornin', sir, but my nennen say no, to go right away before I lose de job. So I put on my hat an' . . ."

"And you went for the job?"

"Yes, sir."

"What time did you leave home?"

"About eight o'clock, sir."

"And what time did you get to the lady's house?"

"About a hour later, sir."

"That would make it nine o'clock. The constable, according to his report, picked you up at around one o'clock. Young woman, did it take you four hours to walk from Woodbrook to the Savannah?"

Malvina was silent.

"Answer de inspector!" said Constable York firmly.

"No, sir," Malvina mumbled, at last grasping the meaning of the lieutenant's question. "De lady did have company an' I sit in de pantry till twelve o'clock. She say she didn' have time to attend to me. An' when she come out she tell me she didn' have no work for me."

These niggers would lie even on their death-beds, thought Lieutenant Lawson. "You expect me to believe that story?" he asked with disgust.

"Yes, sir," was Malvina's simple reply.

Lieutenant Lawson spoke angrily. "You expect me to believe that your god-mother sent you out at eight o'clock to walk four miles for a job?"

"De inspector talkin' to you, young woman!" boomed Constable York.

Malvina began to sob. "I . . . I was tryin' ever . . . ever since I leave Mistress Mars . . . Marsden where I did work as a maid to get another . . . another . . ." she trailed off into silence.

Lieutenant Lawson sat up. He knew the Marsdens well – old Thomas Marsden, leading citizen of the island. Just an hour before he had seen Godfrey, the old man's son, at the club.

"How long did you work with Mrs Marsden?"

"About t'ree months, sir."

"When did she discharge you?"

"She didn' fire me, sir. I leave."

"When?"

"About six months ago."

The inspector raised his fountain pen against his ear and mused for a space.

"Let me have a look at that child," he demanded at length.

York strode up to the lieutenant with the baby in his arms. Some of the women on the benches nudged each other and giggled.

"Very well," said Lawson after a scrutiny, his eyebrows raised ever so slightly. He chuckled, then assumed the proper expression to address the constable. "Take her home and check her story. If it's all right, leave her at her godmother's with the baby."

York saluted smartly and ordered Malvina to follow him. All the women giggled as he marched out with the screaming baby in his arms.

The crests of the northern hills were already touched by the flaming fingers of dawn when a constabulary car, with the policeman at the wheel, drew up beside a dilapidated shack in Maraval. Beside him sat Malvina, the baby held awkwardly in her arms.

A light mist was rising from the green valley. A wooden cart, loaded with provisions and drawn by a donkey, passed by on its way to the market. A mangy dog sniffed at the car, uttered a feeble bark, and ambled off. Across the street, a naked child with a distended belly ran to the communal pipe to fetch a pail of water. A strong stench rose from the street gutter. In the light breeze that had just sprung up, the drooping fronds of the coconut trees on the hillside waved gracefully.

"What is your nennen's name?" York demanded of Malvina as he stalked up to the shack.

"Cecilia. We does call her Ma Cecilia."

The constable rapped on the door. He waited for a while and rapped again.

"Who there?" a voice asked from within.

"De constabulary."

"Who?"

"De police," he replied with authority.

Sounds of shuffling bare feet reached his ears, the door came ajar, and a tousled head appeared. Ma Cecilia was obviously just from bed: her pigtails stood up in all directions, her eyes were bleary, her thick lips were parted as if she were still snoring.

"What you want?" she demanded in a rasping voice – and then she spied Malvina. She threw the door open. There she stood, huge and fat, a voluminous nightdress covering her. Her face was black, but anyone could see that in her early days she must have been a fine specimen of black womanhood. There was a certain dignity in the way in which she held her head.

"Me God!" she exclaimed, flinging up her arms. "What you doin' wit' a policeman, Malvina? An' holy Mary, a baby in you hands?"

Constable York stepped in, Malvina following. The baby whimpered. York ostentatiously took out his little black book and sat down. Malvina rested the baby on the couch beside her. Ma Cecilia, dumbfounded, her fat arms akimbo, took a seat too, her gargantuan person overflowing the chair, her eyes darting from the baby to the limb of the law.

The room was spick and span. Everything was in its place, every piece of furniture spotless, the antimacassars were stiff with starch. Framed and hanging on a wall was a large piece of linen with the woven words "Cleanliness is next to Godliness." The old woman was wont to say: "Dirt is the devil's soap;" and as she was a good Catholic, her little shack reflected the assiduity with which she observed her slogan.

"You is Ma Cecilia?" York began, spreading himself out pompously.

"Who tell you so?" she asked belligerently.

"I'se asking you!" the constable shot back with acerbity.

"Yes."

"You know dis girl?"

"Seeing dat I take her in from de time her mooma an' poopa die on de estate in Couva, seein' dat she live wit' me for ten years, seein' dat I bring her up in de fear of de holy Modder an' teach her not to gallivant at nights but to go to mass every Sunday mornin' an' say her prayers every night, seein' dat . . ."

"I don't want to know all dat. I just wants to know if you knows her."

"Yes, I knows her."

"Who is she?"

"Eh-eh, but look my trouble! I tell you enough already, man!"

"What you does call her?"

"Malvina."

"Malvina Mountjoy?"

"I don' call her Malvina Mountjoy. I does call her plain Malvina."

"What's her last name?"

"She take my name when her parents die."

"De name."

"Mountjoy."

Constable York scribbled in his little book. There were tears in Malvina's eyes. The baby whimpered.

"Now then, Mistress Mountjoy . . ."

"I isn' no mistress," the old woman snapped. "I'se *Miss* Mountjoy."

"All right, Miss Mountjoy. You remember last night?"

"It is still last night!"

"Was dis young person here wit' you last night?"

"She does live wit' me, so she must a been wit' me here last night."

"She didn' go out at all?"

"Of course, she went out."

"What time?"

"I hasn' no clock so I don' know for sure."

"About what time?"

"About eight o'clock, because de church bell up de road was ringin'."

As the constable made some more notes, he remarked as if to himself: "De way you giving your testimony is just as if you knows something an' you hiding it."

"What's dat you say? When you addressin' me, young man, look me in de face, an' don' talk inside you mouth."

"Now then, Miss Mountjoy, why did you godchild go out?"

"She went out to do what all young women should do – find work. I did tired tellin' her dat I didn' have enough to support meself, much less her. Every day she use to tell me . . ."

"You knows where she went for work last night?"

"A lady in Woodbrook. A neighbour come in last night an . . ."

"All right . . ."

"Don' interrupt me, man. You askin' me questions an' . . ."

"Miss Mountjoy, I must remind you dat you speakin' to a representative of de king!"

"Pooh!" said the old woman with scathing contempt.

Constable York glared at her, was about to speak, thought better of it, and made a few more notes in his mysterious little book.

"Now, Miss Mountjoy, did you godchild ever work for Mistress Marsden?"

"You mean de big *bourgeois* lawyer?"

"He self."

"Certainly, we does always work for de best white people."

"How long ago?"

"Holy Father, what all dis got to do wit' dat baby in my . . ."

"We comin' to dat. Answer my question, Miss Mountjoy."

"About seven months ago."

"All right," and York made a final note in his book. It read: "Mrs Cecilia Mountjoy, the witness, tell a lot of lies and a little truth."

"You goin' now?" the old woman demanded truculently.

"I going, Miss Mountjoy, when I finish my business with you." He paused to glance at Malvina. "Miss Mountjoy," he continued, "I here to tell you dat I find your godchild last night attemptin' to abandon her baby in de Savannah."

Ma Cecilia's small beady eyes regarded the policeman with utter astonishment. She stared at him long and hard, as if she were trying to make him *feel* the ridiculousness of the suggestion.

"Man," she said at last in slow, measured tones, "man, maybe I didn' hear you good. Is you accusin' Malvina of bringin' dis infant into de world?"

Constable York rose. With elaborate ceremony, he placed his little black book back into the pocket of his tunic. "All de evidence points to dat fact," he announced in the manner of a magistrate on the bench.

Ma Cecilia rose, her arms akimbo. "Evidence, pooh! Fact, pooh!" She almost spat the words. "Dress up you trashy nigger in uniform, put a police hat 'pon he head, an' he think he's governor of de island!"

"Old lady, I must ask you to respect a representative of . . ."

"Young man, I must tell you to respect my age!" she shrieked at him with concentrated fury and contempt. He blinked. The baby whimpered. The old woman gave it a look of maternal concern, and her eyes softened. "Mister Policeman," she said quietly, "maybe you knows you Bible?"

Constable York was on his guard. "Miss Mountjoy, I didn' come here to answer questions from you."

The old woman disregarded the remark. "If you knows you Holy Book you must know dat Jesus comin' to earth again. But de Bible didn' say nothing about a black Jesus; an' dis baby here, if is Malvina flesh an' blood, must be de new Jesus."

York showed his horror at the blasphemy: his eyes opened wide and white, his thick lips quivered. He didn't know whether to resent the remark as a good Catholic or as a policeman. "Miss Mountjoy," he said, "if you blasphemin' to . . ."

"I'se not blasphemin', young man. I only sayin' dat if dat baby is my god-child's, then it born of virgin."

"I'se a policeman, not a doctor, Miss Mountjoy, an' I has my duty to perform." Then he bade good morning in his best manner and made to leave.

"What about dis baby?" Ma Cecilia demanded, her anger returning. "You can't leave it here, man!"

"Orders is orders, lady. I find your godchil' wit' de baby in her arms, an' possession, as you knows, is nine points of de law." Saying which, he went.

Ma Cecilia gazed at the door through which the policeman had gone, then turned to Malvina. Crossing herself, she raised her eyes to the ceiling and murmured: "Holy Mother in heaven, more weight 'pon jackass back!"

"Oh Nennen, Nennen," Malvina sobbed, going up to her godmother and putting her arms about her.

"Compose youself, Malvina, compose youself. But where you get de baby?"

"I find it, Nennen."

"Look me in de eye, child. What you mean you find it?"

"Dat's how it is, Nennen," and the sobbing girl told her story.

"But look my cross! Oh heavens, why you didn' find money or a piece of jewel instead of finding another mouth to feed? This isn' a toy, it isn' even a dog or a cat dat you can put outside in de street. It have a soul, like you an' me. What we goin' to do wit' it? Answer me dat!"

"I don' know, Nennen," Malvina replied dully.

The old woman came and stood over the baby, gazing down upon it for a long time in silence. Then tenderly she took it into her arms. "It pretty, an it half-white! Is a white man child, of that I sure."

As she stood like that, rocking it gently in her arms, her face took on a far-away expression. After a space, she replaced the infant on the couch and turned abruptly to Malvina. Only her eyes betrayed her excitement.

"Child, how long you work for Mistress Marsden?"

"About t'ree months, Nennen."

"An' you leave about six, seven months ago, not so?"

"Yes, Nennen."

"You know," she murmured slowly, "come to think of it, I did work for Mister Marsden mooma an' poopa long, long ago, when I was about your age." She was silent. Her small beady eyes were keen with suppressed agitation. "Tell me, Malvina, I use to hear you speak of Mistress Marsden son when you was workin' there. What you say was his name?"

"Mister Godfrey."

"Mister Godfrey . . . he was a nice young man?"

Malvina hung her head.

"Out with it, child. What he do to you?"

"He only try, but I wouldn' let him."

"Try what? Come on, speak!"

"De butler too . . . his name was Clifford . . . he try to fresh wit' me."

"Don' mind de butler. What Mister Godfrey try to do?"

"Plenty times he try to hold on to me. An' one night he come to my room in de yard an' try to get into bed with me. Dat was de night I run away an' come home to you."

"Let God an' de good Mother be your witness, child. You'se telling de truth?"

"Yes, Nennen."

An ugly expression crept into the old woman's face. Gradually it wore off, and wrinkles appeared about the corners of her eyes and mouth, and she broke into laughter, high-pitched, raucous laughter, prolonged and almost hysterical. Malvina stared at her with stupefaction, stared at the shaking, obese body, the arms akimbo, the head thrown back, a black Amazon in a mood of roaring triumph. And the old woman fell silent. She looked at Malvina and the infant, and then lifted her eyes to exclaim:

"The Saviour is found in de bulrushes!"

Quickly she recovered her composure. "Child," she said, "we must feed de baby."

By five o'clock that afternoon clouds had tumbled down and the sky was overcast. A drizzle fell. The Honourable Thomas Marsden came down the steps from his office. Despite his sixty-five years, he moved with a sprightly step, his tall, powerful frame immaculately clad in a white drill suit, his head covered with a sun helmet. His face was very red, his hair grey, his bearing haughty. Most of the people he passed on the way to his waiting car doffed their hats to him; he responded with a mechanical half-salute. He glanced up at the sodden sky and muttered: "A pity, a pity!" His chauffeur held the door open for him and he sprang into the car. The next moment they shot forward.

The Hon Thomas Marsden was very happy. He lay back on the seat and took a cable out of his breast pocket to read it for the dozenth time.

PRIME MINISTER ASSURES ME YOUR KNIGHTHOOD SAFE THIS YEAR'S NEW YEAR LIST STOP HEARTIEST CONGRATULATIONS FROM EVA AND SELF SIGNED BASSINGTON

Good old Bassington! He must invite him to the West Indies and return the hospitality Bassington had shown them when they were last in England. Many were the advantages in knowing a peer of the realm: he could show you something of his country when you visited England; he could use his influence to win you recognition. Good old Bassington!

Already it was October. Another few months and he would be Sir Thomas Marsden. "Sir Thomas Marsden, illustrious son of the island . . ." "Sir Thomas Marsden has kindly consented to . . ." In such fine fashion would run the press notices of him. Except for Goodridge, that bounder, editor of the *West Indian Evening Gazette,* his old-time political enemy. What would he not give to be present when Goodridge received the official news of his knighthood! His heart expanded with a mixture of pride in himself and warmth for his fellow-men. Bless him, he would shake hands with Goodridge now, bury the hatchet with him, forget all about the old, bitter struggles between them when they were both members of the City Council. Good old Goodridge!

The car's wheels sang as they sped over the wet streets. Thomas Marsden's heart sang too. His heart sang, his mind sang, his whole being sang. He regretted the dismal heavens, but what was a little rain to a man who was now within grasp of the last of his life's ambitions?

"The club, sir?"

It was the chauffeur's voice breaking in on his meditations.

"Home, Lewis," said the Hon Thomas Marsden. "Home, please. I have fine news for Madam."

"I glad to hear that, sir. Would it be disrespec'ful if . . ."

"Not at all, Lewis, not at all. I am to be knighted this New Year. I shall be *Sir* Thomas and that sort of thing."

Lewis whistled through his teeth, himself feeling fine at working for a Sir. "Congratulations, Sir Thomas!"

"Thank you, my boy." Good old Lewis!

Home, yes. Why should he deprive himself of the intense pleasure of watching his wife's face as she read the telegram – by reading it over the phone to her? Alice, a good woman if ever there was one, a near perfect wife. With what unquenchable anticipation she had been looking forward to the news! How she would rejoice in it! With what implacable determination she had directed his course towards its possibility! Ambitious beyond measure, ambitious in a woman's way, she had not scrupled to discard friendships made in their poorer days, friendships that would have been a hindrance to the realization of their dream. It had all seemed so cruel at the time, this breaking of old relationships, so heartless; but how right she had proved to be!

Mentally he reviewed his life: his early days at the Bar; the long, tedious nights of polishing briefs; his first spectacular success; the press of clients in his expanding offices; the bigwig officials beginning to take notice of him socially; his becoming a member of the most exclusive stag club in the island; the War. The War! It was then that the idea had begun to take definite shape. Already a rich man, with his surplus earnings invested in cocoa and coconut estates, prodded feverishly by his wife, he had set to work, spending lavishly in organizing contingents of the island's young white men for service in his Majesty's forces overseas. His name was in the papers every morning, articles spoke of the great unselfish work he was performing for the Empire in its hour of dire need. That period had brought him an M.B.E. – Member of the British Empire. And he had come to it all from a humble cradle.

"Now, Tom, you *must* listen to me." It was Alice speaking, nearly seven years ago. "You must send Godfrey to Oxford. It's the proper, the right thing to do." For nights they had quarrelled over that. It would be expensive, he objected. "On ten thousand dollars a year? Fiddlesticks!" expostulated Alice. All right, but had he not himself risen high in the world without a lot of highfalutin education? "Nonsense, Tom. You had *me* to push you on." Oxford accent! Of what value would that be in an island like this? "Tom, I sometimes think you're a bit of a fool. Or perhaps you're jealous of what you didn't have, aren't you?"

He had pooh-poohed the idea, but looking back upon it now he had to admit that Alice was again right. Godfrey had gone to Oxford, Balliol at that, and there had been moments when the boy's facile social success had caused him a queer feeling of resentment. He didn't like to think of it, for after all, Godfrey was his son. He liked the boy, but what had he done to show his appreciation of his father's hard struggle for success? Nothing but play tennis, dress for dinner, dress for dances, ask for more money. A regular round of binges, an empty, futile existence. Now, when *he* was Godfrey's age . . .

The Hon Thomas Marsden shook off the unpleasant tangent of his thoughts. He shook it off with a chuckle at the sight of the cable in his hand. This was the consummation of a life of bitter work; this was the reward for a life unmarked by any suspicion of scandal, so frowned upon by the Home Office in London. Where would his knighthood have been had he not unswervingly kept to the respectable path?

The car turned into the driveway of his home. The white colonial mansion stood embowered in trees in which all day long the birds sang lustily. Thomas Marsden, being a busy man, seldom heard them; Alice Marsden was more often than not irritated by their singing during the afternoon siesta; as a boy, Godfrey had delighted in sling-shooting them with stones.

He looked at his home. How well he remembered the time of its projected building, when Alice had insisted on the plans for the larger structure!

"But we've got only one child, m'dear, and this has twenty rooms!"

"You'll need them one day, Tom, and please don't try to argue with me!"

By Jove, again she had proved to be right! With their ever-widening circle of friends, they had thrown parties from time to time which had made the house seem actually small: for instance, the party for Godfrey on his return from Oxford a year ago.

As he entered the house, his butler Clifford came forward and as usual handed him the evening paper.

"Is Madam in?"

"No, sir," said Clifford, his handsome coffee-coloured face, though serious, mobile, with roaming eyes.

"Where is she?"

"She gone to a bridge party, sir, an' she tell me to tell you she'll be back early this evening."

"I have some good news for her, Clifford."

"Yes, sir?"

"A knighthood, Clifford, in the New Year's list. I shall be *Sir* Thomas."

Clifford raised his eyebrows. "Delighted to hear the news, sir."

Good old Clifford!

Mr Marsden ascended the stairs to his room, showered, briskly rubbed himself dry, changed into tropical evening dress, extracted the cable from his pocket, picked up the newspaper and descended into his study to await his wife's return. Sitting at his desk, he opened the cable and carefully placed it beside him.

For a while he sat gazing out of a window. The drizzle was still falling, a thick mist dampened his view, so he turned to the paper with a muttered:

"Let's see what that old bounder, Goodridge, has to say."

Idly his eyes wandered over the front page while his thoughts skipped around the incredible scene of his kneeling before the king to receive his knighthood. His eyes wandered idly – and were suddenly arrested. He stiffened in his chair as he read the black headlines:

ATTRACTIVE YOUNG GIRL CAUGHT
ABANDONING BABY
FORMERLY MAID AT THE HOME
OF THE HON THOMAS MARSDEN

While Constable York was on duty near the Savannah in the vicinity of Dundonald Street this morning at about one o'clock, he was surprised to hear the cry of a baby. Looking in the direction from which the cry had come, he saw a young girl running off from under a tree in the Savannah. With commendable promptness he gave chase and caught the girl, who gave her name as Malvina Mountjoy, and who said that she had been living with her godmother in the Maraval district. The girl was booked at the Police Station and subsequently released on her own recognizance and the promise that she would give her baby the care of a good and loving mother. There seems to be no husband.

With a catch at his breath, Thomas Marsden read on for fifty sickening lines. Then came Goodridge's final dagger thrust:

In social circles it will be recalled that the Hon Thos. Marsden's son, Godfrey, returned to the colony from Oxford University about one year ago.

Marsden's face was flushed darkly as the paper dropped into his lap. His first impulse was to spring into his car, rush down to Goodridge's office, and give him the beating of his life. He sat back, trying desperately to ward off the brutal blow of the article; but the more he tried, the more its sinister implications struck him. Goodridge fled from his mind and Godfrey bounced into it. His face was drained of its blood. His temples throbbed.

He clutched at the paper and slowly, deliberately, re-read the article. Every word seared into him. He was slumped in his chair when Clifford, tray in hand, came in with the customary whiskey and soda. The butler gave him a quick glance, withdrew his eyes and set about calmly preparing the drink.

"Have you seen this, Clifford?" and Thomas Marsden thrust the paper into Clifford's hand.

"Yes sir, I seen it," Clifford replied, quietly laying the paper on the desk.

"Who came here today about this . . . er . . . er . . ."

"A reporter, sir. I speak to him. He only ask if Malvina use to work here. I told him yes. Madam was out at the time."

Thomas Marsden gave his butler a searching look. "D'you know anything about this . . . er . . ." and he pointed to the paper, struggling to appear unperturbed.

Clifford stirred the drink with a spoon and did not answer. Thomas Marsden passed his hand across his eyes; his hand shook.

"Clifford, you *do* know something!"

Clifford avoided his master's feverish look and said in a low voice: "I don't wish to commit myself, sir. I'm your butler, sir, but if you *order* me to talk . . ."

"I do, and at once."

"Well, sir, I regret to say it is true."

Beads of perspiration stood out on Thomas Marsden's forehead; he brushed them away with a nervous sweep of the hand.

"Go ahead," he said quietly. "Hide nothing from me, understand?"

Clifford's eyes were fixed on the gloomy scene framed by the tall French window. The words fell heavily, as if he found it difficult to articulate them. "I speak under orders, sir. All I know is that late one night I was in de backyard putting out the garbage can. Mister Godfrey came into the yard and he look around him as if he was making sure that nobody was about, but he didn' see me in the darkness. Then he creep across the yard to Malvina's room, push open the door and went in. I see him several times after that go to her room an' stay there a *long* time."

"Were you . . . were you spying on my son, Clifford?"

The butler did not reply. His face hardened.

"I'm waiting."

"I may be black, sir," he said bitterly, "But I'se not given to doin' that sort of thing."

"Then how . . ."

"I did love Malvina, sir," he continued in a soft voice. "I wanted to marry her. Mister Godfrey did spoil my chances." There was no acrimony in his voice.

"You realize, of course, what you're saying?"

"Yes sir, but I speak on your orders."

Thomas Marsden closed his eyes as if he were trying to shut out the awful picture of his white son competing with his black butler for the favours of a coloured maid. He took the glass and gulped down the drink. Dusk was creeping into the room.

"Is that all?"

"That is all, sir."

A silence followed. From the lily pond in the garden came the screech of a cricket. The drizzle was falling steadily.

"Is Mr Godfrey at home?"

"No sir."

"Send him in to me as soon as he arrives. Now you may go, Clifford."

"Thank you, sir." The butler went out.

Thomas Marsden got up and walked to the tall French window. He stood there gazing out on the dripping garden, then he began to pace the floor. His face was splotched with livid stains. He went to his desk and poured himself a stiff drink of neat scotch. In the early days he drank gin. Since the tide of his good fortune he had been drinking scotch: a couple before lunch, a couple before dinner, and one before retiring to his bedroom – seldom more. He swallowed the straight shot now. For a moment he stood over the desk, gazing down at the cable. Then he sat and rested his head on his hands. The next minute he was up again, pacing the floor, back and forth, back and forth, his brain a maelstrom. He who had always had to use his mind with the precision of a machine, now found himself unable to think coherently. A critical moment in his life, perhaps the most critical moment in his life, and all he could do was pace the floor, bewildered, numb, lost.

The dusk thickened. He felt the night enveloping him, threatening to choke him. He switched on a light. The sudden assault of brightness hit him in the eyes and he closed them tight. Queer tadpole things began to swim before him, swim through his sea of darkness, performing fantastic dives.

"I must think. I must think," he kept muttering.

He opened his eyes as he heard a voice outside. It was his wife, just come in from her bridge party. Her voice was gay. Pulling himself together, he walked to his chair and sat. He felt a strange emotion swelling within him, something directed against his wife, and for a fleeting moment he gloried in it. He waited for her with the calm of a coming storm.

Alice Marsden opened the door and entered. The first thing you noticed about her was the colour of her hair – raven black. He had remonstrated with her when she had first thought of dyeing it, but as usual she had had her way. In her day she had been a beautiful woman, austerely beautiful. Her face was lined in startling contrast to the youthful gleam of her hair. She held her head high. Her body was still good, tall and erect, her bosom high. Her dress was expensive, but in good taste.

She greeted her husband cheerfully. "Hello, Tom. Been home long? I had a divine afternoon, simply divine. Everybody was there – the governor's wife, Lady Seton-Saunters, Mrs Bellairs . . ." Her chatter ceased as her dancing eyes fell on her husband. "Why, what's the matter, Tom? Anything wrong?"

With a great effort he controlled the desire to rise and strike her in the face. He waited until he was sure that he had himself in hand. Then he said, quietly:

"While you were playing bridge, my life was tumbling about me like a house of playing cards."

The words stunned her for a moment. Then her face opened into a teasing smile, the smile he knew so well. He knew what she would say next.

"Why, Tom, at times you're such a boyish fool. For a moment I thought there was really something wrong."

Silently, afraid to speak, he handed her the cable. He would put her through the horrible experience too. He would delight in her suffering, watch her enact for him what he himself had just been through.

She read while he watched her closely and saw the joy dawn and burst in every feature of her face. Her eyes shone, her nostrils quivered, her thin lips came apart. She read it again, then uttered a little shriek of delight, threw her arms around his neck and hugged him closely to her. He let her have her way. He felt the warm, gasping breath of rapture on his cold neck. Then she withdrew, took a few paces away from him, her cheeks suffused with an ecstatic glow, and with great feeling said:

"*Sir* Thomas Marsden! *My* Sir Tom! Really, Thomas, what a naughty boy you are to play such tricks on me!"

He sat slumped in his chair, looking at her with pain in his heart and yet with relish. The strange emotion was now swelling within him to bursting point, pity mixed with rancour, pain with elation. He sat staring at her. For the first time during their long years of living together, their intimacies, their endearments, her spirit was naked before him. The friendships she had shattered, some of them dear things in his life; the snobberies she had practised; the false front she had presented to the world; her hypocrisies; his own ghastly activities during the War, working for a knighthood under cover of other men's broken bodies because of her proddings; her incessant proddings – he

could see them all now, and feel them too. And her way with the boy: cod-
dling him; spoiling him; making of him the playboy that he was, the playboy
who could, overnight, bring to ruin a whole life's work – all this he was ready
to throw at her now. And what a striking resemblance between mother and
son! This thought nauseated him. He handed her the newspaper.

"Why Tom," she exclaimed without glancing at the paper, "can they really
have got the news already?"

He did not answer, but leaned over and pointed to the headlines on the
front page. As she read it he watched her. At first, the ecstasy of the cable
news coursing through her veins, she did not understand what she was reading. She read it again. He watched her with a malignant joy. He saw her brows
furrow, he saw her eyes narrow, he saw her face turn deathly white. Her thin
lips trembled – and at last the full horror of its meaning broke through her
face and body. Good old Goodridge!

This was the moment when he could stand his own silence no longer. But
she forestalled him.

"How do you know this is true?" she said, too paralysed with shock for her
voice to register any emotion.

"I *know* it is true! Ask Clifford, ask the servants of the house, ask them all.
And this is the last time you will tell me what to think, what to do. It *is* true!
I have all the evidence to prove it."

"It can't be, Thomas, it can't be! If it is, we are ruined!"

"*You* are ruined, not I. I have only just begun to find myself." His mood
was exultant now. The words came surging up from his heart while his mind
was dumb. He flung them at her, a torrent of words that beat down upon her.
She had never seen her husband like this. She cowered before him, terrified.
She put her hands to her ears to shut out his accusations, but still she heard
them. Gathering what little strength was left to her, she pulled herself up, her
head high, her cold blue eyes flashing, and almost screamed at him:

"Thomas, you fool, you've got to listen to . . ."

He shouted her down. He was standing now, frenzy in his eyes. The
splotches had gone from his face which now burned red and insufferably hot.
"I told you so! I told you so!" he shouted, pointing a finger at her.

She retreated from the bruising spate of his words, sobbing now, her hands
held before her face in a hopeless gesture of defence. When she got to the
door, she pulled it open, slid out, banged it shut behind her.

Clifford stood at the far end of the hall. She saw him, drew herself up to her full austere height, her head thrown back in an agony of defiance. The butler did not even look at her as she walked out. Quickly she moved upstairs to the couch in her own sitting room and threw herself on it in a paroxysm of weeping.

Thomas Marsden found himself alone and his anger dropped from him immediately. It was then that he felt his legs shaking beneath him, threatening to bring him down to the floor. He suddenly felt old, broken and old. Leaning heavily on his desk, he worked his way around it and flopped into the chair. His chin rested on his chest. The decanter of whiskey stood before him. He poured himself another stiff shot and gulped it down. The whiskey tingled down his gullet, giving warmth to his cold limbs. He raised his head and looked around. The windows were all open and he could hear the monotonous trickle of the drizzle outside. A moth blundered in, bashed itself against the electric light, and fell to his desk-top, dead. He flicked it off with his fingernail.

As he sat there staring ahead of him, the door opened and Clifford came in.

"There is a woman to see you, sir. She says it is personal and important." Thomas Marsden stared blankly at his butler. "Shall I show her in, sir?" Thomas Marsden was silent. "Are you unwell, sir?"

"I'll be all right. Who wants what?"

"A woman, sir. She say she *must* see you. Shall I show her in?"

The master nodded.

A few moments later she entered: a fat black woman dressed up in her Sunday-best. A bright bandanna was wrapped around her head. The door closed noiselessly behind her and she advanced to the desk and curtseyed.

Thomas Marsden raised his eyes wearily to her. "Yes?" he said.

"You remember me, Mister Tom?"

"I . . . I don't think so."

"You don' remember me, Mister Tom?"

His gaze fixed on her, he shook his head slowly.

"Cecilia, sir."

"Cecilia? Cecilia? The name sounds vaguely familiar."

"Cast you mind back, Mister Tom, to when you was a young man an' I was a maid in de house. Mister Tom, look *good* at me."

He knew her now all right. "Oh, yes," he said, quietly.

"You remember how you make me suffer dat time? You remember how you tell me you love me, how you make me love you, an' then how you kick me into de street? Dat was de time you wanted to marry de white lady, an' you tell lies about me to your mooma, an' she chase me out de house as if I was a dog, wit'out pay, wit'out nothing, because you wanted to marry de white lady. You . . ."

"Please, Cecilia, please . . ."

"You can't stop me now, Mister Tom. I lookin' you in de eye, I lookin' you in de eye at last. God is good an' just. He let me live to see de day when I could hold my body before you, de body you love up and then fling into de gutter like if it was dog. He let me live to see de day when I could face you wit' courage an' conviction, de man who nearly make my heart break when I was young an' helpless, too young for such wicked treatment. As soon as I walk in here, Mister Tom, you should a remember me. De thing you do me should a been on you mind all you life, haunting you, giving you conscience no sleep, no rest, making you life a hell on earth." She lowered her voice to add: "I hold no bitterness, sir, but I can't forget; an' now dat I tell you all dat was in me, I feel better."

Thomas Marsden breathed heavily as he rose and dragged a chair to his desk. "You . . . you must forgive me, Cecilia," he said quietly. "Please take a seat."

"Thank you, Mister Tom," she said, pity flooding her heart for him.

They sat for a while in silence.

"It's a long, long time since . . ."

"Yes, Mister Tom, it's a long, long time. You looks a little old, but you still have de same features, Mister Tom."

He smiled wryly. "And you . . . I wouldn't have recognized you anywhere. You've got fat, Cecilia. How many years ago was it?"

"More than forty, Mister Tom. But I don' want to talk about it again. I don' want nothing for myself. What is gone is dead an' bury. I hold nothing against you, Mister Tom, not now."

"Thank you, Cecilia."

There was another silence, broken only by their breathing and the drip of the drizzle from the eaves.

"Mister Tom," Cecilia began, "I don' know how to start I feel so bad about it, but right is right an' God does see an' know all." She paused to mop her perspiring brow. "Is about Mister Godfrey, sir."

"My son?" he asked with renewed interest.

"Malvina is my godchild, an' she home, in bed, Mister Tom."

Mention of the name set his mind working. His brows wrinkled. Malvina? Malvina? Mal . . . Suddenly he rose, picked up the paper from the floor, resumed his seat and sat gazing at the headlines for a while.

"It's all in the newspaper," he murmured at length.

"Me God!" she exclaimed. "I too, too sorry, Mister Tom. I didn' want nobody to know about it."

"I understand, Cecilia. It's too late now. The whole island is laughing at me by this."

The room was very still. At last Cecilia said:

"The mills of God does grind slow, Mister Tom. He let you get away once, but He catch up wit' you. Two times is too much, Mister Tom, too much." She paused, and then asked: "What yu goin' to do now?"

"I don't know, Cecilia, I don't know – yet. You must give me a little time to think it out."

The door burst open and Godfrey, in white flannels and open shirt, bounced into the room.

"What's all this?" he demanded of his father. "Mother has just been telling me . . ." He stopped as he caught sight of Cecilia.

"This is Cecilia Mountjoy, Godfrey." He turned to the old woman. "This is my son, Cecilia."

A tense silence followed. Godfrey regarded the woman with undisguised fury. The father's eyes were fixed on the son. Cecilia sat up.

Marsden addressed his son. "Mrs Mountjoy is the godmother of the young woman, Malvina. She has come to find out what I intend doing about it."

"About what?"

"About your child," he answered calmly.

"*My* child? Have you gone crazy, Dad?"

"No, Godfrey, I have not gone crazy. It's no good trying to deny it. I *know* it's your child. Mrs Mountjoy here assures me that her godchild . . ."

"It's a bloody lie!" He swung on the black woman. "You damn liar! You filthy, scheming nigger! Get out of here before . . ."

"Godfrey!" There was no anger in Marsden's voice, only a note of elation. "I'd advise you to be more respectful. Mrs Mountjoy might very easily have been your mother."

Godfrey went taut, the blood rushing to his face and neck. "You . . . you . . ." he cried, raising his clenched fist and moving towards his father.

Cecilia rose as quickly as she could and grabbed the boy's arm in her powerful hands. "Young man," she said, dignity in her voice and posture, "when Adam banish Cain from him for disrespec' an' murder, God did look down from heaven wit' satisfaction. An' Cain, de murderer of his own flesh an' blood, wandered over de face of de earth wit' sorrow in his heart all de rest of his days." She released her hold and Godfrey's arm fell to his side. He lowered his head, turned on his heel and quickly left the room.

Marsden picked up his pen and held it in his hand for a few seconds. Then he opened a drawer in his desk, took out a sheet of writing paper and his cheque book, and began to write a note. He wrote slowly, trying to form the letters in his usual bold style. Then he wrote a cheque. Folding both with care, he addressed an envelope and enclosed them.

"You know Mr Harvey-Read, the manager of the bank, Cecilia?"

"You mean Mister Bob, sir?"

"Mr Bob. He lives in the big house up the road."

"I know it, Mister Tom."

"Go straight away with this to him." He sealed the envelope and handed it to her. "Tell him I shall phone him presently. Understand?"

"Yes, Mister Tom."

"But go straight away. Go *now.*"

"Yes, sir."

"I shall phone to make sure that you are there and to explain further. Good-bye, Cecilia," and he rose.

"Good-bye, Mister Tom. I did feel God would show you de way, sir." She made a low curtsey and shuffled out the door.

The drizzle had ceased. She walked down the driveway and into the deserted road. The heavens were still overcast. The air was damp. She shuffled along, her feet unaccustomed to the shoes. Filled with curiosity, she began to wonder how much the cheque was for. "Perhaps is fifty dollars," she muttered. "I did know Mister Tom would do de right thing by me. Is late, but better late than never. Fifty dollars! Poor man, he did look so old an' broken down, like de thing hit him hard. Funny how I did feel for him, seein' him again after all these years, sittin' face to face wit' him. I didn' think I could feel tender for him again, after all he do me. If is fifty dollars I goin' buy clothes for the baby, an' a new bureau, an' a dress for meself, an' one for Malvina too. I wonder if is fifty dollars?" She approached a street lamp. Inside its circle of yellow light innumerable insects dashed about. As she got to it, she held up the envelope to its glare. She held it away from her, then drew it slowly to her eyes. She held it away from her again.

"Eh-eh," she muttered, "it look like a one and two noughts. Dat is a hundred. A hundred dollars! De Lord be praised! I goin' to pay off de mortgage on de shack. Free for de rest of my days in dis vale of tears. Holy Mother, one hundred dollars!"

When she knocked at the back door of Mr Harvey-Read's residence, the butler appeared.

"I wants to see Mister Bob," she said acidly, instinctively impolite to another of her colour.

"You can't see de gentleman now. He at dinner wit' friends."

"I *must* see him. Tell him is important."

"Important?" the butler sneered. "What it is?"

"It isn' your business, man. I come wit' a message – dis," and she thrust the envelope under his nose.

"You can wait here while I take it in to him if you like."

"You don' put you black hands on *dis* envelope," she said with scorn.

"Who it from?"

"De Honorable Mister Thomas Marsden."

The butler looked at her sceptically. "How I know you tellin' de truth?" he asked.

"You t'ink because you does lie, everybody else does lie too? See for yourself, you common man," and again she thrust the envelope under his nose.

He read the printed name on a corner of the envelope. "All right," he said reluctantly. "Wait a minute."

A few seconds later she handed the envelope to Mr Harvey-Read.

"Mister Tom send me to you, sir."

Mr Harvey-Read took his glasses from the pocket of his dinner jacket and tore open the envelope. He glanced at its contents, raised his eyebrows, looked at the woman and then at the cheque, and finally said:

"Come with me."

Cecilia gave the butler a contemptuous glance as she went in.

He led her into his study and waved her to a seat. She sat. Mr Harvey-Read went to his desk and, reading the note again, eased himself into a chair. Then he held the cheque before him, scrutinizing it for a space. Not satisfied, he re-read the note.

"What is your name?" he asked.

"I'se Cecilia Mountjoy."

"My good woman," he said at last, incredulously, "d'you know what this is?"

"I has a idea is a little money, sir. I . . ."

"Little money!" Mr Harvey-Read laughed.

The thing was . . . the thing was . . .

"Madam," he said at last, "this cheque is for . . . for *one hundred thousand dollars!*"

He waited to watch the effect on the black woman's face. He expected to see her spring up and shriek with astonishment, with joy, with anything. She did nothing of the kind. She kept her seat and stared at him, uncomprehendingly.

Mr Harvey-Read, growing more and more puzzled, said: "This note instructs me to set up the money as a trust fund for yourself, your godchild and your godchild's baby. Can you sign your name, or do . . ."

The telephone bell rang.

Mr Harvey-Read snatched up the receiver from its cradle.

"Yes, yes? That you, Tom? . . . Yes, she's here. But hell, man, what damn-fool business . . . Yes, I know you're a rich man, Tom, but one hundred thou . . . Can you really be serious? . . . Very well, I'll follow your instructions to the letter, Tom, but it does seem to me preposterous that . . . True enough, you can't expect me to know your private business if you don't tell it me, but still . . . Yes, yes, I give you my word, no matter what happens . . . But why all this fuss when I can see you tomorrow and arrange . . ." An explosive report broke in the instrument. Cecilia jumped. Harvey-Read rattled the receiver frantically. Then he threw it against the desk.

"My God," he said, striding to the door and leaving Cecilia Mountjoy sitting with her hands folded in her lap. Quietly she sat like that, her mind a whirl of thoughts. On the desk lay the note from Mr Marsden – and the cheque. She picked up the note and read it through moist eyes. Then she studied the cheque and sat with both bits of paper in her hand, her face giving no sign of the tumult in her mind and the agony in her heart. "Forty years ago," she thought, "forty years an' now this . . ." Deliberately and slowly she tore the cheque into small pieces, scattered them on the desk, took Mr Harvey-Read's pen and scrawled at the bottom of the note with a steady hand: "I don' want payment fo' de love I give an' de love I take. All I want is a hundred dollars for Malvina baby" – and rose and slowly walked out of the room.

Neighbours

In Port of Spain it is always with a certain amount of trepidation that you move from one house into another. This is quite understandable when I tell you that the town must harbour representatives of every blood in the human family. When it is remembered that your social standing is governed, more or less, by the colour of your skin, you will understand further why I say that one moves from one house into another with trepidation. I do not mean this to be a generalization, for the more well-to-do folk can always control the matter of where they shall live; I refer to those white folk with prestige in the island who are too poor to be able to select; and also to those slightly coloured families that seek to associate themselves with people more fair than they but who, again, have not money enough to allow them to be choosers.

Well, my wife and I are Portuguese, our grandparents having found their way from Madeira to this island some seventy years ago. We pass for white in the island, although I know there is a drop of Moorish blood in our veins. I have read that the Moors belong to the Mediterranean stock of races, so I feel satisfied that our social position is not based upon a wrong premise.

But the matter of my social position does not worry me in the least, though it does my wife, for she is after all a woman; and my experience tells me that women make much ado about whom they shall be seen talking with, dancing with, and visiting. I have other aims in life that adumbrate the social one, and make it seem ridiculous and futile.

When we first moved into our present house, my wife blamed me for not having discovered before that our neighbours were coloured people.

"But, my dear, I don't see that that matters so much," I said. It is a remark of that sort that upsets my wife a lot.

"You have no ambition!" she said heatedly. "If you have no concern for yourself, then have some for me. You bring your coloured and black friends into the house without even consulting me. What will people think of us?"

"But, my dear, you know very well that the white boys take no interest in books. I find congenial friends amongst the black and coloured boys in town and I don't see why you should expect me to sacrifice my pleasure in talking about books to this silly whim of yours."

As usual, one word provoked another until there was a row in which my wife got the better of me. She always gets the better of me for she has an astute mind and a sharp tongue; but for all that she has never been able to convince me that she is right and I am wrong.

At first it was very amusing to watch Mrs Carlton, our neighbour, making overtures of friendship to my wife. She would pass in front of our house in the evenings, all dressed up, and look in at my wife seated in the gallery, with an expression that said as plainly as ever, "Good evening," until one afternoon, my wife's face being perhaps more pleasant than usual, which Mrs Carlton must have taken for an inviting sign, she very gracefully gave the greetings of the day. My wife, of course, replied, for despite her colour prejudice she does not like to hurt anybody's feelings. One thing led to another, as it always does, and in a short time Mrs Carlton was visiting us and my wife was visiting Mrs Carlton. Sometimes on a Sunday when I was at home I would hear them talking to each other from across their windows, for the houses stood only about fifteen feet apart.

"So I see you've got friendly with Mrs Carlton?" I said one night at dinner.

"Yes," my wife said. "After all, if I suddenly fall sick one day, whom can I appeal to but my neighbours? It's just as well to make myself affable."

I held my silence, for I knew that if I opened my mouth to say what I was thinking, my wife would grow angry with me.

Very soon I got to know quite a lot about Mrs Carlton. As is the way with women, whenever Isabella (that is my wife's name) and Mrs Carlton got together, they would discuss all manner of things: their husbands; their own past histories; their ideas in regard to how a woman should react to a discovery of her husband's infidelity, and so on; and, as is the way with most wives, Isabella would pass on to me whatever she thought would interest me concerning Mrs Carlton.

It appeared that Mrs Carlton was the illegitimate daughter of a rich white Barbadian planter and a black woman. Her father had settled on her at her marriage to Mr Carlton, a large-boned coloured man, some property which made her independent. She would say to Isabella:

"Manzy" (that was her husband's nickname) "carn' do as he like wit' me. I got me own income an' he got to be careful."

But what interested me more than anything else was what Isabella told me one morning over our coffee.

"You know, dear," she said, "Mrs Carlton was telling me last night that her husband is not faithful to her. He seems to be very fond of women."

I was not surprised, for I know very few men who are faithful to their wives.

"And how does she take it?" I asked.

"Oh, she says she doesn't mind as long as he gives her everything."

I looked up from my coffee and Isabella must have read in my eyes the bewilderment that I felt, for she said:

"You see, it's like this, from what I can make out. As long as he doesn't deprive her to give to other women, she still feels that she is mistress of the situation."

"That means," I said, "that she regards her husband's fidelity in terms of dollars and cents?"

"Well, I suppose so, if you put it that way. Niggerish – that's what I should say. As long as she can gloat over her husband's women by letting them see that she keeps a nice house, with two servants in it, dresses herself and her children well, and goes to all the shows, she's satisfied."

Some time after that Isabella brought me the news that Mrs Carlton was not visiting her coloured friends in the district any more. The fact of her visiting us gave her too much prestige with us and the other white families around for her to wish to continue. I was not a little disgusted with the woman's stupid snobbery, and said so. My wife could not help but agree with me this time.

Well, one night about six months later, we were at dinner. I heard Mrs Carlton say loudly:

"Don' be rude to me, woman. I know you take it; why the hell you don' say so, enh and be done wit' it?"

I looked inquiringly at my wife.

"She's quarrelling with her cook," Isabella said, preparing herself to listen by not eating. To me that was nothing unusual, for Mrs Carlton had time and again sacked her servants to the accompaniment of rowdy words.

"I tell you I ain' tek it, Madam," the cook said.

"Well, who the hell take it if it ain' you, enh? I put the twelve cents on the sideboard just now, there, and now it gone. You goin' say . . ."

"Madam, I tell you I ain' tek you twelve cents." The cook's voice was harsh and threatening. I glanced over my shoulder, for we could see into their dining room. The cook, a fat Negress, was standing by the table with her arms akimbo. Mrs Carlton was seated at the head of the table, her face wearing an angry expression. I could not see Mr Carlton. His silence made me think that perhaps he was not there, for always when his wife was having trouble with a servant he would interfere with a strident voice, and either order the woman out of the yard or beat her out of it, and then refuse to pay her a cent of the money due her. Of course, the woman would always take him before the magistrate and the magistrate would invariably order him to pay.

Words grew higher and higher until I felt sure that we were in for one of Mrs Carlton's domestic scandals. The cook at first protested her innocence in a mild way, but then began to be rude and boisterous. Mrs Carlton's voice rose, and "damn" and "hell" and "fool" and "nigger" fell from her lips noisily. And still Mr Carlton was silent.

"Madam, I tell you lef' me alone. You goin' mek trouble foo youself."

"If you ain' take the twelve cents, who the hell take it, enh, you old nigger-thief? An' you, man" – this must have been to her husband – "why you carn' shut the blarsted woman up wit' a cuff? Why you sittin' there for lookin' on, enh?"

I could hear Mr Carlton say something in an undertone, but I failed to catch the words.

"Is Mr Carlton sick?" I whispered to my wife.

"I don't think so."

"He's not saying a word: strange!"

Isabella looked contemptuously at me, but said nothing.

Then we rose and went to the back, for by this time Mrs Carlton and the cook were in the kitchen going for each other like two furies. I looked out into the alley that runs at the back of our house and saw a crowd collected there. All the neighbourhood was enjoying the altercation.

"You'se a low, nasty woman!" the cook shouted. "Dat's foo why you carn' keep no servants. You too darmn low."

Mrs Carlton was getting hysterical. She always gets like that when she's sacking a servant. She began to scream. Then she called her husband a coward for leaving her to fight the battle alone. Some of the children began to cry. The cook was by this time thoroughly enraged. She banged the pots about the kitchen. My wife and I were looking over the wall that separates our house from theirs. We saw Mr Carlton come into the yard. He stood looking on, like one who is undecided what to do. The cook, seeing him, rushed into the yard and shouted at him:

"I tell you, Mr Carlton, tell you wife to keep quiet. She lookin' foo trouble, an' I go gie she. Tell she shut she darmn mout', or be Chris', de whole blarsted neighbourhood go hear me voice!"

"Come, come," Mr Carlton said, laying his hands on his wife's shoulders, "what you making this noise for? She say she ain' take the money. Leave her alone."

But that only helped to infuriate Mrs Carlton further. She pushed him aside and rushed at the cook with clenched fists, screaming. They came to grips, and before you could say "Holy Moses!" they were both on the ground, rolling over each other. And still Mr Carlton was inactive. I made an attempt to scale the wall, but Isabella held me back.

"Stay where you are," she whispered sternly.

And then the cook rose, and this is what she screamed:

"You darmn arss you! Whey you t'ink you husban' standin' dere for an' he ain' sayin' a blarsted word? Look a' he, look a' he! Ask he when I gorn – and be Chris' I goin' wid dis! – ask he when I gorn why he man enough to protec' you now! You darmn arss, ask he whey happen between he and me!"

And with that, she laughed aloud and stalked out of the yard like a savage queen.

My wife, turning to me, smiled contemptuously and said:

"Only niggers can behave like that!" And that night she swore an oath never to let me choose a house again.

Laura's Return

As the S.S. *Camito* was steaming through the second Boca, Laura woke. Raising herself on her elbows, she looked through the port hole and saw land sliding gently past. The illusion was very intriguing to her. It seemed just as though the land was moving and the steamer stationary. The only indication of the steamer's motion was the reflection of the rapidly advancing water on the glass of the port window that was swung up and hitched by a short chain to the ceiling of her cabin. That also was strange, and she had noticed it all through the voyage out from England: how the steamer, judging from that reflection, appeared to be moving in the opposite direction to the one it actually was. Another illusion.

Was all life an illusion? For most of her experiences, she was beginning to realize, were not quite as she had once thought them. What if her two children in the bunk below . . . She leant over and saw that they were sleeping. They, at any rate, were real. Nothing illusive about them. Unless, perhaps, it was her feeling for them. But no. That was *elusive,* something which she could not exactly place in relation to any of her other feelings.

And yet, might not life itself be one huge deception, a chimera, a dream in which objects might be imaginary? If that were so, God, or whoever or whatever the power was, was having great fun with her, cruel fun. But supposing God himself were a myth, a myth among many other myths created in the minds of men? Strange, inveigling fancy! Imaginary beings creating imaginary powers! Imaginary mortals creating imaginary immortals . . . She lay back tiredly on the pillow and closed her eyes.

But, of course, sleep now was out of the question. As a matter of fact, she had had very little sleep that night, the last of the voyage out. Fourteen days of sea and sky, sky and sea, until she had got to detest the smell and lash of the salt breezes, the sight of the impending, concave sky. They had become too much part of her existence. They had grown too familiar, and the familiarity had bred, within her, contempt for them.

Even her acquaintances of shipboard had palled. She loathed them all. The circumscribed area of their activities had brought out and shown up the smallness of their natures. Fourteen long, unending days of them! Ugh! With their insipid laughs, their idiosyncrasies, their conversational *clichés*. It was more than she could bear with equanimity.

And yet, perhaps, they were thinking the same of her. In what characteristic could she have revealed herself to them? Perhaps she had shown too much concern for her children. Modern mothers were not quite so – maternal. There was Mrs Chadwick, for instance, returning to her husband after an absence of three months with her little boy. One didn't see *her* fussing over her boy. Oh no! One saw her sitting at nights in dark corners of the deck with the second officer. Very cosy they would be, talking in undertones . . .

Once the first officer had tried to be fresh with her, and how she had resented it! How she had hated the sight of him after the incident! That was four days out on the voyage, and she had since then only vouchsafed him the usual civilities . . . or perhaps she had talked too much of her husband, whom she had not seen for a year. Each passenger in turn must have had a good, quiet chuckle over her queer, out-of-date notion of fidelity. On more than one occasion she had let them know what her opinions were . . .

She was a fool! Of course she was, and yet she couldn't help it. After those letters she had received from him! They had been enough to upset any woman's balance, to reverse any woman's feelings, desires. Even her aunt, to whom she had shown one of them in her London flat, had cast a look of pity on her. Now she remembered well what her aunt had said to her, and the words flowed over her memory with an overwhelming force:

"My dear child, he's not worthy of your affection!"

Dear, simple Aunt Eliza! Little did she know what pain the remark had caused her then! And how it had rankled in her mind since! More so than ever now in the quietude of her cabin, when the meeting with her husband, to which she had been looking forward so long, was at hand. She tried to visualize what their reunion would be like. Utterly impossible! He had receded from her life, immeasurably distant, not because she had ceased to care for him – God knew that could never happen – but because when she read his letters, she seemed to be reading the words, the cruel, heartbreaking sentences of one she did not know, had never known . . .

She found herself standing on the deck, in a light, flowered dress, her two little girls on either side of her. She felt blissfully happy. There was a cool breeze sailing from the land over the placid surface of the gulf. It reached her with a gentle touch on the cheeks, reminding her of sunflowers, the bougainvillea vine that arched the gate of her bungalow, the humming-birds that sucked her garden-roses in the mornings.

In the distance not two miles off lay the mist-covered town of Port of Spain. She tried to distinguish landmarks; the mist was too thick. But wait! Ah yes! There, faintly visible, was the Sacred Heart Church tower; and there, to the left, on the water-front, the Power Station, and a little further in, the Queen's Royal College tower. Back once more to the island which eight years before had seemed so exotic to her! How well she had accustomed herself to it, had even grown to love it in a subtle sort of way! And then she saw Robert, her husband, coming towards her, his brown face smiling, coming towards her eagerly with quick steps, and she put her arms out to take him within them . . . She opened her eyes, heard her heart thumping against her breast, and wondered where she was. But only for a minute.

She had been dozing. Another illusion! Land, water, her husband. How vivid the dream had been! Or was this the dream? The cabin fan above her, still; the life-belts wedged in between the ceiling and a wooden rack; the large screws binding the steel plates together: familiar surroundings for fourteen days. She had even one night, when she could not sleep, tried counting the number of screws in the ceiling of the cabin . . .

She turned over on her side and looked at her wrist-watch, which she had been in the habit of strapping over the rail of her bunk. A quarter to six. Much too early to rise. She had done all her packing the day before, and now there remained only to dress herself and the children. It was strange that she had no desire to go on deck and marvel once more at the beautiful islands that lined the ship's passage up the Gulf of Paria.

How different from eight years ago! Then, it was she who had awakened

Robert before the cabin was quite bright with day and had persuaded him to dress and accompany her on deck. How she had delighted in his naming of each tiny rock island, each with a gaily painted bungalow and some with several: Huevos, Chacachacare, Monos, Gasparee, Carrera, the Five Islands! Chacachacare, Gasparee – lovely words, she thought. And he had seemed so pleased over her ecstasy on that far away morning, eight years ago! She remembered they had been the first to arrive on deck, and he had kissed her passionately during one of her happy exclamations of delight until, elated, she had gasped for breath, only to be once more excited as another island slid by them, the wash of the sea against the sides of the ship breaking the stillness with a gentle splashing sound.

But now she was alone, miserably alone; and the nearer the pulsating ship took her to Robert, the farther away she felt from him. Four thousand miles away in England, she could reconcile herself to his distance from her; now, a few miles from him, in another two or three hours with him in the same house, under the same roof – intolerable! Unless some miracle could come to pass, and the smiling, eager Robert of her dream a moment since . . . A moment!

Her dream had seemed to last one long, sweet hour, and yet it could not have been more than a minute or two. Life was something like that, she thought; or, more accurately (she couldn't think coherently this morning), all the happinesses of it were crammed into short, fleeting moments, and the wide, gaping years were drawn-out epochs of apathy; and if not apathy, misery.

"My dear child," her Aunt Eliza had said. Child. Yes, her Aunt Eliza had thought she was a child, else why had she used the word? Now, in the quiet of her cabin, she revolted against the use of the word in connection with her. Hers was a woman's sorrow because her realization of loss was appallingly deep. Never more would the old sense of security return to her. No child's dream could steal into her and dispel the fog that had settled over her spirit so stealthily; stealthily because at first, with the arrival of his letters, she had tried to coax herself into believing that that was his way with her, knowing all the time that Robert was not like that, could never be like that, unless . . .

She rubbed her eyes smartly and yawned. She pressed her hands tightly down on her naked breasts and yawned again. She thought of awakening her children, but they had fallen asleep so late the night before, excited over seeing their father once again, that she decided to let them rest a little longer. Poor little things! They were hers and yet not quite, with one arc missing in the circle that should have enclosed their oneness. Phyllis, Isabella: how Robert and she had joyously contended over the names! Robert, wanting to perpetuate the name of his mother; she, giving in eventually as long as her second child could be named by her. And what a fuss they had made over this arrangement! . . . Isabella: queer that she, an English girl, should have a child with so foreign-sounding a name! And yet it had been natural enough . . . She tried to reconstruct in her mind how she had come to marry Robert.

The time seemed infinitely remote, like a dream . . . ugh! That word again, creeping into her thought-vocabulary, taunting her with the effervescence of things, mocking her like a little imp with a tiny red-hot fork, which every now and again he prodded into her sensitive brain, laughing at her the while! She could almost hear his laugh!

Yes; the time receded into the misty distance, as though it belonged to another one of her lives, another incarnation . . . What silly ideas leapt into her mind this morning! Incarnation: she who had a simple faith, the Victorian faith of the poet laureate of that time, with its heaven and hell and anthropomorphic god, now thinking naively over the possibility of having lived on earth before! Absurd! But how else could she put it to herself?

The memory loomed up from so long ago, not only as though from another life, but also from another world, despite the worldliness of the surroundings . . . It was during the war, the war in which she had lost her brother and her father. There was someone else too; she would admit it to herself: her first lover. He had been killed in Flanders, and though she had sorrowed at the time, the sorrow had been short-lived. For her mild affection for him she had been thankful, for she knew her capacity for pain over the death of anyone she loved. Her father, her brother: not even now could she think of them without that lump rising in her throat and threatening to choke her unless she cried. *That* did not seem so long ago; indeed, she could remember as though it were yesterday, her mother ringing her up at the office and asking her to come home.

And when she had got home each time, she had known the truth without having been told anything. First her father, then her brother . . .

It was at the Ministry of Food that she had first met Robert. She was a typist. Robert came into the office one morning to do some checking. It was so long ago she could not remember how he had got into conversation with her. She had looked up at him as he walked in, his discharge badge on the lapel of his well-cut coat (she learnt afterwards he had been gassed so badly as to be unfit for further active service), and noticed his swarthy, foreign face. His face had amused her for the moment – long, narrow, with a hooked nose: it had reminded her of a bird's. Evidently, others had thought as she had thought, for she had observed some girls nudging each other and giggling at him . . .

And then, before she had realized where she was, he was asking her to marry him, and she was consenting. How like a strange comet he had come into her life! Impetuous, irresistible! He had told her, soon after their engagement, that his mother and father were Portuguese, but that he had been born in Trinidad. He had told her that he was a barrister-at-law, and that if she consented to marry him she would have to go out to his native island to live with him there . . . Oh, so long, so long ago!

There was a knock on her door. She started. Could she have arrived without realizing it, and could this be Robert knocking now? The ship still shuddered and the reflection on the glass of her port-window still gave evidence of motion. A knock again.

"Come in," she said, and the sound of her voice startled her. The black steward entered with a tray on his hand.

"Oh, good morning, Steward." She watched him lazily as he rested the tray on the settee: her early morning cup of coffee, a habit that had taken possession of her since her residence in the tropics.

"Steward," she asked, as he moved towards the door, "when do we drop anchor?"

"Not before an hour, Madam. And then it will take an hour for the doctor to come on board."

"Thank you." The steward went out.

It was really time for her to rise, she knew, and waken the children to dress them, but she felt so enervated that she could not even decide to make the effort necessary to reach her coffee. Why had she not asked the steward to hand it to her? Now, it would have to wait.

She stretched out her hand and turned on the electric-fan switch, for now that the ship had entered the land-locked Gulf of Paria, her cabin was close and hot. The soft, purring noise of the revolving fan was soothing to her nervous, mental tension. The sudden rush of air brought back life into the cabin; it cooled her hot forehead; seemed to enter into her seething brain and cool that too. It was a delicious relief. Why had she not thought of the fan before? The air rushed over the top of her night dress and down her stomach, her limbs. It was almost as though she felt a baby sucking at her breast again. It passed long fingers over her body: Robert's fingers when his eyes are glowing in the darkness of their bedroom and he is wanting her. It touched her lips, like a kiss: Robert's kiss . . . it whispered into her ears softly: Robert's words . . . ugh! Another illusion. The land, the sea, Robert, and now, her body, all conspiring against her better knowledge, to make a mockery, a scapegoat of her.

Did she not know that Robert no longer cared for her? How had this thing come to pass? How could she have left him just at the time when she had begun to suspect his growing fondness for that girl? It had been difficult for her to assimilate one particle of its truth, knowing Robert as she did, with his intelligence and his admiration of it in others, his seriousness, his utter con-demnation of fickleness found in so many married men.

He had always told her that, apart from her pretty face and tempting fig-ure, he believed he had married her because of her intelligence. And that other girl? Shallow, empty, simple in the extreme, with her irritating smile and nasal intonation of voice, acquired from a few months' residence in New York. It was this that had kept at bay the slightest acknowledgment of the truth – this incongruity of his affection falling on such a type of girl. It was a strange thing that she found herself now in no way harbouring ill thoughts for her. She should be hating her, but she wasn't. This girl who had insinuated herself into her most sacred life – she would hate her, cultivate hatred for her, so that if . . .

"Mummy!"

Her thoughts cracked into a thousand pieces and fell, scattering to the floor in loud confusion.

One Day for John Small

John Small sat up on his bed and rubbed his eyes. The room was still dark, but he could hear the cocks crowing, and he knew that dawn would not be long in breaking. Striking a match, he took an Anchor cigarette from the box that lay on a little table by his bedside. On waking every morning he did that; and sometimes at night, when he lay awake thinking schemes out for making money, he would smoke. Everybody who knew him thought him an inveterate smoker.

Lying back on the pillow, he puffed for a while, wondering if Felix had arrived as yet to help him with the cocoa. He listened, trying to catch any sound in the yard, but he could hear only the hens cackling and the cocks crowing. He hoped that Felix would not be late this morning as he had an order for five hundred cocoa-sticks for Lee Sing, the Chinese shopkeeper. He had worked up to twelve o'clock on the job the night before, and as Lee Sing had told him that he was wanting his order filled today, he had made arrangements with Felix, a young coloured fellow, to come up to his place at five o' clock so they could continue on the job. And he had calculated on having the five hundred sticks finished and packed by seven o'clock. Often he did that; and ever since he had started manufacturing cocoa-sticks, Felix had been working with him. He felt he had done a good thing in taking him on, for

Felix was one of those unfortunate fellows in Port of Spain who could seldom get a job; and even when he did succeed in getting one, it was always temporary. So that Felix, usually penniless, would work well and be satisfied with a couple of shillings per week and meals.

Of course, Ethel, the woman John Small was living with now, could not be expected to be always available for helping him with this little sideline; otherwise he felt sure that he could have managed with her alone. Ethel had her domestic duties to attend to. She did all the marketing in the mornings, and when she returned home, it was to cook and wash and clean the house out and sew for herself. Sometimes, however, she would make time to help John by standing at the table and cutting off the lengths of rolled cocoa as they came from the machine which John was manipulating. But that was seldom.

What made matters worse for John Small was that he had only one hand. All his friends and even the merchants in town knew how he had lost it. It was a pleasure for him to relate how, in the water riot of 1903, he had been shot at, the bullet smashing his wrist. The wound was so bad that the doctor had amputated the hand. Although he had grown quite accustomed to the loss of the hand, still, at times he regretted that he did not have it, especially when he was working in his cocoa-room, for turning the handle of a machine was all he could do.

He liked to think that he had made a success of his little cocoa venture. True, it didn't give him much. He never was sure of how much he was making, for he didn't keep books; but he felt that it couldn't be less than five or six dollars a week, money enough to pay his rent and Harry's schooling. One day he hoped to extend the business by buying a motor to do the work. As it was, he often had to refuse orders which he could never hope to execute; but his good customers – like Lee Sing – he must keep in favour with, by accepting all orders received from them and delivering to time. It would never do to allow them to get into the hands of the two or three merchant-manufacturers in town. In fact, Lee Sing and Chow Fat and the others had told him that his cocoa-sticks were better than anybody else's.

"But yes, man!" he would say, "Nobody can make cocoa like me. I got a secret which nobody else got. I learn it in Demerara from an old Po'tegee man."

John Small had never been to Demerara, but he liked to impress his customers. A lie was not a lie when it was for your good.

When he had smoked his cigarette to a small stump, he threw it to the floor. Then, making the sign of the cross and pressing the fingers of his one hand against the stump of the handless arm, he mumbled:

"The Lord is me shepherd. Goodness and mercy shall follow me all the days of me life and I will dwell in the house of the Lord forever."

Every morning and every night – that is, when he was sober – he mumbled this prayer. He was not a Roman Catholic, but his mother had been one, and as a child he had imitated the habit she had of making the sign of the cross; and never had he been able to rid himself of making this gesture whenever he prayed. Ethel was a Roman Catholic. John Small had found that the Roman Catholic girls of the island were safer to choose from than the Protestant. The priests had filled them with dread for the consequences of sin, and that, added to their superstitious natures, made them docile. Not that John had any definite ideas concerning sin and virtue, and none at all about religion. All he cared about was the fidelity of the woman with whom he lived, for it was something below his dignity to have his friends gossiping about his keeper's sexual lapses. The five or six women with whom he had so far lived, he had broken with because they had made him appear a fool in the eyes of his friends.

"Wha', I goin' support a woman to make a arss of me with her dirty ways? Chut man, I ain' no fool!"

He would often remember Tina, a Negress from St Vincent and the first woman whom he had taken as his mistress. He couldn't help remembering her for she had left him a child who was now a big boy of twelve years. These low-island women, as the women from the northern islands are popularly called, were no good, John always said after his experience with Tina. He had chased her out of the house one night because Carabache, his friend, had told him during the day that he had overheard Joe Brown, the butcher in the Eastern market, boasting of how he was in the habit of visiting Tina at nights when John was out on his sprees. That had enraged him, not against Joe Brown, for Joe Brown was still his friend, but against Tina. And that night he had purposely delayed going home in order to turn Tina out at an hour when he knew it would be difficult for her to find shelter for the night. He liked to think that she had suffered for the humiliation she had caused him.

He still saw Tina now and again, but only to speak to. Once he was finished with a woman, he was finished with her for good. Occasionally Ethel would dress little Harry Small in his best suit and send him to see his mother. But Harry never enjoyed these visits. He said that his mother asked him too many questions and never gave him any sweets or pennies. He always would end up by saying to Ethel:

"You is a better mooma."

When John finished mumbling his prayer, he rose and lit the oil-lamp that stood on his dressing-table. He saw a few sweepstake tickets lying on the dressing-table and remembered putting them there the night before. Taking them up, he scanned them closely by the light of the lamp. He murmured:

"Which is the winning number? Gord, if I got it here now!" But he didn't like to think of the possibility of winning, for he had been buying them now for nearly twenty years and he had never even come near the winning number. Folding them up carefully, he opened the drawer and placed them in it.

"Ethel!" he said softly.

Ethel stirred in the bed but did not wake.

"Ethel," he called again.

Ethel turned, rubbed her eyes, and sat up.

"Is getting late, Ethel, an' I got that job to finish."

"Yes," she said. "Felix come yet?"

"I ain' hear him. But he mus' be there. Lemme see the time." He picked up his watch from the dressing-table.

"Is after five – five pas' five."

"Is late yes, John."

Ethel knelt beside the bed for a few minutes. In the meantime John took off the old pair of drawers in which he had slept, donned a merino and a soiled pair of pants, took a frayed towel from the bed-rail, and went out into the yard to wash. He found Felix in the yard, waiting for him.

"You ready, Mister Small?" Felix asked.

"I go be ready jes' now. Go an' ask Miss Ethel fo' the key and open the door and get everything ready."

John washed, took a few mouthfuls of water, spat them out, rubbed his face and neck dry, and went back into the house. He found Ethel already dressed. She was wearing a plain white dress that reached to her knees, and it showed off her figure to advantage, for it was close-fitting. Ethel's figure was a very fine one. John Small was a connoisseur in the matter of women's figures; and as Ethel had some Chinese blood in her, her hair was long and frizzly, her skin a pale brown, her features more refined than John's. John was deeply coloured, and yet he was quite handsome in a crude sort of way, for his nose, though large, was not bridgeless, and his mouth was full but well-shaped. As he was nearly bald, you could not notice the kinky state of his hair.

"You goin' make some coffee, Ethel?"

"Yes. Bu' I got to hurry up fo' market, because it late."

John invited Felix into the house to have a cup of coffee. In a few minutes Ethel had the water boiling on the Etna stove, and in a short time the coffee was before John and Felix.

"Harry ain' wake yet?" John asked Ethel.

"No. I put his corfee in the cupboard. Gie it to him when he wake up, and tell him to wear his check-suit for school." And with her swinging gait, Ethel walked out of the house with a basket slung over her arm.

By this time dawn had almost broken, so John doused the lamp. Going to the cupboard, he took a handful of corn and threw it to the fowls in the yard. Then he went into his cocoa-room and started to work. In a few minutes he was perspiring, but he always considered the work from two angles: first, it increased his weekly income; and secondly, it gave him exercise and helped him to keep fit. He was a big-boned man and tall, nearly six foot. He prided himself on having a fine figure and was wont to think that it was his figure that was attractive to women, so he always clothed it well.

"Well, Felix, whey you doin' today, enh, me boy?"

"I ain' know, Mister Small. Dat is fo' gentlemen like you, wid money, to t'ink about."

John's face was suffused with a smile. "But boy, wha's wrong with you, you carn get a job? Somebody put *maljo* on you or you gerl working *obeah* on you?"

"I ain' got no gerl, Mister Small," Felix murmured, bending over his work.

"Maybe that's why you got bad luck. You ever had a gerl?"

Felix was silent. John rested by leaning on the table and looked at Felix. Then he repeated his question.

"Yes, I had one, but she was wut'less and I lef' she."

John looked at Felix sympathetically. "Man," he said, "don' let that worry you. All women is the same, and they goin' kill you if you start worryin' about them so young."

They worked for a few minutes in silence. John was very adept, even with his handless arm, for he used it as often as he used the other.

"You got people here, Felix?'"

"Whey you mean, Mister Small?"

"I mean you mother, you fa . . ."

"Dey dead long ago, in Grenada. I come from Grenada."

"I tol' Miss Ethel so once because of you speech. An' you ain' got no people here now, then?"

"I got a sister, but she seein' hell sheself wid eight children."

"Then why you carn get a job?" John repeated in a testy tone.

"I get one sometimes bu' it don' last."

"You too darm lazy, Felix. You like wuk that ain' got much in it, like this job."

Felix said nothing, but continued turning the handle of the mincing-machine slowly. He was a big fellow, though not quite as big as John, and perhaps he was twenty or twenty-one. His complexion was very much fairer than John's and his features less coarse. Once he had told John that he had Portuguese blood in his veins. But looking at him working now, you could see he was lazy. His movements were ponderous and slow. When he stooped for more panfuls of cocoa with which to feed the machine, he stooped with a heavy slowness. John's movements were quick, and they gave you the impression of being light, in spite of his hugeness.

John gazed at Felix and smiled. It amused him to think that Felix was gone on Ethel. He had known that for a long time now, for John's experience was enough to let him know without his being told anything when a man was gone on a woman. But he didn't mind that so much, for he knew Ethel well enough to realize that her religion held terrific sway over her. And even if he discovered one day that there was something between them, he persuaded himself that he would not worry about it as long as they kept it quiet and did not set anybody talking about them. That would mean his appearing a fool in the eyes of his friends; and that, above everything else, John loathed and dreaded. And besides, Felix worked for him steadily and was satisfied with little remuneration because of Ethel. Indeed, John felt a certain pride that Ethel was comely enough to attract the attention of other men. Oh yes, he was quite satisfied with things as they were. Ethel was young, about Felix's age, and young, pretty women with good figures would attract men anywhere. That he took as a natural state of affairs. Once or twice he had spoken to Ethel about Felix's infatuation. From her replies he had judged that there was nothing on her side.

"Felix," John said, "I think you in love. You wuking long enough with me to tell me yes or no."

But Felix applied himself suddenly to his work, turning the handle of the machine faster than ever, and said nothing. John laughed aloud at his confusion and told him anybody could see he was a fool in his dealings with women.

A few minutes later little Harry came into the yard and asked for his coffee and bread. He was very tall for his age and was almost black. John looked up from his work and said:

"Harry, you wash you face an' hands yet?"

"No, Poopa."

"I ain' tired tell you to do that before anything else in the morning?"

"I fooget, Poopa."

"Fooget? Go an' do it now."

Harry walked off, sulking.

John and Felix worked for a few moments in silence. Harry reappeared soon after, and John told him where to find his coffee and what suit to put on for school. Every morning Harry woke before John and Ethel, but this morning he was late in rising because the night before he had been playing with some boys in the street, and had retired later than usual.

When Harry had gone into the house, John said:

"I think that boy goin' do well in school. He got good brain an' I ain' goin' stint him edication. Is wha' I never had, and is wha' I goin' gie Harry."

"Yes, Mister Small."

Sometimes John would speak to Felix about matters that were of great personal concern. It wasn't as though he expected any intelligent criticism from Felix; he spoke more to himself than to Felix, and the matter of Harry's future was of paramount importance to him. Indeed, John's feeling for his son was the only unalloyed feeling he had ever known. He had never loved a woman in his life. His relationship with women was kind and forbearing, given the conditions he desired, and he liked to have a woman in his home because life would be too lonely otherwise, he thought. He liked company, especially women's company, and he regarded them as necessary adjuncts in more ways than one. With Harry it was different. Harry was his obsession. He delighted in visions that showed him Harry a grown man, practising a profession in Port of Spain, a profession that would give him prestige and would make him a respected member of the community.

"I goin' sen' Harry to St Mary's College, Felix, not Queen's Royal College. You know why?"

"No, Mister Small."

"I don' walk aroun' town with me eyes shut, me boy. This town is three-quarters Roman Catholic an' all the big stores got bosses who is Catholic. As you know, St Mary's is the Catholic College, and these Catholics like to help people who is Catholics. The fus' thing they want to know is wha' college you been to. That is, of course, if I carn' afford to make Harry a lawyer, or a doctor, or something like that. You see the point, Felix?"

Felix said: "Yes" and they continued working in silence.

Ethel returned from the market at about half-past seven with her basket laden. John had completed his job and was dressing to deliver the parcel to Lee Sing and then to go to town to see what he could pick up. Going through his wardrobe, he chose a light-coloured palm beach suit, cut in the latest American fashion. In a few minutes he was dressed, and although John was forty, he looked ten years younger. He sprinkled some perfume on to his handkerchief. He asked Ethel to make a neat parcel of the cocoa-sticks for him, and although she was tired – for John and Ethel lived in the L'Hospice over the bridge, which was some distance from the market – she made up the parcel without saying a word. Felix was sitting on the back doorstep, resting from his morning's exertions. Harry was getting ready to go to school.

The house contained four small rooms: one was used by Ethel and John as their bedroom; another was used by Harry; the front room giving to the street was the drawing-room; and the back room adjoining it was the dining-room.

John rented from his friend, Carabache. Ever since he had known himself, he had been friendly with Carabache. They had had misunderstandings but had always quickly patched them up, for John and Carabache were both of the opinion that life was too short to permit men to row with each other and harbour resentment against each other for any length of time. And from Carabache he had got the house cheap: ten dollars a month. Any other owner would have charged him at least fourteen dollars a month. But then Carabache knew that his rent was safe with John Small, which was more than could be said of most men in Port of Spain in John's station of life.

Harry came out from his room, ready for school. Looking at John, he said:

"Poopa, I wan' a bicycle. When you go gie me one? All the boys in school got bicycles."

"All right, Harry. I go gie you one fo' you Christmas if you do good with you lessons."

Harry walked out of the house with his bag slung over his shoulder, and went down the road whistling a popular tune. He knew that when his father made a promise he would stand by it.

Before leaving the house John called Ethel to strap on his false hand for him. After the amputation of his hand at the Colonial Hospital the government had given him the option either of choosing a false hand or a sum of money, and John had chosen the former. It would never do for him to walk about the streets with a handless left sleeve. And women too, he had reflected at the time, would prefer to see him with a cork hand than with no hand at all.

Ethel strapped the hand on, after which John went to the mirror, puffed a little powder on his face and rubbed it in. He opened the drawer and took two dollars and a pack of cigarettes from it. He lit a cigarette, then went into the yard and affixed the parcel of cocoa sticks to the rear of his bicycle seat with a piece of twine.

"You goin' stay here, Felix?"

"Yes Mister Small. De yard wan' sweeping. I goin' sweep it fo' Miss Ethel."

"All right. An' clean up the mincing-machine, you hear?"

Felix said, "Yes."

"I goin' Ethel," John called out. Ethel appeared at the door.

"All right, John. You comin' home fo' breakfas'?"

"I ain' know. If you ain' see me by twelve o'clock, you know I ain' comin'. So long."

John wheeled his bicycle out of the yard and was soon cycling down the street. He made up his mind to go straight to Lee Sing's shop in Tragarete Road. It was a long ride, but the sun was not hot as yet. He looked up at the sky to the east and saw that it was a clear morning. There was a cool breeze blowing and the street was filled with hurrying pedestrians, all on their way from the market. Now and again John saluted an acquaintance with a merry wave of the hand and a cheery: "Mornin'."

As he cycled, he began to think of what he would do for the day. He hoped Lee Sing would have enough change in the shop – for it was early to pay him for these five hundred cocoa-sticks. He foresaw a heavy morning, for this was the cocoa-crop, and he had written to one or two customers of his in the country to bring down their cocoa this week as the market was good. He would have to hurry in order to catch the arrival of the train. He was a bit hard up now and it would never do to miss Jugmansingh and Jagai and Chow Lin On and others for whom he sold cocoa on commission and whom he was expecting this morning. If he missed them this morning, that would necessitate his having to make a draw on his bank-balance of some two hundred dollars. That was the last thing in the world he wanted to do, for he had started off this savings account since the previous year's crop, for Harry's future. Indeed, he called it "Harry's account," and as such he had no desire to touch it.

He began to go over in his mind how he had thrown away money. He remembered the year of the cocoa-boom, when everybody had made money and when he himself had cleared, for the six months of the crop, at least two hundred and fifty dollars a month. Every cent had gone in sprees that very year, but he did not regret it. He felt he was in good company, for even the merchants were fooled into believing that profits would flow in forever as they did in that year, and went to Europe and the States on costly trips. John knew that that was why many of them had gone to the wall. He had done what they had done, only on a very much smaller scale.

But things had changed since then. Prices had fallen considerably and for the past three or four years he felt that he had not been making more than a hundred and fifty dollars a month during the cocoa-crop. The crop had only just started and he would have to be careful this year.

Of course, there were other sources of income. During the black-eye peas season he made good money too, again on a commission basis. Unfortunately – John complained that troubles never came singly – for the past two years the crops had been spoilt by the excessive early rains, and he had known many an Indian planter around Peñal, ruined by these elemental happenings. And again, whenever he had a few dollars to spare, he would lend small sums out on interest rates of between one hundred and one thousand per cent. But with that form of making money he had to be extremely cautious, for several times men whom he had thought his friends had swindled him of the amounts borrowed.

When he arrived at Lee Sing's shop he rested his bicycle against the curb of the sidewalk, untied the parcel, and stepped with it into the shop. The shop was empty of purchasers and Lee Sing was standing behind the counter, with his back to John, gazing at his well-stocked shelves and making mental notes of what articles he would have to buy to replenish his stock.

"Mornin', Lee Sing," John said in a bright voice.

Lee Sing turned round quickly as though he had been caught in some covert act, and said:

"Mornin', Mister Sma'."

Lee Sing was very small with a little yellow face and hair sticking up on his head like pieces of wire. It was impossible to tell his age.

"You bling de cocoa?" he asked, leaning over the counter.

Small began to untie the parcel on the counter. These Chinamen would never accept your word for anything; they wanted to see everything for themselves whenever they bought.

When John had undone the parcel and had placed the ten packets of cocoa on the counter before Lee Sing, Lee Sing said, screwing up his eyes in a peculiar way:

"You know, Mister Sma', de last sticks was too short. You no make dem long as you make dem once. Why?"

John was accustomed to this kind of fault-finding.

"No make them long like I make them once? Wha' you sayin', Lee Sing. You know you talkin' darm lies, because is the same measure I got since I selling you cocoa."

Lee Sing shrugged his shoulders and held one of the packets up to the light as if he doubted the number of sticks in it and would count them in this fashion.

"Cocoa ain' like glass, Lee Sing. You carn' see through it," John remarked in a chaffing voice.

A few seconds elapsed while Lee Sing gazed at the ten packets on his counter. Then a woman walked in from the rear of the shop with a brown-faced baby in her arms and stood beside Lee Sing.

"Mornin' Felicia," John said with a fine smile on his face. John knew Felicia well. She was Lee Sing's woman. She was a well-shaped, voluptuous woman of Venezuelan extraction. Once or twice he had tried to make advances to her, but he had never followed them up for fear of arousing Lee Sing's suspicions.

"Mornin', Mr Small," Felicia replied.

"An' how is the baby?" John asked, crooking his finger at the little brown thing in Felicia's arm.

"He all right, t'anks, only he got a little col' and cough."

Then Lee Sing said:

"You cocoa goot, Mister Sma', but oder man selling cheaper dan you."

"Who?"

Lee Sing thought for a moment. "Alick Blown," he said.

John had never heard the name in his life. He looked closely at Lee Sing and saw that he was lying.

"Lee Sing, I carn' sell me cocoa cheaper than the last price. If you can buy cheaper from this Alick Brown, buy from him," and he made to gather up the packets from the counter. The baby began to cry and Felicia walked indoors with it.

"All righ'," Lee Sing said. "It goot cocoa an' me take it. You wan' de money now or you come pack later for it?"

"I wouldn't min' the money now," John said, "you too far fo' me to come back."

Lee Sing pottered across to the till, counted some money, then brought it and placed it on the counter, counted it again and handed it to John. John had watched him count it and so he placed it in his pocket without bothering to check it. Lee Sing cast an apprehensive glance at John and said:

"Suppose money wrong, no come pack to me. You no count it."

"Is all right," John said. "So long, Lee Sing." He looked around for Felicia but did not see her. Then he went to his bicycle and in another minute was cycling down the road.

When he got to Antonio Gomes's rum shop he stepped in for a shot of vermouth. He always had a shot of vermouth on his way down every morning. It bucked him up and set his brain in action. He looked at the clock on the partition and saw that it was half-past eight. Gomes was in the shop and John asked him how business was.

He answered in a sing-song voice:

"Bishinzh izh bad, me boy. I never see it so bad since I come to dish island from Madeira twenty yearzh ago. Izh de darn government an' de tax dey put on we. Dey not wan' peoplezh foo dhrink rum again."

John agreed with him and said it was a damn shame the way the poor rum-shopkeepers were being taxed. Then he tossed off the drink, paid, and walked out of the shop.

As he was cycling down Charlotte Street he remembered that it was a long time since da Costa (popularly known as Jumby, because one Carnival day, years and years ago, he had disguised himself as a skeleton and walked through the cemetery for a wager of one dollar) had bought his cocoa-sticks. As he still had some time to spare before the arrival of the train, he thought he would stop in and try and make a sale with Jumby. After a lot of talk, Jumby gave him an order for a thousand sticks. Jumby was a big shopkeeper. His shop was next door to the market and so all day long he was kept busy with his four clerks behind the counter. It was rumoured among the black people that he was a wealthy man, and John thought that there must be some truth in the rumour, for Jumby had shops located all over Port of Spain.

When he left da Costa's shop he rode straight down to the Standard Grocery, deposited his bicycle there, and walked across to the railway station. The train fumed into the station soon after and John took up his position outside the third class exit. People began to pour out from the large gate. He knew several of them, and he was saluting and shouting greetings all the time. Then he spied Jugmansingh in the crowd. He called him loudly and went forward to meet him. Somebody bumped into him and the impact knocked the cigarette out of his mouth. Taking out another, he lit it, and in another moment was standing before Jugmansingh and greeting him with slaps on the back and hand-shakes. Jugmansingh was an old Indian with a long flowing beard. John knew that he was rich, for he had large cocoa properties Rio Claro way; and Jugmansingh's son had mentioned once to John – he was sweet at the time – that his father had sixty thousand dollars in the bank. Jugmansingh wore a voluminous *capra* or loin-cloth and a head-cloth done up on his head like a tower.

"Salaam-ho, Jugmansingh!" John cried out as he shook hands with him, the old man blinking in the sunlight.

"Salaam, Monsieur Small. How like cacao-price today? Me bring-am fitty bag."

"Hah, boy, I go get good price. You get me letter?"

"Haen. Dat's fo why me come, an' me got-am one case court-side."

"You got sample an' cacao receipt?"

The old man fumbled in his pocket and pulled out a small parcel of cocoa-beans which he handed to Small. Then he gave him the receipt for the cocoa which the railway authorities had given him and left John to do the rest.

It was like that, that country-customers trusted John Small, and John was more than proud of the implicit confidence these country-people put in him. He guarded their interests as though they were his own. It amused him to hear some of the larger merchant estate-owners talk of him as a cocoa-scorpion, meaning that he stung whenever he got a chance to sting. Jugmansingh and the others knew him better than that. And even sometimes the merchant cocoa-proprietors would seek his aid in selling their cocoa on the local market, for John was popular with the cocoa-buyers and he could always manage to squeeze an extra ten cents per fanega out of them.

He stood for a few minutes after Jugmansingh had left him, but saw neither Jagai nor Chow Lin On. Perhaps, he thought, they would come down tomorrow – and he walked off to see what offers he could get on the fifty bags of Jugmansingh.

John walked into the cocoa department of A.L. Lupton and Company. He saw Mr Devenish, the head of the department, sitting in his office reading the *Port of Spain Gazette*, for Mr Devenish was a Catholic, and the *Port of Spain Gazette* is the Catholic organ in the island. Mr Devenish looked up from his morning paper and said:

"Hallo Small. Anything today?"

"Yes borss, I got fifty bags; but you got to make a good offer or I give them to Mr McCarthy." Mr McCarthy was in charge of the cocoa department of Others and Company.

"You have an offer from him already?"

"Yes borss, an' a good offer." John knew that Mr Devenish was short for the shipment due to leave for the New York market in a day or two, according to contract. John could tell you what contracts each firm had made, at what prices the contracts had been made, how much money they stood to lose or make, and so on. He kept his ears open and had a way of asking questions that elicited information without the informers realizing they were letting out secrets. And, too, what helped him considerably was this: every cocoa-buyer in town liked him.

"How would fourteen-thirty do, Small?" asked Devenish, puffing clouds of smoke from his cigarette and rising.

John chuckled. "Ah, borss, you clean out of it this time. You don' know that Mr McCarthy anxious fo' this lot today?"

"Yes, I did hear him say something about not having his quantity for the *Maraval*. But still, I don't think he can make you a better offer. The market in New York is not so firm today, you know."

"All right, borss," and John made as if to go.

"Wait a minute, Small. Let's have a look at the sample."

"Fus' class estates, borss," said John, handing over the sample to Mr Devenish. Mr Devenish looked at the beans, took his penknife from his pocket and cut one in half, and looked at the two halves closely to make sure that worms had not taken possession of the cocoa.

"All right," he said at last, "the best I can do is fourteen-forty."

John took the sample from Mr Devenish and left, saying he would let him know in a few minutes.

As he walked down South Quay, he determined to see if he couldn't do better with Mr McCarthy at Others. He hadn't known before seeing Mr Devenish that Mr McCarthy was short for the *Maraval*. That would help him a lot in forcing Mr McCarthy's hand.

He strolled in to Others and Company cocoa store, calling out greetings to the head-porter and the clerks. De Souza, one of the clerks, asked:

"Well, Small, going on the sands today?"

John's face wrinkled into a broad smile.

"Going to the seashore today, borss, singing: 'I'm forever blowing bubbles,' with some gerls and champagne."

De Souza and some other clerks laughed. Every day they heard John say the same thing, but every day they were amused by it.

Then John asked for Mr McCarthy. De Souza said that Mr McCarthy was upstairs on the cocoa-shed looking at some cocoa which the labourers were dancing, as it had got a little mildewed. John mounted the stairway and found Mr McCarthy where de Souza had said he was.

"Good morning, borss," John said, tilting his hat.

"What, you? Morning, you rascal. What do you want up here?"

"Ah, borss, not rascal. I only come to offer you some cocoa, fifty bags."

"Plantation?"

"Yes, borss. Jugmansingh estate. Look the sample."

Mr McCarthy took the sample and cut a few beans and smelt them, and gazed at them.

"Had any offers as yet, you rascal?"

"Plenty."

"Good offers, I mean?"

"You can go higher, borss. You is one of the bravest buyers they got in this town. That's why I always leave you fo' the las'."

John knew his man well. McCarthy's face assumed a heroic expression, and he puffed his chest out. He pinched his pince-nez on his nose and fixed it, though it didn't need fixing.

"Let's see, now. What'll get it? I want it, you know, Small."

"I know that, borss, an' I prefer to let you have it before anybody else in town. Some of the others is all right, bu' I prefer you to get it, because I know you want it; an' when you want a thing I like you to have it."

Mr McCarthy thought for a moment. Then he said:

"Fourteen-fifty."

John opened his eyes wide.

"You shame me, borss," he said, glancing at the coolie women dancing the cocoa. "You got to go higher."

Mr McCarthy scratched his head. His face was very red in the sunlight.

"All right," he said, "I'll go ten cents more," and he turned aside to signify that that was his final offer. John followed him down the steps. When they got to the office, John said:

"Make it five cents more, borss, an' I gie you the fifty bag. You want it an' you can pay five cents more. You know I always bring you cocoa when you want it."

Mr McCarthy, lounging back on his desk-chair, looked at John and smiled.

"You're a rascal, Small," he said, "to be fooling me this early morning."

"I ain' fooling you, borss. Is Jugmansingh cocoa an' he ain' goin' sell unless he get fourteen-sixty-five. You know what these coolies is. They ain' like you an' me."

Mr McCarthy looked at John and thought how impossible it was to resent anything he said. After a second's reflection he agreed to take the fifty bags and added:

"I'm taking it only because it's you, Small. For anybody else not a damn cent more than fourteen-sixty."

John smiled a fine smile, handed Mr McCarthy the railway-receipt to get delivery of the cocoa, and walked off whistling and smoking. As he strolled down South Quay, he decided to go and have another vermouth. He calculated mentally that this deal would yield him, as commission, between seven and eight dollars. That, coupled with his sale of a thousand cocoa-sticks to Jumby, represented already a good morning's work. He felt happy. His straw hat, cocked at the back of his head, gave him a debonair appearance. His jacket, unbuttoned, flew open to the wind. He puffed at his cigarette and spoke to all the carter-men as he walked.

As he was passing Meucci and Company, motor-car representatives and garage-owners, a firm that had been established over fifty years ago by a Corsican, he heard somebody call out his name. He looked in the direction from which the sound came and saw young Joe Meucci beckoning him.

"Morning, Small," young Meucci said as John approached him.

"Mornin', Mister Joe."

"How? The sands today?" asked young Meucci, slapping John familiarly on the back.

John said what he knew Mister Joe liked him to say. He knew young Meucci well in business. His father had been a well-to-do cocoa estate-owner, but since his death young Meucci and his five or six brothers had been having a high old time with the money they had suddenly come into. They belonged to the best set in Trinidad, the *élite,* and although young Meucci was married, every night he was at some dance or the other, without his wife, or at the club, or at the Queen's Park Hotel playing billiards and drinking martinis. He was a good-looking fellow with straight black hair and beautifully chiselled features, so he was a favourite among the girls.

"I want to ask you a favour, Small; that is, if you can grant it."

John guessed what the favour meant, as it wasn't the first time he had been asked by Mister Joe to grant him a favour. It was a pity, though, he thought, that Mister Joe was spending so much money. He liked Mister Joe.

"Certainly, Mister Joe, if I can do it."

Young Meucci led John to the back, away from his brothers and the clerks.

"You think you can lend me a hundred dollars? I'll give you a note, as I always do."

John thought for a moment. He thought of the two hundred odd dollars he had in the Government Savings Bank for Harry. Lending Mister Joe was like lending the bank, John reflected. Oh yes, the money was safe right enough.

"Bu' Mister Joe, you ain' think you spending too much money?" John asked, feeling that he must give some sort of advice.

"That's all right," young Meucci said, with a wave of his hand. "You can lend me the money? I don't mind increasing the interest to fifteen dollars for the two months."

John thought this an opportunity not to be lost.

"All right," he said. "When you want the money, Mister Joe?"

"Tomorrow'll do. Thanks, old man, thanks." After a few more words John left.

As he mounted the stairway of the Standard Hotel, he was thinking of how funny it would be if Mister Joe's friends should ever get to hear that he was in the habit of borrowing money from a man like John Small.

When he got to the bar there was nobody there. He glanced at the clock. The clock registered half-past ten. It was an awkward hour for anybody to be at a bar. At round about eleven o'clock there usually flocked in a group of commission-agents to have a chat and cocktails before going home to breakfast. Now and again John found himself in their midst and they would ask him to join in a cocktail. Very few coloured fellows in town could say that they had had the privilege of drinking with white men. John made no mistake in letting his friends know that he was in the habit of drinking with the white commission-agents in town. The fact gave him prestige.

Albert, the black barman, said:

"Mr Carabache been here lookin' fo' you, Mr John."

"What he wanted me fo'?"

"He didn' tell me, but he say he was goin' look fo' you. He ain' fin' you?"

"No," said John, and called for a vermouth. After he had drunk the vermouth, he said to Albert: "If he come back here, tell him I at Others and Company weighing some cocoa there."

"All right, Mr John," Albert said, pocketing the tip of six cents.

John decided to go up Henry Street, turn up Marine Square, and so back to Others and Company to weigh the cocoa. He thought it a foolish thing to take the same road twice when you were on the look-out for business. All sorts of opportunities could be missed by taking the same road twice. As this thought was working itself through his brain he saw Mr Mendes standing at his store door with his hat and jacket on. Mr Mendes was a medium-sized man with a dark-red face and greying hair. It was wonderful, John thought, the way the Portuguese had managed to amass wealth in the island. They had first arrived only about eighty years ago, penniless, and yet here they were, owning perhaps one half of the island's wealth. John knew their history, for some of the Portuguese clerks had told him quite a number of things.

"Mornin', borss," John said, tilting his hat as he came up to Mr Mendes.

"Morning, Small. How's cocoa?"

"You still have that hundred bags, borss?"

"Yes. What do you think you can get for the lot?"

John had nicknamed Mr Mendes "the bull" because Mr Mendes was always wanting prices for his cocoa which were above market-value.

"I can get fourteen-sixty-five, borss, an' I'd advise you sell today. This is only a false price because the boat goin' tomorrow and dealers is short in their contracts. The market in New York falling, borss. Look Mr Devenish jes' tell me that."

"Fourteen-sixty-five?" Mr Mendes was silent for a moment. "Leave it till this afternoon. I'm just going out."

But John felt that to put it off was to lose his chance of making the sale. He could see that Mr Mendes was in a good mood.

"Borss, don' put it off. Sell now. The market go drop after breakfast. Tell me you lowes' price."

"If you get fourteen-seventy I'll accept."

"Good, borss. You goin' out now?"

He told Mr Mendes, as he was going out, to leave instructions with his head-clerk about the cocoa. Mr Mendes turned to Gouveia and said a few words to him, after which he walked off.

John, smiling, said to Gouveia:

"Mr Bobby, if you wan' me you'll find me at the Union Club. I goin' there now to have breakfas': turtle soup, crab-backs, petit pois and curried shrimps." Gouveia laughed and told John he was a damn fool.

John hurried to Others and Company. He didn't feel as though he was walking on earth. A run of luck was his way this morning, and he would make the most out of it. He wondered what Carabache could be wanting to see him about. He hoped it wasn't to scold him for not attending the last meeting at the lodge. He was too tired that night to go anywhere.

He saw Mr McCarthy sitting where he had left him, writing.

"Well borss, I bring you another hundred bags. Grand View cocoa."

"I'll give you the same," said Mr McCarthy.

"You carn' add five cents? Mr Mendes say he want fourteen-seventy."

"That's my best offer, Small," and Mr McCarthy resumed his writing. John thought for a minute and decided to take five cents out of his ten cents per fanega commission and add it to his fourteen-sixty-five offer. He often did that.

By twelve o'clock all the cocoa had been received and weighed, and with the two cheques in his pocket he went off to Mr Mendes's office and gave him his cheque. Then he went to the merchandise department of Lupton and Company and deposited Jugmansingh's cheque with the cashier. That was a standing arrangement between himself and Jugmansingh.

He calculated mentally how much he had made for the morning: about fifteen dollars as commission on the two lots of cocoa, fifteen dollars interest on the loan to young Meucci, and the profit on the sale of cocoa-sticks to Jumby. That was a splendid morning's work. He decided he wouldn't do another stroke of work for the rest of the day. And just as he was turning into Henry Street, he butted into Carabache.

Carabache was a squat coloured man of about the same age as John. His features were coarse and very ugly, and he spoke with a rasping voice. The sentences fell from his mouth in jerks; so much so that, if you didn't know him well, you would have thought he stammered.

"I been lookin' all about fo' you, John."

"Tha' so, Albert?"

"You fo'get what you got comin' to you now?"

John could not remember what he had coming to him this morning and told Carabache so. For answer, Carabache put his hand in his breast-pocket, withdrew a roll of notes from it, counted out twenty-five dollars from the roll and handed them to John with the laconic statement:

"You sou-sou money. This week is you han'."

John took the notes and gave a soft whistle. He had forgotten all about this sou-sou and its unexpectedness sent a sudden shiver throughout his frame. His hand had turned up earlier than former sou-sou hands, for he had only paid in his dollar a week for four weeks now. His luck had placed him fourth when the order of payment was being drawn for, Carabache told him. Out of twenty-five, fourth place wasn't so bad.

"Albert," he said "we goin' dong Carenage this afternoon. We goin' ask – lemme see, Lilla an' Jess; no, Jess came with us last time. Who you want, enh? I want Lilla."

Carabache thought for a moment. Then he said:

"I know a new gerl. Darm fine gerl, man. Her name's Phyllis."

"Darm fine name, too." John commented. "Bu' now I hungry. Let's go get somethin' to eat. I make some good commission this morning. Mister Joe make a borrow from me again this morning: a hundred dollars, an' fifteen to boot."

"That boy is a darm fool. His father would turn in his grave if he knew all this."

John agreed and they both wagged their heads like wise men. John was sincerely sorry for Mister Joe, but that did not prevent him from doing business with him that was profitable. His sympathy was one thing, his business another, but the latter was more important by far.

John stepped into the Standard Grocery and asked the man in charge to keep his bicycle for him until the following morning; and turning to a porter who was nailing up a box, he tossed him a sixpenny piece and asked him to clean the bicycle properly for him.

As they walked up along Henry Street, John said:

"How about Kwong Tong, Albert? For a change."

"A change? I like that Chinese food, man. I like it better than Creole food. Creole food ain' got enough pepper in it, man."

"You ain' know wha' you talking about, Albert. Creole food ain' got enough pepper? You ever taste a good pélau that make by a Bajan woman? If you ain' taste that yet, you ain' know wha' food is, man."

"Phyllis is from Barbados."

"Phyllis? Oh, that gerl you talk about jes' now."

All along the street, up to Marine Square, carts rattled by on iron-bound wheels. Carter-men shouted oaths and greetings and cracked their whips with ear-splitting noise. Motor-cars rushed by with horns blowing. The sun was at its zenith and beat down on the road with rays of burning light. Chinese, Indians, Negroes and whites jostled each other on the pavement. As Carabache was stepping past a cart unloading some boxes of onions on to the side-walk, the carter-men threw a box down and struck him on the foot.

"Why the hell you carn look at wha' you doin'?" he asked indignantly.

"To hell with you again, man! Look whey you gwine!" shouted the perspiring carter-man at Carabache's retreating figure.

When John and Carabache arrived at Kwong Tong's restaurant in Charlotte Street, they found a few black and coloured fellows having breakfast in the main room. They were engaged in a heated debate over a sweepstake ticket. Carabache made to interfere, but John, knowing how easy it was to arouse his friend's temper, pulled him away and led him into one of the private rooms. During the meal they made plans for the afternoon's outing. Half-an-hour afterwards they were both in a car going up Belmont to meet Lilla and Carabache's new girl. John was wondering what sort of girl she was. He hoped she had a good figure.

Lilla was at home when John knocked at her door. He called out loudly:

"Lilla, Lilla, we com' fo' you."

Lilla opened the door. She was a plump coloured woman of about twenty-five years. There was no haste in her movements and she had perfect control over her feelings, for though she knew why John had come to meet her, she showed nothing of the excitement that fluttered in her breast.

"We goin' dong Carenage, gerl. Go an' get dress. An' the coal-pot: tell the boy put the coal-pot in the car we got outside. I buy a fowl in the market jes' now. We goin' make a pélau when we get dong there."

"Who else goin' wid we?"

"Albert say he got a new gerl. He say she's a darm fine girl: Phyllis I think he say her name is."

"Phyllis?" The corners of Lilla's heavy mouth drooped with sarcasm. "A darm fine woman, she? Well, you go see fo' youself. I know she well. She ain' much eether."

"Wha' you mean? She whorin'?"

"I ain' sure; bu' she ain' goin refuse money, dat I can tell you."

Lilla prided herself on taking no man for money.

"Hurry up, Lilla. We ain' got much time."

Lilla walked slowly indoors. When she walked she showed you all the charms of her body. In a few minutes she reappeared dressed in a smart flowered dress reaching to her knees. She wore no hat. Her coarse hair was gathered up at the back of her head into a large coil. She smiled her lazy smile and asked:

"I look good?"

"You look too sweet, gerl," John said, admiring her through half-closed eyes.

"Sweeter dan you woman?"

"Plenty!" John said, laughing. When they reached the front gate he reminded her about the coal-pot.

"Enh, enh, look me nuh, I fo'get all about it!"

That was Lilla's chief fault, John thought as he watched her moving away from him to fetch the coal-pot: she was too lazy even to remember what she must do.

Ten minutes later the car drew up at a little house giving on to the street. Carabache alighted and knocked at the door. John bent down, curious to see what Phyllis would be like when she appeared. But when she opened the door she did not expose herself. Carabache stepped in.

"Enh ben, Phyllis. A frien' an' me goin' dong Carenage now on a little spree. You don' know him. He's a nice boy an' you goin' like him. We come to ask you to go with us. We goin' have a fine time, gerl."

"Dong Carenage?" Phyllis asked. "All right. Oi gwine dress quick. You'se a dear to tink o' mer, nuh," and she skipped out of the room.

Phyllis was a small woman; perhaps she was the same age as Lilla. She was very slight, but there were graceful curves in her body. She, too, was coloured. Her hair, bobbed, gave charm to her brown, oval face, and there was no mistaking the vitality that flashed from her large brown eyes. She had arrived in Trinidad from Barbados about two years before, and Carabache had met her one night at a dance, had taken a fancy to her, and had danced with her all night. Once or twice he had seriously considered making her his mistress; but each time his natural inclination for freedom had dissuaded him, as it had done all through his life, "from tying himself up to any woman," as he put it. Carabache liked women under certain circumstances, away from which, he feared them and said they were dangerous. Once, in his young days, he had got a girl into trouble. The girl's parents had brought into play every argument and pressure they could think of to force him into marriage, but Carabache had evaded them all and had escaped scot-free. He often would boast of his astuteness to his friends and say that it took a clever fellow to get out of a difficulty such as he had happened to be in at the time. He didn't mind making presents to Phyllis once in a while, on the clear understanding between them that they were only presents.

"This is Phyllis," he said to John as they stood by the car.

John doffed his hat with a fine grace, shook her hand, and said he was very pleased to meet such a pretty girl. Phyllis giggled, got into the car, and nodded familiarly to Lilla. Lilla's face was scowling, and John, noticing that she was beginning to be jealous already, paid her more attention than he would otherwise have done; for he argued that it would never do to create discord in the company before they had even set out on the outing. He knew Lilla well enough to realize that she would become affable as soon as she had had a few drinks.

They all sat on the rear seat, Carabache at one end, then Phyllis, then John and Lilla at the other end: a tight fit, but that was what they wanted.

The car raced down Four Roads and turned into the Carenage road. John and Carabache took off their hats and jackets and began singing: "I'm forever blowing bubbles," a favourite air with them. Lilla and Phyllis soon joined in. The street was deserted, for it was afternoon and a week-day, when nobody thought of seeking the seaside resorts. John suggested a drink. Phyllis said:

"Sure t'ing. Oi feelin' t'irsty already."

Lilla kissed John on the lips as recompense for the suggestion. Carabache stooped down, withdrew a bottle from the basket that lay at the bottom of the car, pulled out the cork with his teeth and offered the bottle to Phyllis.

"Dis is rum?" she asked, holding the bottle before her to the light and looking at it with parted lips and a sparkle in her eyes.

"You carn' tell rum when you see it, Phyllis?" John said, thrusting his hand out playfully and pushing the bottle to her mouth. Some of the liquid fell on to Phyllis's lap. She laughed thinly and they all joined in.

Phyllis took a swig at the bottle.

"Dis is great!" she said, smacking her lips, and forthwith she burst into song, a lewd carnival refrain that went:

All the young men got gerls tonight,
All the young men got gerls tonight,
All the young men got gerls tonight,
Sans humanité.

The others drank and began to sing, too.

The bathing-houses were deserted when they got down to the beach. The old, bearded Negro who was in charge of them (he was nicknamed Napoleon because he had been something of a tyrant amongst his own people in his early days) led them with shuffling steps to the finest one of the lot and charged them eighteen cents an hour.

"Napoleon," Carabache said, wagging his finger, "you overcharging us. I goin' tell Mr Figuera when I see him." Mr Figuera was the Portuguese owner of the beach-houses.

"Don' talk darm foolishness, Albert." John said. "This ain' the time to talk about foolishness like that."

Old Napoleon grinned and showed two rows of teeth that were startlingly white against the black background of his wrinkled face.

When the basket, ice and other parcels had been deposited just outside the bathing-house, Lilla and Phyllis locked themselves in and began to undress. John and Carabache knocked at the door, but the girls wouldn't let them in. Old Napoleon stood a few feet off, looking on and enjoying himself immensely. He was remembering his younger days, when he did the same sort of thing, and when life was something which gave; now it only took. He smiled sadly and shambled off to sit on the beach a little further down. He drew unrecognizable figures on the sand with his shaky finger, to while away the time. How he wished he was young again like Massah John an' Massah Albert! But, he reflected, John and Carabache would get like him one day. He would be in his grave then, sleeping the eternal sleep.

When Phyllis and Lilla came out from the bath-house they were wearing bright-coloured bathing-suits. You saw now the massive, sensuous curves of

Lilla's body and the *petite,* graceful outlines of Phyllis's. They all had a drink, after which John and Carabache went into the bath-house to change and the two girls set about making the coal-pot ready. Lilla took hold of the fowl and, handing it to Phyllis, asked her to kill it. Phyllis shuddered.

"Oi carn' kill a fowl, Lilla; oi ain' make fo' dat koin' o' t'ing."

Lilla's face screwed itself into a contemptuous laugh without any sound coming from her mouth. She took the struggling fowl from Phyllis, held its neck with her right hand, and began swinging the fowl round and round. Phyllis screamed. John poked his head out of the bathing-house and asked what was wrong. Lilla said:

"Dis gerl ain' a woman yet. She only a chil'. She fraid to kill a fowl."

Phyllis, seeing that the men were gazing at her, for Carabache had by this time opened the door and was standing beside John, as naked as he was born, laughed aloud to hide her confusion. Then she ran into the water and plunged headlong. Lilla shouted at the top of her voice:

"Hai, gerl! Whey you t'ink? I here to cook food fo' all you and you ain' goin' help me? Whey de hell you is? Madam an' me de cook? Come out an' get de rice ready, gerl, or I lef' de whole darm t'ing!" Lilla was angry. She stood with her rounded arms crossed over her breasts, looking at Phyllis in the water through narrowed eyes. Phyllis dashed the water over her head, taking no heed of Lilla. Lilla turned to the two men who were still standing at the bath-house door watching the scene, and said:

"Whey all you bring dong here? A lady? I have a darm good min' to dress meself an' go back to tong."

John put on his bathing suit and came out to Lilla.

"Don' get vex, Lilla. She never come with us before and she don' know wha' she got to do." Placing his hands over his mouth, he shouted to Phyllis to come out and give Lilla a hand. Phyllis waved her hands above her head, laughed on a top note, and ran out of the water. John looked at her figure approvingly.

"Come, Phyllis," he said, making an attempt to be stern for Lilla's sake. "Gie Lilla a hand with this pélau. When you get it goin' we can all bathe together and enjoy ourselves."

When they had the fire going and the pot on it, they all went into the water. Half-an-hour passed during which they had two drinks more. Lilla's sulky mood was beginning to pass away under the influence of the drink. The sea scintillated in the sunlight. Wisps of bodiless cloud raced across the sky, and in the offing a few sailing vessels could be seen careening to the wind. The coconut trees that bordered the shore hissed and slapped their pendulous leaves. Carabache put his arm around Lilla and danced on the sand with her. John thought this an opportunity not to be lost, and ran across to Phyllis, caught her up in his arms, and began dancing wildly with her, away from Carabache and Lilla.

"You got a fine figure, Phyllis, " he said, gazing at her lewdly. Phyllis giggled and wound her body to the rhythm of John's feet. He held her more closely to him. Her right hand grasped the stump of his left arm. She was looking up into his face, her large brown eyes opened wide, her nostrils quivering.

"We goin' have a fine time, gerl, before we lef' here tonight, enh?"

"Yes, we gwine have a foine toime. Oi glad oi get to know yuh."

"True?"

"True," she said and giggled again.

Old Napoleon was lying on the beach, the sunlight beating down fiercely on his sleeping form. A few flies buzzed about his ebony face, but they failed to waken him. He had had a drink with the others a few minutes before.

As Lilla stooped over the pot, stirring it with a large tin spoon, she hummed:

> Woman sweeter dan man,
> Woman sweeter dan man,
> A t'ing I carn' understan'
> Is why dey say woman sweeter dan man.

Lilla knew all the carnival song-skits, for every year she would join a band organized by John and Ethel, and through the streets of Port of Spain the thirty or forty of them comprising the band would skip, singing until they all got hoarse and caught cold from the drizzle that seems to make it a point of falling every year during the two days of Carnival.

John was in the sea with Phyllis. Carabache stood beside Lilla and offered her a drink of vermouth. She refused the vermouth and asked for rum instead.

"The pélau nearly ready, Lilla?" Carabache asked, drawing his arm across his mouth.

"It nearly ready," she said, standing and smiling inanely.

"John an' Phyllis having a high ole time. Look a' them."

Lilla scowled and said nothing.

"You ain' goin' in again?" he asked.

"I feel col'." She left him and went into the bathing-house. He followed her in and found her lying on the wooden seat. Bending over her, he kissed her on the mouth, and she drew him down to her with her plump brown hands.

In the meantime, John was giving Phyllis swimming lessons.

"You mean to say you carn' swim an' you come from Barbados?"

"Oi lived on a sugar estate, far from de sea, dat's why oi carn' swim."

She splashed about for a few seconds, lying across John's supporting arms. Now and again his arm slipped up to her breasts. Once he held her and she screamed, with laughter in her voice. Pulling her to him, he kissed her on the lips. His eyes were heavy with drink, but he wasn't feeling even tipsy as yet, for John could carry a lot without its having any effect on him. Phyllis's eyes were bright with an unnatural brightness. She saw and felt everything moving round and round her, as though the world had turned suddenly into a huge merry-go-round.

Still holding her, he said hoarsely:

"Albert and Lilla disappear. Where they gorn to?"

"Oi knows," she said in a lively voice. "Dey in de bading house. Oi see dem gorn' in jes' now. Le' we go an' see."

They waded through the water, out on to the beach, and walked stealthily up to the bath-house. Phyllis peeped round the corner of the door and burst into high-pitched laughter.

"Get away!" John heard Carabache say in a half-throttled voice. John caught Phyllis by the waist and pulled her with him into the coconut plantation until they reached a sequestered spot. There he coaxed her and played with her until, giggling, she surrendered herself to his compelling embrace.

When they emerged from the shade of the trees they saw Carabache and Lilla a good way off, evidently looking for them. Phyllis hailed them loudly and waved her arms. John saw Lilla wheel round and advance towards him with a slow, firm stride. He sensed trouble, and searched his mind to see what excuse he could give.

"Whey you been?" Lilla demanded of John in a strident voice. She was breathing heavily. Her manner angered him.

"Wha' the hell tha' got to do with you? Ain' I see you in the bath-house with Albert jes' now, with me own two eyes?"

"Dat ain' none o' you darm business. Albert is an ole frien', an' you knows

116

it darm well. Whey I wan' to know is whey you been wid dat little whore!"

"Whore? Who mo' whore dan you, nuh?" shrieked Phyllis, suddenly coming to life and rushing at Lilla with bared teeth, and fingers curved for scratching. But before she could get her nails into Lilla's face, Lilla swung her arms around her frail body, and the next minute they were rolling on the sand. Lilla snarled with pain, for Phyllis's teeth were fixed in her left breast. John pounced on the struggling figures and had much difficulty in separating them because of his handicap. Old Napoleon still snored some distance off.

When they were separated, the two women glared at each other. In her rage, Lilla was calm, but Phyllis shrieked at her stink curses, and then began to cry hysterically. Carabache held Phyllis, saying:

"Don' make a arss o' youself, gerl."

John led Lilla to the surf and washed her wounded breast, on which the marks of Phyllis's teeth were red and angry-looking.

"Tha' gerl got a hell of a temper," he remarked.

Lilla said nothing.

"You shouldn't a' call her a whore, Lilla," he ventured quietly. "Tha' make all the trouble."

Still Lilla was silent.

"Come, le' we see if we carn' make it up. Don' le' we spoil our spree, Lilla," he urged, drawing her away from the surf, towards Carabache and Phyllis.

Lilla felt cowed. She hadn't for a single moment thought that Phyllis could have given such a good account of herself. Lilla was accustomed always to have the upper hand: the only word, the only blow. Because of her size and silent, deliberate way, every woman of her acquaintance was afraid of her. Phyllis's attack was something new in her experience and it left her dazed.

Phyllis had calmed down just as quickly as she had flared up. She was sorry now that she had lost her temper and bitten Lilla so cruelly. She went up to Lilla impulsively and held her hand out without saying a word. Lilla took it reluctantly, wondering if she was giving in too easily. Her breast pained her, but that didn't worry her much. She knew she had been wrong in calling Phyllis by such a name, but she couldn't blame herself entirely for the incident. When a drink was suggested, she agreed, and they all drank together. Then they went into the sea and behaved as though nothing had happened.

An hour later, as the sun was sinking, making the Five Islands look like dark blue shadows on the sea, and pelicans skimmed the surface of the water looking for food before night fell, they sat around the pélau-pot, helping themselves from it with their hands. They were all tipsy. Now and again they would break into song and scare away the birds settling to roost on the coconut trees. John called out to Napoleon, but Napoleon did not move. And the sun set.

On shaky legs they went into the sea for the last time, naked. The dusk would hide their nakedness. They splashed about, and screamed and sang and laughed drunkenly. The moon rose and the sea sparkled in its bright light. The sky was empty of cloud and a few stars twinkled. They hailed the moon with raucous cries and unintelligible words. John mocked the priest's duties at mass by genuflecting to the moon and making the sign of the cross, mumbling in a sonorous sing-song fashion the while. The others laughed and splashed handfuls of water on him. He ran around and they ran after him, falling as they ran. Soon after, Carabache led Phyllis into the bath-house and Lilla and John were left alone on the beach, embracing each other and whispering lewdly into each other's ears. They lay on the sand in the full light of the moon.

The tooting of a motor-car horn awakened them to the fact that the car had returned for them. John remembered that he had told the chauffeur to return at eight o'clock for him, so he supposed it was round about that time now. They dressed as fast as they could, helping each other to button and pin and fix. Once a pin pierced the stump of John's handless arm as he was clumsily attempting to fix it into Lilla's dress. The sharp pain almost sobered him.

A few minutes passed, and then John heard the chauffeur talking loudly outside in the moonlight. He wondered why he was talking so loudly and making such a noise. He looked out, swaying slightly on his feet, and saw him approaching in a half-run.

"Wha's th' matter?" John asked, blinking in the moonlight. The chauffeur's form was blurred before him, like a shadow.

"Borss," he said, and his voice betrayed his excitement, "Napoleon look as if he dead. I carn' get he to speak an' he face col' like ice."

John swayed, not comprehending. He heard what the chauffeur said, but the words were all jumbled up in his head and conveyed no meaning.

"Who you say dead, nuh?" asked Phyllis. She was the most sober of them all.

"Napoleon, Miss. It look like if he dead"

"Dead? Gord!" And Phyllis shrieked. The others came to their senses and began to realize in a vague way what had happened.

"Bu' how you know he dead?" asked John, hiccoughing.

"I ain' sure, borss, but he col' an' I carn wake he!"

"Le' we go an' see," said John.

But nobody moved. They could see the dark heap of Napoleon on the beach about fifty feet off. Phyllis shuddered. Carabache coughed to break the silence. Lilla held Carabache's arm. John stood, undecided what to do.

"Louis," he said at last to the chauffeur, "go an' tell Mr Figuera wha' happen quick."

Louis hurried away.

John turned to the others, cowering at the door.

"Wha's matter? All you 'fraid o' dead people? When you dead, you dead, I always say." He hiccoughed. "Is livin' people you ought to be 'fraid of," and with that he straightened himself and walked unsteadily towards old Napoleon, who had died as the sun was setting, quietly, in contrast to the stormy passage of his life.

John placed his hand over his heart and felt no beat. He called the others. They approached, one behind the other, Carabache leading, Phyllis last.

"He dead." John told them. Phyllis was about to shriek again, but Lilla, who was watching her and dreading the shriek, said:

"Fo Chris' sake, shut you darm mout'!"

They all stood over the dead body, their hair dishevelled, their faces scared in the moonlight, swaying slightly and whispering to each other as though the sound of their voices was something to frighten them. When Mr Figuera arrived with three or four men, they slunk off from the little crowd gathered round old Napoleon and had two drinks, one after the other. On the way down in the car they drank and sang, and drank again until they all got drunk. Louis dropped them off one by one, helping each out of the car into the house.

When John arrived home, Ethel was sewing by lamplight in the dining-room and talking to Felix, who squatted on the doorstep. She undressed John without saying a word, put him to bed, wet his head with bay-rum, and returned to the dining-room to talk to Felix.

Sé-sé

Sé-sé lived in a three-dollar room in Prince Street with her mother. "Sé-sé?" the mother would say. "Sé-sé too good fo' dis worl'. Is only Satans dat live happy in dis vale o' tears."

And indeed, Sé-sé was a good girl. Although already past twenty-one, no neighbour had ever succeeded in even inventing scandal to her discredit: Sé-sé's goodness was so apparent to everyone. Seldom was she seen in the streets after dusk. She had never been seen with a young man, not even with Popo, who was her cousin. She made her living by washing, and knitting alpagarta-tops. Every morning she rose at four o'clock and went to mass. In the yard shared by all the barrack-yarders, Sé-sé's voice was always quiet and unoffending. She interfered in none of her neighbours' rows, and the wonder was that she could be so unconcerned in the midst of the most furious altercation. The young men stared at her tall, comely figure with envious eyes, and remarked among themselves that "that nigger gerl" had no blood in her veins. The young women said of her that she was "all stuck up wit' herself." The old women were wont to ask their wild daughters why they were not like Sé-sé, forgetting that in their youth they had been wild themselves.

Sé-sé was not conscious of the beauty that lurked in her small black eyes, the black satin skin of her face, and her large, luscious mouth. She dressed in simple prints, did her kinky hair in a simple fashion, and walked with a

120

demure, though firm, step. She had no friends, and yet everybody, with the exception of the young women, who were scared of her, was willing to befriend her at any time.

And one night Sé-sé's mother fell down in a fit that left the right side of her body paralysed. Sé-sé attended to her without making any fuss, murmuring every now and again that it was God's will, and accepted the misfortune with resignation and prayer. No longer would her mother be able to help her with the washing, the marketing and the cooking. Sé-sé did all without complaining.

But every hour of the day the mother lamented her condition, saying feverishly that she wanted to get better, she wanted to get better, she wanted to get better. Sé-sé at first listened to this reiteration with composure, then with timidity for her mother's safety, and at last with a keen sense of sorrow for her mother' s sufferings.

Of this was born a desire to see her mother well. The neighbours said that a doctor should be called in. How much would that cost? Sé-sé wanted to know. And knocking their old heads together, they told her that it would cost perhaps five dollars, perhaps ten dollars with medicines. Sé-sé didn't know what to do, for she had no money. What she made went in the bare necessities of life; and it was all she could do daily to put aside a little so that the end of the month should not find them without shelter from the sun and the rain. And she began to blame herself for not having saved in the past, and asked God to forgive her for her sin.

Her lamenting mother filled her with grief more and more as the days went by; and when her mother began to reproach her for not wanting to get married to some man who would help in the illness, Sé-sé knelt down behind the screen that hid her from her mother's sight, and for the first time in her life knew that she was weeping. In her simplicity she cast about in her mind for a possible husband, and the only man she could think of was Popo, who she knew to be wild like the forest deer and improvident like the river-lappe. Still, she went in to her mother and said she was quite willing to marry Popo if her mother desired it; and her mother, grown irritable from long suffering, rebuked Sé-sé, saying, among other things, that if she wanted to get ten dollars she could get it from any young man in Port of Spain because of her prettiness and her virtue.

Sé-sé left the room and, not understanding, wept again. And as she wept she repeated softly to herself that she wanted ten dollars, and begged God so often to send it to her that at last she thought she saw two five dollar bills shining like two golden images before her moist eyes.

And one bright morning it happened that Popo, dressed up to the nines, swaggered into the yard to offer sweepstake tickets. "Only two shilling a ticket," Popo said and shook the book open before Sé-sé's slumberous eyes. Sé-sé thought for a moment, hesitated, then thought for another moment, and at last told Popo to return the following morning. Popo, his black face shining in the sun, swung his cane and strolled over to another part of the yard.

And all that day Sé-sé wondered if it was a sin to buy a sweepstake ticket; and the following morning went early to confession and told her confessor that she had bought such a ticket. And the priest, being a man full of wisdom, told her that it was quite all right, as every businessman in town conducted his business on much the same principle, and did Mother Church condemn them, he asked himself aloud.

And Sé-sé, later that day, bought a sweepstake ticket off Popo. Carefully folding it up as if it were a new dress, she put it away in her box. And every night Sé-sé prayed that it would bring her ten dollars; and if not ten dollars, then five: with that amount she would be satisfied. Every mass she attended, she remembered the ticket and she remembered God. Eventually she came to look upon the small piece of paper as something sacred like her string of beads, and touched it with reverence. Her mother's lamentations no longer filled her with disquieting grief. Again and again there came to her the vision of the two notes, shining before her eyes like two golden images, and her spirit glowed with a more intense light each time. In four weeks she made four stations-of-the-cross. And although sometimes, in her gentle kneeling from effigy to effigy, the figure of Christ was metamorphosed into a five dollar bill, Sé-sé's spirit was untroubled by this phenomenon.

The day arrived when Popo came hot-foot into the yard to tell Sé-sé that she had won the first prize! Quietly, Sé-sé made the sign of the cross. But when Popo went on to say, all the wide-eyed barrack-yard women standing around and uttering little obscene exclamations of surprise, that the prize was ten thousand dollars, Sé-sé murmured in pained astonishment:

"Holy Mary, moder of Gord!" and straightway went to her room and fell on her knees, and said indignantly with her face lifted up to the ceiling:

"Oh Gord, I didn' ask you for ten t'ousand dollars. I ask you only for ten – or even five!"

Shango

"**B**oss, remember what I tol' you on Tuesday?"

Not for the world of me could I remember what Harry, the coloured chauffeur of his own taxi, had told me on Tuesday.

"You fo'get already, boss! The Shango."

Of course! Fancy forgetting the Shango! Just what I had been longing to see danced since I had heard about it from a fellow clerk at the bank.

"Well, you fellows," I said, turning to my two companions, "after this drink we are off to San Juan. Agreed?"

"Isn't it rather late?" put in Frederick, the young Negro whose acquaintance I had made soon after my arrival in the island about a year ago, an acquaintance that had ripened rapidly into friendship because of our mutual interest in literature and art.

Frank had taken out his watch. "Eleven o'clock, boys," he said.

Harry, the chauffeur, interrupted with: "The dance start at twelve o'clock, boss; midnight."

"Heaps of time," I persuaded. "However, let's have our drink, and then, San Juan."

We had just come from the theatre where we had seen *The Fanatics*, staged by a travelling English repertory company. During one of the *entr'actes* I had met Frederick Burton at the bar. One or two remarks he had casually let drop had aroused my curiosity concerning his opinion of the play and its production, and I had invited him to accompany me home with the intention of drawing criticism from him. I was doubly glad now that he had come, for I felt sure he would know something about the Shango, enlightening me as to its significance and its mysticism.

"Whiskey, rum?" I asked as we stood in the room which I occupied in a certain boarding house in the city of Port of Spain.

"*Crême-de-canne*," Frederick answered, using the colloquial expression for rum, adding: "I always take rum," as though I had not known that fact before. Frank's was whiskey and so was mine.

In the glare of the lighted room, Burton cut a strange figure. He was tall, perhaps six foot, with a graceful stoop of the body that made him appear to be shorter than he really was. Despite his coal-black skin, his expression was extremely pleasant, two beady eyes looking out from an intellectually broad forehead above which clustered, closely cropped, the crinkly curls that are common to the black race. The way he stood, the quality of his voice, his manner of address – his whole person spoke unmistakably of refinement and culture.

Frank, like myself, was English; and Frank, like both Frederick and me, was deeply interested in contemporary literature. In fact, our interest had manifested itself through the medium of composition, for though Frank had so far not succeeded in placing any of his descriptive sketches, Frederick had had a short story published in the *Saturday Review*, with the proceeds of which we had all three run a binge, and I had had some verse accepted by one or two of the better-class English magazines. We were arriving, slowly but surely.

"By the way, Frederick," I began tentatively, "you were telling me something about *The Fanatics*."

"Was I?" he questioned nonchalantly.

"Not so badly acted," Frank commented.

Frederick looked at him sharply. "You are always giving me occasion to tell you, Frank, that you will never be a critic of the drama or short story." He rubbed the back of his hand across his nose irritably, a way he had of expressing disapproval. "The play was acted damnably. I read the book some months ago, and the impression I received from reading it was entirely different from the one I got from seeing it acted tonight."

"One understands that," I interposed, "for the interpretation which you may have given . . ."

"Interpretation or no interpretation," Frederick interrupted peevishly, "the play was damn badly done. This is no *Hamlet,* my dear fellow, where subtle distinctions can be made that give rise to all sorts and conditions of contrary opinions. This is straightforward, plain sailing, sociological drama. The man who acted the part of the father, in my opinion, made an ass of himself, fussing and fretting about the stage like a setting hen instead of being what the author intended him to be: a staid, dignified, Victorian gentleman condemning the ultramodern eccentricities of his children in a staid, dignified, Victorian manner."

"Of course, Frederick," I said, "you have the advantage over us of having read the book."

"But still, didn't the father's behaviour seem extraordinary to you?" he asked pettishly, rubbing the back of his hand across his nose violently. "A sort of caricature of an irate old father! Chut!" I agreed.

"Of course you must agree," he continued with a wide, outward sweep of his arms. "And the son – good Lord! When he became inspired in his denunciations, when his diction should have been most distinct, it was then that words followed on the heels of each other in such a helter-skelter fashion that one was hardly distinguishable from the other. You heard a roar, a prolonged roar that was really facetious – and at the same time exasperating."

There was a short silence, broken by Frank's thin voice saying: "The opening of that second act was beastly. Like a Sunday-school class discussing a problem in morality."

"Ha, Frank," Frederick said with an argumentative twitching of his thick lips, "I see you're improving, though I can't put all the blame on the cast there. The play starts with a terrific burst of action, if you remember, in the first act, and calms down to a sluggish flow from the second act onwards. Lopsided, that's what it is. Like promising a child a train, and you give him instead a treatise on its mechanism. Naturally the child is disappointed. Furthermore, what was there so very clever and epigrammatic in what the characters had to say of modern conditions of life? Nothing that I could see. Chut! The play lacked even dramatic dialogue. It wasn't worthy of the success it had in London."

"I suppose that accusation can be levelled against most of the plays running in London today," I said. "The unsophisticated public is not very discerning in the matter of the stage."

"Time's moving, you fellows," chimed in Frank, looking at his watch. "Twenty-past eleven. It takes twenty minutes to get there, remember."

We had another drink and left.

As we drove through the cool night air I questioned Frederick about the Shango. He was sitting next to me, for Frank sat in the front seat with the chauffeur. I could get very little out of him at first. He gave me the impression that he knew all about it and was unwilling to tell me much. I remember thinking at the time that perhaps he was ashamed to have us witness a demonstration of one of the atavistic ceremonies of his people. For though he was educated, well read, a product of Western culture, they were still his people. To have himself brought face to face, in the presence of Frank and me, with a dance like the Shango, might prove to be more than he could bear with equanimity.

"I believe it to be a sort of sacrificial rite," he was saying at last as we sped through Laventille.

"Sacrificial?" I said, interrogatively. He was silent. "What exactly do you mean?" I urged.

"Well, in the event of ominous illness," he replied, with a ruminating slowness of speech, "the dance is offered to appease the wrath of the gods, and thus save the life of the victim. It is said, too, that no full-blooded Negro, observing the performance of the ceremony, can resist its gravitating influence. He must, perforce, participate." He ceased talking for a moment. "Of course, superstitious rot!" As though it were an after-thought, he added: "I am a full blooded Negro. Ha, fancy me . . ." and he burst into loud laughter that echoed a nervous note to my ear.

When we arrived at the scene, everything was excitement. Everywhere there was an air of preparation. The crowd was forming itself into a ring, in the centre of which stood a group of Negroes, men and women, chanting a low, mournful incantation, the women wearing bright-coloured neckerchiefs, a quaint touch of the anachronistic, which they held out from them like wings, the men bare from the bellies up, only a pair of trousers covering their loins and legs. Suddenly a loud thud sounded above the monotonous chant. It was only a preliminary sound, like the striking of a middle A before a concert piece. Now and again I could hear the crackle of burning logs, for four huge wood-fires had been set going to give light to the proceedings. There was not a breath of air. The trees cowered around like crouching animals ready to spring upon us.

And then rub-a-dub, rub-a-dub, rub-a-dub from the tom-toms, like a terrific storm of noise sweeping over an island that has been silent since the creation, throbbing, throbbing, catching at my heart with faint pangs of pain, thud chasing thud through the startled air like a stampede of prairie horses. The central group gradually, with weird, graceful sweeps of the arms, disintegrated itself, forming a wider circle, slowly, rhythmically stamping their bare feet on the ground, turning just as slowly, just as rhythmically as they rotated in an ever-widening circle.

Frederick was on my left, Frank on my right. I glanced round at the ranks of black faces, over which played the reflection of the swaying flames, giving them a hideous cast of savagery. I shuddered, not so much from fear as from excitement. I dared not look at Frederick. Why, I do not know.

By this time the dancers had worked themselves up into a frenzy. They wriggled from the hips, bent rapidly down then straightened themselves up with a perfect precision, quickening their movements and chanting more loudly all the time as the deafening rub-a-dubs of the tom-toms rushed far and wide through the night.

My attention at that moment was distracted by a disturbance a few yards away from me. I saw a short black man being held back by stout arms gripping him around the waist whilst others held him by the wrists. I understood. A victim to the alluring influence of this primeval jungle-rite.

Time went by. I don't know much of it, for my heart was beating to the rhythm of forest-syncopation, and my blood was running through its veins with a savage fury.

Suddenly I felt my left arm gripped as by a vice. I looked up and saw Frederick staring down at me, a wild, demoniac expression in his eyes, his face puckered up into wrinkles, his nostrils dilated, breathing stertorously.

I shuddered, this time from some unknown fear, as I heard him saying in a hoarse, harsh whisper:

"God! For Christ's sake, let's go!"

We walked away with rapid steps, towards our waiting car.

Three Rebels

"Life's boring," Helen Lee Choy said, and yawned.

"You mean you feel bored," Toni said.

"All right, I feel bored. And you?"

"Oh, I feel bored too. It's the heat."

Arthur, sitting on the floor in one corner of the room, chuckled audibly.

"You bored, Arthur?" Toni said.

"Bored? I always feel bored, except when I'm working."

"Life's boring for you then," Helen Lee Choy said.

"No, life's not boring. Life's a big adventure in work. When I'm working, especially on something difficult, I'm alive. No, life's not boring."

"Well," Toni said, "I don't work, I have no special interest in life, I'm not an artist. But I don't find life boring. You know why?"

"Why?" Arthur and Helen Lee Choy said together.

"Because my life's a work of art. I'm bored now because of the heat. Yes, I'm sure it's the heat."

"Come back to what you just said about your life being a work of art," Helen Lee Choy said. "What do you mean by that?"

"I mean that I'm free, I mean that I do as I want, that I'm not a respectable person, that I have no responsibilities. I don't work, but that doesn't prevent me from living. Some days I have nothing to eat. What the hell! Some days

I have lots. And life's an interesting adventure because there's lots of things to do for him who doesn't care what he does. Everything out of the ordinary that the respectable person does, he does it in the dark, behind back-gates and lamp-posts and behind God's back. To hell with that! I believe in what I do, so I do it all in the open, right flop in the bright burning open."

"Hear, hear!" Arthur said from his corner.

"Does that make your life a work of art?" Helen Lee Choy said.

"Sure. Art is an untrammelled thing. A work of art is a spontaneous creation."

"Rats!" Arthur said. "Look at that canvas I was working on last month. It gave me hell. I struggled and struggled with it, passing sleepless nights thinking of it. Helen, are your canvases spontaneous?"

"No, but I think I see what Toni is driving at. It is difficult to put into words, but what he means is this. He means that every work of art must have life in it. And life, significant life that is, is nothing if not spontaneous. And his life is a work of art, Toni says, because it is spontaneous."

They were silent for a while, Arthur thinking: she's talking damn nonsense, but he said nothing. It was too hot to argue. The room in which they were, was a large one in the upper story of a house overlooking Marine Square. Two candles, stuck into bottles, gave a feeble yellow light. There were two easels in the room, one chair and two large katias – an East Indian sort of bed. Helen Lee Choy, a slim, good-looking Chinese girl, sat in the chair. Toni, a tall white boy, lolled on one of the katias. He was very handsome: a perfect Roman nose, a shock of fair curly hair and a high, broad forehead. He boasted descent from the early aristocratic French settlers in the island. Arthur was also white, but short. His face was thin and ascetic-looking. His eyes moved restlessly and his hands too.

The walls of the room were plastered with finished and unfinished pictures. Some were Arthur's work, some Helen Lee Choy's. On one easel there was an unfinished watercolour which Arthur was doing. On the other easel there was an oil painting of a luscious black woman striding down a country lane with a tray of fruit on her head. Helen Lee Choy had that afternoon put the last touches to it.

"How do you like my fruitseller?" she said.

"It's got life all right," Toni said. "It's got movement."

"My watercolour isn't worth a damn," Arthur said. "I don't care. When you are doing a commission, you don't care. If stupid society women who don't know art from their bottoms want to pay for a picture, that's their business. Let them. I have to live, so I give them what they want."

"Christ," Helen Lee Choy said, yawning, "you bore me with your foolish talk about money."

"Ho, ho!" Toni ejaculated. "I don't like money. Or rather, I hate people with money. They bore me stiff because they're all fools. Ever heard this?

When God perceives a man who does not care
To have the gift of tongues or love or healing,
A man who has no wish to do or dare,
For science no regard, for art no feeling,
A man whose soul knows neither heaven nor hell,
Whose heart is empty both of milk and honey,
When God sees this he says to Gabriel:
Give the poor fellow lots and lots of money.

"Ha, ha, ha!" Arthur roared.

"I see nothing to laugh at," Helen Lee Choy said. "It's clever, but I see nothing to laugh at. We shouldn't disrespect money."

"Hear her using that funny word 'disrespect'!" Toni said to Arthur. "Helen, in this matter you're a petty *bourgeois*. Your sense of values is all wrong. Will we never convert you to communism?"

"I believe in individualism," Helen Lee Choy said. "I believe . . ."

"For Christ's sake," Arthur said, "you bore me! Shut up, you two. Leave me alone with my inertia."

"Sounds like a vamped up title of a Rudy Vallee song," Helen Lee Choy said.

"Both of you bore me stiff," Toni said.

"I'm bored," Helen Lee Choy said.

"Shut up, you two!" Arthur said. "Christ, shut up, will you!"

They sat in silence. Helen Lee Choy was wearing a short blue serge skirt, a red jumper and a pair of fancy shoes with the stockings turned down over them. Her hair was bobbed. She puffed clouds of smoke into the warm air and had her legs crossed in masculine fashion. Toni was wearing a pair of baggy trousers made of black silk and a blue shirt open at the neck, with a large batik neckerchief falling down past his stomach. His hair was untidy and his lips were rouged. Arthur wore nothing.

The three had been living together now for over a month. They were living together because they were birds of a feather; or rather Helen Lee Choy and Arthur had the painting taste in common. Toni lived with them because he was Arthur's lover. All Port of Spain was agog with talk of the two crazy boys always seen together in Frederick Street. Toni and Arthur were crazy because they wore unconventional garments, because they were social rebels. They were not only crazy, respectable Port of Spain said; they were also immoral because they practised an "unmentionable vice". The police, respectable Port of Spain said, should clap them in jail for being what they were. But Toni and Arthur went about in their bright alpagartas and gaudily strange clothes, uncaring. Sometimes they had nothing to eat. "What the hell!" they said.

Arthur worked hard and found happiness, the ecstatic happiness only artists know, in his work. Toni found happiness everywhere and anywhere and anyhow: when he was drunk, when he was sober, when he was hungry, when his belly was full. Helen Lee Choy worked in a newspaper office. She believed in order and organized religion and big business; she believed in these things not for herself but for other people, the great unwashed *canaille*. She despised unintelligent people and divided the human race into two classes: the intelligent, a small minority, and the unintelligent, well, almost everybody. Very often she argued with Toni and Arthur in support of her beliefs and, like all young women of twenty-three, often talked nonsense. Sometimes Toni and Arthur talked nonsense too, but then they also were like all young men of eighteen and twenty.

A few in the island recognized that Arthur had talent. A very few said that he would one day make a far-reaching reputation for himself as an artist. Helen Lee Choy's work was not considered as good. Though born in Trinidad, she had lived abroad for a number of years and had only recently returned to the island of her birth. Most people said that Arthur's talent would be ruined by his relationship with Toni. Helen Lee Choy and a few others did not think so. Wasn't Toni showing Arthur the sights of the town, so to speak?

Arthur had tried his hand at a job, only to find that he could not brook its restraints and inhibitions; and soon after he chucked his job, his father discovered his affair with Toni and promptly put him out of the house, saying that he did not recognize his own son in Arthur. Arthur, glad enough that he had cut himself adrift from his family, went and lived openly with Toni. Sometimes they behaved like two love-birds, it didn't matter who the devil happened to be present. Indeed, Toni was proud of his inversion and often boasted that the best artists had always been "like that".

"Say something, somebody, for Christ's sake!" Helen Lee Choy said. "The silence is getting on my nerves. I shall scream in a minute."

"Scream," Toni said. "Do you good and us two, too."

Arthur yawning, asked: "What about a drink? Any rum in the house?"

"Any rum, Helen? Any *crème-de-canne*?"

Helen Lee Choy clapped her hands. "Bravo, Arthur, you thought of a drink and neither of us thought of that."

She rose and went to the little room at the back. While she was away Arthur got onto his feet and began to dance around the room in imitation of a ballet dancer. The white skin of his naked body was like water before dawn in the yellow light. Toni looked on, admiring Arthur's white and robust body. Arthur's hands moved about restlessly as he danced, and his eyes too. When Helen Lee Choy returned, she took no notice of Arthur's performance. Arthur stopped his dancing to drink. They all drank and sat in silence. The night was hot and the trees in the square were spreading themselves out to get whatever air was going.

"This rum's not strong enough," Toni said. "Let's have another."

They had another. Five minutes went by in silence.

"It's the heat," Toni said suddenly.

The others sat up.

"Heat?" Helen Lee Choy said.

"It's the heat that's boring us."

"Oh!" Helen Lee Choy and Arthur said together.

"It's the heat that's boring us," Toni repeated.

"Hell must be a boring place then," Arthur said.

"You two will know in time," Helen Lee Choy said.

"That's an old joke," Arthur said, "and unworthy of one belonging to your small minority, Helen."

"We can't be on pedestals all the time. We must come down now and again."

"Right, right!" Arthur said.

"It's good to be stupid now and again," Helen Lee Choy added.

"Oh, dry up!" Toni said. "Let's have another drink."

"There's no more," Helen Lee Choy said.

"Good God!" Arthur and Toni said together.

Helen Lee Choy turned the empty bottle upside-down and threw it on the katia on which Toni was reclining. Toni snatched the bottle and hurled it through the window. Helen Lee Choy and Arthur put their fingers to their ears. The bottle crashed on the pavement below. Helen Lee Choy ran to the window and looked out.

"Toni, you're a damn fool," she said. "Supposing you had struck somebody?"

"What the hell. I'm bored."

"You'll be having the police up in a minute."

"You and your police," Toni said, flinging his arms into the air. "I want another rum, that's what I want."

"No money, no rum."

"Any money, Arthur?" Toni asked.

Arthur made the motion of putting his hands into his pockets. Toni and Helen Lee Choy laughed. Then there was silence that lasted for five minutes, and during that time Arthur's restless hands moved about his naked body and his restless eyes looked through the window into the dark night, then at Helen Lee Choy and at Toni. Sometimes they looked at the pictures hanging on the walls. Toni lolled on the floor and stared up at the ceiling with thoughts running through his mind like little imps. Helen Lee Choy puffed smoke into the hot air, her legs crossed in masculine fashion. Suddenly she cocked her head and looked at Toni and Arthur out of the corner of her eye.

"I've got it!" she said, slapping her knee. Then she threw her cigarette end and it fell on Toni. Toni sprang up *toute suite*.

"Christ, you've burnt me!" he said. "What the hell . . ."

"I've got it!"

"Got what?"

"Look, this is my idea. You are bored, Arthur is bored, I am bored. All right. We want to do something exciting, something that will buck us up. All right. This is my idea. Toni, you go into Marine Square. Arthur, you take Victoria Square. I will take Brunswick Square. Now, this is my idea. Each of us must find somebody and bring our finds here. What about it?"

"Great," Toni and Arthur said together.

"And, let me see. Yes, there must be a time-limit for doing the job. Half an hour, I suggest. What's the time now?"

There was no clock in the room so Toni ran out into the street to get the time from a public clock. When he returned he said it was just eight o'clock.

"All right. We must all be back here by a quarter to nine. Bring in whom you like, man or woman, black, brown or white."

Arthur quickly slipped into some clothes. Then they all went out. The sky was spattered with stars. In a hotel opposite there was a dance on. Arthur, Toni and Helen Lee Choy could see the couples dancing and hear the music.

"Well, Toni," Helen Lee Choy said, "you're lucky. Your hunting ground is right here."

"You take Marine Square," Toni said to Helen Lee Choy.

"No, I'm going to Brunswick Square."

"You take Marine Square. I insist."

"Yes, Helen, you take Marine Square," Arthur said. "So long and good luck."

"So long, Helen," Toni said. "And good luck."

"So long you two," Helen Lee Choy said.

Toni and Arthur walked up Frederick Street. When they got to Brunswick Square, Arthur kissed Toni goodbye on the lips and went on to Victoria Square.

. . . . .

"But why not?" Arthur was saying. "I tell you, you're quite safe. There's nothing to get the wind up over. Come on up."

"I ain't coming," the black boy said.

"Is that you, Arthur?" Toni called out from the window upstairs. "Is that you, Arthur? Time's nearly up."

"Right." Arthur called out. "But my boy won't come up. He's scared."

Toni came lumbering down the dark stairway, then he came to the gate and saw Arthur standing on the pavement and a little farther on, a black boy.

"Is that your find?" Toni said.

"Yes, but he's scared stiff."

"Hallo there," Helen Lee Choy called out from the window upstairs. "Hallo there."

"Who's dat?" the black boy asked.

"That's a nice, nice lady upstairs," Arthur said. "I'm sure you'll like her."

"Won't you come up, sweetheart?" Toni said.

The boy still stood irresolute. Toni made a dash at him and, catching him round the waist, lifted him and ran through the gate and up the stairs with him, the boy screaming all the time. Arthur glanced up and down the street, and seeing no policeman in sight, followed on up the stairs.

"Come, come little boy," Helen Lee Choy said. "Nothing's going to happen to you. We only want you to pose for us so we can draw you and paint you."

The boy was crying and muttering that he wanted to go back home, that his mother would beat him when he got back home.

"No, no, your mother won't beat you," Helen Lee Choy said. "Tell her that a nice lady met you in the street and asked you up to her house."

The boy stopped crying and Helen Lee Choy, taking him gently by the hand, led him into the large room.

"So this is what you picked up," she said to Arthur.

"That's my catch, a nice black-velvet boy. He gave me hell, that nice black-velvet boy."

"And what's your name, my boy?" Helen Lee Choy asked.

"Timot'y."

"A nice name, Timothy."

"Dey does call me Sonny."

"Sit down Sonny." Instead, Sonny's scared eyes searched the room. Then he went to the window and looked out.

"What's your age?" Helen Lee Choy asked.

"I don' know," Sonny said.

Arthur came into the room with Toni and saw the other two strangers. One was white, the other coloured.

"This is my friend, Mr Cohen," Helen Lee Choy said, introducing the white man. Mr Cohen was short, fat and Jewish. He bowed to Arthur in an abstracted manner.

"Here's my friend, Arthur," Toni said. "Mr Theophilus Montague, barber at the Belle Vue Hotel. His friends and I call him Theo for short." Theo was very tall, very thin and very brown. His features were distinctly negroid and his hair, although kinky, was plastered down upon his skull with an extravagant amount of vaseline. He was dressed up like a dandy. He said: "Pleased to meet you," to Arthur and shook him by the hand.

"I picked up Mr Cohen just as he was about to go off with a black woman in Marine Square," Helen Lee Choy said.

Mr Cohen looked at her with an alarmed smile and fingered his gold watch-chain slung across his vest.

"I guess this dame nearly took the breath out of me when she came up to me," Mr Cohen said. "But say, folks, what's this game you're playing?"

"From New York, Mr Cohen?" Toni asked.

"Yep, from the Big City. But say, folks, what's this game you're . . ."

"Ever been in Trinidad before, Mr Cohen?" Toni asked.

"Mr Cohen has never been here before," Helen Lee Choy put in. "He's here on business, staying at the Queen's Park Hotel. He's here on big business."

"Are you a communist, Mr Cohen?" Toni asked.

Mr Cohen looked horrified. "Nope siree!" he said with emphasis. "I've seen enough of what they've tried to do back in the States and heard enough of what they're trying to do back in Russia to remain what every respectable business man should be, a . . ."

"Ever heard of Mr Mike Gold, Mr Cohen?" Toni asked.

"We've got a young man with that name in our New York office; but not Mike. He's Joshua. But say folks," and Mr Cohen looked around the room, "is this a stoodio?"

"You've said it," Toni said.

"And who's the painter-boy?"

"The painter-boy," Toni said, pointing to Arthur, "and the painter-wench," pointing to Helen Lee Choy.

"Has your big business anything to do with pictures?" Arthur asked. "Or shall I say, are you in the market for paintings, Mr Cohen?"

"You've said it, big boy. I tell the world how much my wife likes good photographs and such work of arts."

"Hear, hear, Mr Cohen," Arthur said. "These are all work of arts."

"But say, this light is kind of dim to see the . . ."

"You don't have to see them now, Mr Cohen," Arthur said. "Come tomorrow. Come in the morning. Come any old time you like."

"Sure thing, sure thing. And do you live here?"

"Sure thing," Arthur said. "All of us."

"And that young man too?" Mr Cohen said, pointing to Theo.

"No," Theo said. "I work at the Belle Vue Hotel. I am a barber at the Belle Vue Hotel. This is the first time I been up here."

"Got a cigarette, Mr Cohen?" Toni asked.

Mr Cohen offered cigarettes around. Even Sonny took one. He had been smoking since he was ten and now he was fifteen. He was plump, was wearing a ragged suit, and had no shoes on his feet. Sonny had no need to dress well for he was a yard-boy and breakfast-carrier.

136

"Say folks, what about a drink?" Mr Cohen said.

"We have no drink, Mr Cohen," Helen Lee Choy said, "and we have no money either."

"Perhaps Mr Cohen would like to treat us all?" Toni said.

"Sure thing, sure thing." Mr Cohen put his hand into his breast pocket and produced a roll of notes. Toni's eyes rolled. Mr Cohen passed a five-dollar bill along to Toni who immediately ran off to buy the drinks.

Helen Lee Choy was sitting on the floor with her back against the wall, and Arthur too. Mr Cohen was sitting on a katia. Sonny was leaning against the window. Theo sat on the other katia.

While Toni was away, Mr Cohen kept glancing at Helen Lee Choy. He tried to attract her eye, but she was not looking his way; she was looking at Theo who appeared to be very embarrassed. Mr Cohen's face was heavy and his eyes burned with lust as he looked at Helen Lee Choy, appraising her body. Arthur's hands moved about restlessly and his eyes shot from Theo to Sonny, from Mr Cohen to Helen Lee Choy. He saw the flaming desire in Mr Cohen's eyes and he loathed him, but he liked Theo's tall body. Yes, he decided, he liked Theo's tall body. He wondered about Theo, and while he was wondering, Mr Cohen was trying his best to catch Helen Lee Choy's eye. She knew that, but she kept on looking at Theo. She wasn't really seeing Theo at all, she was wondering how the evening would end, what new light it would throw on life for her.

When Toni returned he handed the bottles of rum to Helen Lee Choy. He didn't give any change to Mr Cohen. Helen Lee Choy prepared the glasses and in a short while the bottle was being passed around.

"I don't want a drink," Theo said.

"What?" Toni said. "You must drink, man. Even Sonny is having a drink."

"I don't drink," Theo said.

"All the more reason why you should have one," Toni said. "It will give you a new slant on the world."

Obviously against his will, Theo poured out a drink for himself. Sonny refused. They made an attempt to persuade him but Helen Lee Choy said no, to leave him alone, that he was really too young to drink.

"It ain't dat, Miss," Sonny said. "Sometimes I does take a little."

"Hear, hear!" Arthur said as Sonny poured himself a drink.

"Here's how!" and Mr Cohen held up his glass to Helen Lee Choy, looking at her over its rim.

Arthur, while drinking, had his eyes on Theo. Theo sipped and coughed.

"That's not the way to drink rum, man!" Arthur said. "Swallow it down with one gulp."

Theo swallowed with one gulp and began to splutter and cough.

"Looks like the first drink you've had in your life," Toni said, "and at your age!"

Theo said nothing. He felt the rum searing its way down his gullet and began to feel a suffocating sensation. It soon passed off, however, and he began to feel a strange exhilaration coming over him. It was the first time he had ever had a drink. He had been reared by parents who were pious non-conformists, and taught to be respectable and well-behaved. Theo had so far succeeded in being respectable and well-behaved, but his struggle against clamouring desires of the body had been a severe one. He had just turned twenty-one. Why he should have accepted Toni's invitation in Victoria Square he could not have explained even if asked. All he could have said was: "I liked the man. He was tall and his head was beautiful." It was the first time he had ever broken his homeward journey after work. My mother must be wondering where I am, he thought – and rose and said that he was leaving. Toni and Arthur and Helen Lee Choy protested and Theo sat down again without saying a word. Suddenly he felt that he wanted to laugh. His head felt amazingly light and carefree. The little guardian angel that was always in it to keep him respectable and well-behaved left him alone to take care of himself. Theo, in short, was happy and slightly tipsy.

Mr Cohen smacked his heavy lips. "Say folks, this cane-juice sure beats everything I ever tasted," he said and smacked his lips again.

"Hear, hear," Arthur said. "I know a man who, some years ago, came to Trinidad for the first time. A one hundred per cent American. He had been all over the world before he came here. He was looking for what he called the elixir of life, for he was a philosopher. He found it here. It was rum. Any old time you care, you may see him loafing about the squares in old torn clothes, unshaven and haggard. When he came here he was all right, had a good job with some big American house or the other. He stayed right here to continue drinking rum, his elixir of life. I've talked to him often. He tells me that he is happy, the happiest man in the world. Moral: never judge a man by his appearance."

"That's an A-one story, Mr Painter, an A-one story," Mr Cohen said.

"And I knew a man," Toni said, "who, tasting rum, said: 'It's too good a thing to be true' and fled from the island that very night."

Mr Cohen laughed. "That's an A-one story. But what about another drink?" and he glanced across at Helen Lee Choy.

"Hear, hear!" Arthur was feeling fine. He kept trying to catch Theo's eyes.

"You shouldn't drink any more, darling," Toni said to him. "You know how you behave when . . .'"

"Rats! I don't behave worse than anybody else."

"You remember what you did the last time, darling?"

"Rats! I'm all right, Toni, I'm all right. Never mind about me for tonight. Mind about Sonny. He's your boy for tonight."

"I didn't bring him."

"I brought him. You can have him. Exchange is no robbery."

Toni scowled but said nothing.

"Oh shut up, you two!" Helen Lee Choy said. "Mr Cohen's offered us another drink."

"Sure thing, sure thing!"

"And afterwards I want to sketch Theo, naked," Arthur said.

Theo looked across quickly at Helen Lee Choy: he remembered how she had tried to defend Sonny against drinking.

But Helen Lee Choy said: "Why yes, that's a good idea, Arthur."

"Hear, hear!" Arthur said. His hands were restless.

Toni scowled but, the drink coming along, he gulped it down. He didn't like the way the experiment was shaping.

"But say, folks!" and Mr Cohen smacked his lips. "What's the big idea? What's the game?" And turning to Helen Lee Choy, he asked: "Why did you bring me here?"

"Wait, my dear. Have patience. Your fate's in the lap of the gods."

Mr Cohen smacked his lips and leered at Helen Lee Choy. She gave him one of her sweetest smiles. He wanted to rise there and then and take her in his arms, but he repressed the desire and sat still, filled with an anticipatory bliss.

Helen Lee Choy rose and began to prepare her easel. Arthur followed suit. Theo, sitting on the edge of his katia, held his hands together nervously. He found it impossible to face anyone. At last he glanced around at Toni in a helpless manner. He couldn't believe they were wanting him to take off his clothes. He had never exposed his body to anyone, not even to his mother.

"Come along, Theo," Helen Lee Choy said.

"Me? No, no!" He blurted out, utterly confused.

"Why, what's wrong?"

"No, no!" was all he could find to say, his fingers interlocked.

"Nonsense, man!" Arthur was annoyed. "Ashamed of the body God gave you? Isn't your god a good god? Would he give you something to be ashamed of? Nakedness is good, if only because it is natural, the natural state of man. Fornication is good, murder is good, everything is good." Arthur was a little drunk, and whenever he was drunk he talked like that.

"Not so fast, kid, not so fast!" Mr Cohen said, lifting his heavy eyes in shocked surprise. "Moider? Even moider?"

"Sure, Mr Jew, sure!" Arthur's hands and eyes were restless. "Didn't your people murder Christ? And doesn't the whole edifice of Christianity rest upon the foundation of a murder committed by your people two thousand years ago? No murder, no dying for the sins of the world, no sacrifice of God the Father, no Christianity." And then, more drunkenly than ironically, he added: "Distance lends enchantment to the view, even the view with a cross in it and a bleeding body on the cross."

Mr Cohen was silent, his heavy eyes and his heavy mouth half-open. Helen Lee Choy and Toni had heard Arthur speak like that every time he was drunk, so they took no notice of him. In any case, Toni was scowling and thinking of something else.

"Rats on this talk!" Arthur said, suddenly calming down. "Let's draw and drink. Come, Theo darling. Take off your clothes."

Theo did not move. He was looking down at the floor.

"All right," Arthur said. "Look at me." Rapidly he took off his clothes and threw them into a corner. His white body, in the yellow light of the candles, glimmered like water before dawn.

Mr Cohen glanced uncomfortably across at Helen Lee Choy. He was surprised to see her take Arthur's nakedness so nonchalantly. He had never before seen a man strip himself naked in the presence of a woman. Immediately his suspicions of her were confirmed.

Theo averted his eyes from Arthur's pale nakedness. He felt the blood rushing to his cheeks, making them insufferably hot.

"You want to paint me?" Sonny suddenly asked.

"Come along, Sonny, come along," Helen Lee Choy said; and in a moment

Sonny's clothes had dropped from him and he was swaying in the middle of the room. Arthur's body grew whiter beside Sonny's black body.

"Sonny, you're drunk," Helen Lee Choy said.

Sonny grinned.

"The boy's getting drunk," Toni said. "Take charge of your boy, Arthur. Put him to bed."

Arthur went and placed Sonny against the wall. "Now try and be quiet," he said. "We're going to draw you."

Arthur and Helen Lee Choy began to draw the black boy. Mr Cohen rose from his chair and went across to where Helen Lee Choy stood. He stood over her and watched the charcoal lines taking shape and form on the white paper. Helen Lee Choy felt him over her and, every now and again, his hot breath on the nape of her neck. Her insides turned, but she said nothing. She wanted to see what new light the evening would throw on life for her.

Theo was extremely embarrassed and wanted to leave, but he was afraid to make the attempt. He was afraid to rise and so become the centre of attraction. He sat quite still, looking at nobody. He couldn't understand how these people could be so unconcerned with Arthur and Sonny naked, and he couldn't believe that they were serious when they had asked him to pose naked for them. The idea alone so unnerved him that he felt like making a bolt for it. He dreaded that Arthur would again begin to ask him to take off his clothes. He didn't like Arthur very much. He liked Toni. He liked Toni's beautiful head and tall body and he liked Toni's manner. He had seen Toni before in the streets in his queer getup and had liked him then. He had heard people in the barber shop discussing Toni and Arthur and could never make head or tail of what they were saying. And now here he was, with them, in their room!

Sonny collapsed to the floor while Helen Lee Choy was in the midst of her work. Arthur, who worked very much faster than Helen Lee Choy, had already completed his sketch. Everybody laughed at Sonny except Theo, and Arthur lifted him and placed him on one of the katias. Theo's heart began to beat violently for he knew that he would be asked to take Sonny's place. Arthur was already looking at him.

Mr Cohen was getting impatient. He wondered how much longer Helen Lee Choy would waste her time sketching when she could be making love with him. He wondered how much she would charge him, or would she do it for love? The mere fact of her having picked him up in the square was proof enough that she fancied him.

The spirit of boredom had fled from the room. Helen Lee Choy was on tiptoes with excitement, waiting to see what would happen. She could see Toni brooding in a corner. She saw that he was working himself into a belligerent mood. Drink always had that effect on him; and now, added to that, was his jealousy of Arthur. Lines began to show on his face and beads of perspiration stood up on his forehead. He called for another drink and the bottle was passed around. He took a heavy shot and so did Arthur and Mr Cohen. Helen Lee Choy avoided the bottle. Arthur poured a heavy shot for Theo and took the glass to him. Toni, furrowing his forehead, glared at Arthur. He heard Arthur trying to persuade Theo to have the drink. Once Theo looked across at Toni and, noticing the sour expression on his face, thought it was meant for him. He gulped down the rum and again spluttered and spat, but the burning sensation in his gullet soon passed off and he began to feel light in the head and amazingly happy.

"It's your turn now," Helen Lee Choy said to Theo.

"Say, kid," Mr Cohen said to Helen Lee Choy, "what's the big idea? You haven't finished the nigger yet and you want to do the high-brown? I guess that's going some."

Sonny, on one of the katias, was groaning. Nobody took any notice of him. Toni, heavy with anger and drink and jealousy, brooded. Arthur's restless eyes were no longer restless: they were fixed on Theo.

A clock in the neighbourhood struck ten. Now and again, from across the still square, strains of dance music slid into the room. Nobody heard them except Helen Lee Choy. She was sober and full of awareness, her narrow eyes quick to take in everything.

And now Theo, growing bold with the last drink, gave in to Arthur's importunities and took off his clothes. Arthur's eyes were bright and again restless. Moving beside Theo, he passed his white hand along the brown back down to the buttocks. Theo, not knowing what to do, stood perfectly still and gazed across at Toni. Theo's brown body had some of the graceful curves of a woman's. Helen Lee Choy began to sketch. Toni reached across for the bottle and helped himself to a drink. Then he watched Arthur, who was standing beside his easel gazing at Theo. Then Arthur lifted his right hand with the stick of charcoal held daintily between his fingers, held it poised in the air for a moment, and then began to sketch with rapid movements. But suddenly he did a surprising thing: he put on his clothes. For a long time there was silence while the two sketched: a silence that was broken only by Mr Cohen's breathing and Sonny's groans. The drink raced through Theo's body and gave him a tingling sensation, but he stood still and gazed at Toni whose eyes were fixed in a bleary stare on Arthur.

Suddenly Theo realized that he was naked, and in some strange fashion he saw in Helen Lee Choy his mother, and he was dreadfully ashamed. Yet he dared not move. He felt just as if he were riveted to the spot, but all the time there was something rising in him and taking shape, something rebellious against his nakedness.

In the meantime, Mr Cohen took up his position behind Helen Lee Choy. No longer could he resist the desire to touch her, and pretending to wish to see the sketch nearer and better, he leaned forward and rested the fat palm of his hand on her shoulder. Helen Lee Choy's insides turned and twisted and her sketching began to go all wrong.

"Please don't, Mr Cohen," she said, quite politely. "You're disturbing me," and gently she took his hand from her shoulder. Mr Cohen was flattered by the gesture and what she had said. He felt now that it was only a question of time and decided not to spoil his chances by being too precipitate. So he moved away and helped himself to another drink, after which he sat on the edge of the katia on which Sonny lay. He offered Toni a cigarette and in a moment smoke was curling from their lips in slow, lazy spirals up to the ceiling.

Arthur stood away from his easel to survey his work and found it good. Helen Lee Choy examined it and said: "It is very good." And just as she was about to give her attention to the resumption of her own drawing, Theo reached for his clothes and began rapidly and excitedly to dress. Helen Lee Choy called out to him to give her another five minutes, but Theo was in a frenzy of haste and took no notice of her. His one desire now was to be dressed and then to bolt for it. But Arthur, with restless hands and restless eyes, ran up to restrain him, whereupon Toni sprang to his feet, leapt across to Arthur's easel and, snatching the sketch, tore it to bits.

For an instant Arthur stood as if he couldn't believe his eyes, but the next minute he threw himself on Toni and his nails were scratching away at Toni's face. Toni, livid with rage and jealousy, screamed as the blood trickled down his chest. Mr Cohen stood. Were it not for Helen Lee Choy and the promise of her, he would have run out and away. He didn't like fights: they put the fear of God in him. Now he saw the two men rolling on the floor and heard them snarling at each other, interlocked and scratching like two women. Helen Lee Choy shouted out to them to come to their senses. It was only when Theo, jacket over arm, was slinking along the passageway to the door, that Arthur tugged himself away from Toni and ran after Theo. Toni also got to his feet, saw what was happening, and gave chase. A moment later Mr Cohen heard the wild scampering of the men down the stairway. And then there was silence.

And Mr Cohen realized that, but for the drunk-sleeping Sonny, he was now alone with Helen Lee Choy. His heart did a quick pit-a-pat of joy.

Many times before had Helen Lee Choy witnessed scenes of violence between Toni and Arthur and she had learnt to take them as they came. She knew that they would be all sweetness to each other in the morning, but she was now hoping that they wouldn't get into trouble with the police in the streets. Once before that had happened and she had been the one to stop the matter from going to the Magistrate's Court by tips to the police. She stood now thinking of that and hoping against hope – and suddenly realized that she was alone with Mr Cohen.

The pieces of Arthur's sketch littered the floor. An unopened bottle of rum stood in a corner. The other bottle had been thrown over in the scuffle and now its contents stained the floor dark in the candlelight. Sonny still snored. No sound of footfall or passing car came up from the street and the music across the square had ceased. A faraway cock crowed and others answered the night-challenge. Some cigarette smoke still hung about.

"Some guys!" Mr Cohen said. The nasal twang jarred on her nerves.

"They often do that," she said pleasantly.

It had all happened so suddenly. Now Helen Lee Choy saw in a flash that she had made a mistake in not following the others. And yet, on second thought, she didn't think it was a mistake. The situation was exciting, it would put her wits to the test. She saw in Mr Cohen's eyes and his hanging under-lip not only what he wanted of her, but what he expected of her.

Mr Cohen approached a step and said thickly: "What about a drink, huh?"

"Haven't we had enough?" she said, playing up to him with a saucy look in her eyes.

"Sure not, sure not!" Mr Cohen said – and came a step or two nearer to her.

"I have," she said, standing her ground and looking him straight in the eyes.

He blinked and said: "Well, I guess this is fine. Enough is as good as too much. Fine, fine!" and he began to take off his jacket.

"No, no," she said, quickly and apprehensively, "not in here."

"Huh," he said, his small eyes bright with the anticipation roused in him by her mellow "not in here".

"The others might come back at any minute." Her voice and manner assumed an intimate tone.

"Then . . . say honey, you know a good place with a nice cosy little room, in a hotel, maybe?"

"Sure I do," said she. "Not far from here."

"Come along then, honey, come along." With which he came up to her and she allowed him to kiss her, struggling ever so slightly in his short, fat arms. Then she led him to the stairway.

"Wait for me at the bottom," she said in a mellow, calm voice, "while I get ready and put the light out."

He stumbled down the steps. When she knew that he was at the bottom, waiting for her, very gently she drew in the door and turned the key in the lock.

Two minutes later she heard his knock at the door.

"Yes?" she said.

"Aren't you coming, honey?" he said.

"Go away, man, or I'll call the police from my window!" she shouted at the top of her lungs.

After a while she heard him stumble down the steps again, and then his heavy, retreating tread on the pavement below.

Béti

They called her Béti. She was young and as pretty as any East Indian girl in Trinidad. She was born on a coconut estate in Cedros, where her father worked as a picker. He could climb the tall, slender boles of the trees with the agility of a monkey: indeed, in all Cedros there was none to compare with him. He had never married Béti's mother, for it was not the custom of his people, earning at the most two or three shillings a day, to indulge in the expensive ceremony of marriage: their poverty precluded that kind of indulgence. After their fashion, they had been happy together in their little thatched hut, built under the coconut trees, within a stone's throw of the beach.

Time and again Ramdeo – for that was his name – had been offered a room in the barrack-building of the estate. Always he had refused the offer, for the simple reason that he was more comfortable where he was than he could ever be in a crowded barrack where there was no privacy, where cheap gramophones blared Indian music day and night, where neighbour quarrelled with neighbour, where tongues of poison spread bad feeling from room to room, and where there had even once been a murder.

Ramdeo would never forget that dark Saturday night. All the workers on the estate were East Indian and every weekend throughout the years of their bondage to the soil, they celebrated their temporary respite from toil and

146

sweat by drinking rum. On such occasions they drank copiously, recklessly, *flambeaux* lighting up the black night under the coconut trees; and while they drank, they danced in the clearing hard by the compound, to jazz music, cracking the night from the gramophone resting on the ground. Always on those Saturday nights, when they were maddened by the humid heat and the alcohol steaming their brains to bursting point, there were rows, jealousies and fights flaring up in the yellow light of the *flambeaux*. And on this particular night the fight ended in murder.

Ramdeo was standing on the outside of the large circle of people, looking on at the dancers gyrating in the centre. As was his habit, he had had nothing to drink. He seldom took anything strong. He had left Soomintra in the hut with Béti, a baby at the time, and had come out to view the prancing couples, to catch something of the perfervid atmosphere created by the bacchanalian abandon of the plantation labourers. To see them in their orgies, with all the work discipline of the week thrown aside for the night, brought back to him the fact that he was one of a herd, that he was not in an empty world, solitarily breathing the breath of life. These Saturday nights filled his vacuum with noise, movement, and the sinister cross-currents of passion that at any moment could explode into violence and savagery. Like all human beings, and as long as he was himself not involved, for Ramdeo was a timid man, acts inspired by the baser instincts of man fascinated him. To see the cutlasses glinting in the thin rays of the *flambeaux*, to hear the primeval cry of pain in the night, to smell the blood of the victim cut from ear to ear – these things gave him an eerie thrill. And this is exactly what happened as he stood there on this Saturday night on the edge of the throng.

The din was deafening – and all of a sudden the only sound rising into the air floated from the gramophone resting on the ground. And hideously, it was to this accompaniment of jazz music that the cutlass slashed through the neck of Ali's wife, severing the head from the body. Eight months later Ali was hanged in the Royal Gaol.

As Béti grew up with her parents in the little thatched hut near to the beach – an only child – she had often heard Ramdeo and Soomintra discuss the story of the murder; so much so that the details had become familiar to her. Ali's wife, Rampatia, had been perhaps the most attractive of the hundred or so young women working on the estate. Indeed, it was her very beauty that conspired to bring her brief life to a tragic end. The evidence presented to the court had proved that Ali's suspicions, while true in so far as her propensity for flirting went, were unfounded in so far as her assumed infidelity was concerned. This, of course, told heavily against the accused with the jury. And when a verdict of guilty was announced by the foreman and Ali realized that he would die by the hangman's rope, he had taken the sentence of death without a quiver of emotion.

But alas, the dead parents had left behind a boy of six – an orphan to be taken care of by the charity in strangers' hearts. He had been born in the barrack-room occupied by his father and mother and knew only the estate life. He was a silent little fellow, almost taciturn, with a mop of black, curling hair, jet eyes that seemed to stare at you without seeing you, with nothing of the effervescence of the child. You never saw him playing with any of the other children, who ran and romped and uttered shrieks of delight all day long about the compound. Childless neighbours took him in, and from the day his parents disappeared from his sight, he never asked for them. His name was Ramish: for short they called him Ram.

From the first cry of each as they entered the world, Béti in the thatched hut and Ram in the barrack-room – it was ordained by the mysterious powers that decide these matters of the human family that love for each other should grow in the hearts of these two. In the fullness of time, it did.

As a girl of fifteen, Béti was as harum-scarum as an agouti. She was irrepressible. She was a tomboy, a *coquette*, a laughter-loving dryad of the trees. If you missed her at all, you had only to raise your eyes to the fruit trees growing in the compound, and you would see her perched precariously on a topmost branch, swinging her legs beneath her. Her parents could do nothing with her, the truth being that they were too fond of her to scold her, let alone to punish or beat her. Some mornings she would dive into the sea and swim out, her mother on the beach frantically screaming to her to come back, and Béti would take no notice, but go on swimming out, like a brick-brown porpoise sporting in the sunlit water. She was then already a woman, carefree and uninhibited – the legacy of a simple life, born and bred in the midst of a coconut plantation and workers who had no knowledge of the proprieties and respectabilities of urban existence.

Even now she was already in love with Ram – and was aware of it. And as for Ram, he was now twenty-one, thickset like his father before him, and his face was like the face of his mother. His taciturnity still sat heavily upon him. He seldom spoke, he had never played with the children of his age, he was alone with whatever strange thoughts crept and crawled through his mind.

No one knew if he held any memory of the tragedy that had orphaned him so many years ago, but all felt that in some occult way it had indelibly branded him. He had long since been working on the estate and he did his work well.

He had been in love with Béti since she was twelve. He seldom spoke to her and as seldom had been seen with her. You spied him wandering along the beach as the sun sank down the western sky. And then, if you had wind of what was happening, you saw Béti approaching him in the deepening dusk from the opposite direction. And night fell and you saw nothing more – unless the moon's light was full enough to reveal the silhouettes of the two figures moving slowly and solemnly along the beach.

But soon Ram noticed that there were other young men on the estate like himself, labourers' children grown to maturity, who could not help but observe the beauty that shone like a blinding light in Béti – and he grew afraid. The barrack-dwellers saw what was happening and gossiped amongst themselves about it, some saying that the mark of Cain was upon Ram, and others that Béti's loveliness would drive her to perdition, and yet others that Ram's father had been hanged for murdering Ram's mother. The whispers gathered momentum and the hum was like an evil cloud hanging over the colony of barrack-dwellers. And some of the whispers seeped through to Ram's ears – and the fear grew bigger within him.

It was at this time that Ram and Béti vanished from the plantation, vanished as if they had been drawn up into the sky.

Some years had gone by when one day salesman and collector Peter Farley was driving his car along the main road between San Fernando and La Brea. The sky was blue and bright and the sun filled the world with a heat that raised Peter's thirst. Peter was not fond of strong drink, and just now an irresistible ache for coconut water took possession of him. He considered this for a moment, and it occurred to him that the prospect he had in mind might have had something to do with this strange desire for coconut water that had so suddenly seized him. Not yet had he even learned her name. In driving by on his daily rounds of selling and collecting, he had noticed the tiny thatched shelter sitting alongside the road, and the young woman standing under it in the midst of great heaps of coconuts. The glimpses he had caught of her told him that she was an East Indian and that she was pretty. Often Peter had observed cars drawn up on the verge of the road, their drivers standing near the hut with their heads tilted back and upwards to the sky, coconuts to their mouths, their Adam's apples rhythmically bobbing up and down as the sweet, cool liquid gurgled down their throats. On more than one occasion he had seen cars of his fellow S/Cs there too.

Peter Farley had not long been with Singer, but he had had a great deal of experience in selling and collecting for other firms. He was tall, and although he constantly wore a surly expression, he had discovered early in his life as a salesman that women were attracted to him. Indeed, his clients were almost exclusively women, as men appeared to fight shy of him, and were even inclined brusquely to dismiss his overtures. They disliked him at sight and never failed to show it. Because of these idiosyncrasies which were part and parcel of himself and over which he had no control, he had in time won the reputation of being a ladies' man. He was now thirty and had never married. His cynical "Why pay when you don't have to?" had tended further to alienate him from his fellow-men, for Peter could not perceive that his attractions for women were envied by members of his sex.

His brooding dark eyes set in sunken orbits, his olive skin, his close-cropped black hair, taken together with his surliness: all these things gave him an odd quality of remoteness, of being difficult to get at, to understand. An aura of mystery hovered about him.

His car was now approaching the coconut stall and he made up his mind to stop for a drink. For some unaccountable reason, unless it was that flair of his which could always spot a possible purchaser, he had decided that the young woman under the thatched shelter was a prospect. Indeed, Peter Farley regarded all women as prospects: black, brown or white; poor or rich; ugly or pretty; from whatever walk of life – they were all grist to his selling mill – as they were for him grist to his other mill. And had he not known that men instinctively recoiled from him, they too would all have been potential customers.

He thought of the times he had spotted his fellow S/Cs drinking coconut water beside the stall. He was quite sure that not one of them had even thought of the young, pretty woman as a person to whom a sewing machine could be offered, let alone sold. She looked desperately poor, so why waste time with her? That kind of defeatist attitude was all right for others, but not for him, Peter Farley. And in any case, it was an illogical argument. No one was too poor to save money by making her own clothes. In fact, the poorer the person, the greater the need for a sewing machine. That was how he looked at it, and he could sit down with you and produce figures to prove his point. Even with women of ample means, the need was equally paramount –

but for a different reason. "My dear lady," he would say to such a person, his sombre eyes burning in their sockets, "all of us take a pride in doing things for ourselves. It satisfies an urgent need within us, the need to create. With a Singer machine in your house, the encouragement is there to make your own beautiful frocks to adorn your . . . your . . . well, I hope you won't think me rude . . . to adorn your own beautiful body." The surly expression would for a moment give place to a sardonic smile. "The dignity of the human spirit is enhanced by work," he would continue, "and remember, Satan doth find mischief for idle hands to do. Boredom, my dear lady, especially domestic boredom, is a dangerous thing." It sounded almost pompous, but invariably it worked. Or was it Peter Farley himself, the allurement women found in him?

He braked his car to the side of the road near the coconut stall, alighted, and walked up to the young woman. Her sleek hair fell down her shoulders, every now and again the wind blowing it about and across her face. Peter was astounded. Not for a moment had he realized how beautiful the girl was. You had to be near to see the classic cut of the features, the large, lustrous eyes, the glowing brown skin, the perfect lines of the body. She was ravishing. And as he looked at her, her face broke into a smile that revealed two lines of white, perfect teeth. Her laughter rippled into the bright morning air like the song of a bird.

"A coconut please," he said.

She gave him a quick, bold look as she picked up a coconut and expertly slashed off the top with a cutlass.

"I see you passin' in your car once or twice," she said, "but this is the first time you stop."

He was flattered, but the surly look remained in his eyes. He drank another nut and began to talk to her.

Her name was Béti and she had been "married" for ten years. Her husband's name was Ram and they had a little girl who was six years old and at school. She lived with her husband and child – and pointed to the thatched hut standing on the little hill behind her stall. Her husband owned a cart and donkey and every morning, including Sundays, he drove down to the nearby coconut estates and bought the nuts for their stall. As a matter of fact, she expected him back at any moment now. No, she did not have a sewing machine and no salesman had ever offered her one, although she knew many of them because they were in the habit of drinking coconut water at her stall.

While talking to Peter, and obviously without restraint, she would now and again shake her head and the long tresses would swing from shoulder to shoulder like dark, eddying water. Yes, she did all her own sewing, even her husband's pants and her little girl's dresses. She would indeed be glad to see a machine if all the things Peter had said about it were true. Oh no, she didn't have to discuss a matter of this kind with her husband: she need only tell him about it . . . and at that moment she spied Ram driving his donkey cart towards them. While Peter was drinking his third nut, Ram drew up the cart alongside the stall, and without a word began to off-load the nuts.

Peter watched him through the corner of his eye, interested to see the kind of man this beautiful girl had married. He was struck by his good looks, but wondered why he wore such a bitter expression. There seemed to be no joy in the man, and he could not understand how the two could ever have come together, let alone live together for so many years.

"Bring a machine this evening an' show me," she said in a light, gay voice.

"Right," he said, and drove away.

That very evening, after night had fallen, Peter was in Béti's hut demonstrating a machine. An oil lamp, set upon a small deal table, cast a sickly glow in the room. Béti, clad in a loose gown, stood nearby looking at Peter as he worked the machine. Ram was not around and Peter began to wonder at his absence. The little girl, he assumed, was asleep in one of the adjoining rooms. A couch stood astride one corner. The hut was larger than Peter had thought it to be at first.

Outside, the mating calls of the frogs soothed the still air and two cicadas shrieked at each other. Dampness pervaded everything as it had rained heavily, late that afternoon. The sky was still overcast and there were no stars in it.

Peter began to feel uncomfortable, even a little frightened. A strange suspicion had begun to creep up on him, a suspicion so incredible that he tried to shake it off. There was little, if anything at all, to keep the suspicion alive: but some mysterious sixth sense in him kept throbbing on his consciousness, throbbing with the fatal regularity of a clock's tick-tock, tick-tock, tick-tock. At once he became alert to the warning, and every nerve in his body was strung taut. With a great effort of will, he revealed nothing of the agitation stirring within him, but continued with his demonstration in low tones, describing the machine in detail and reciting what it was capable of doing while the woman, clad in a loose gown, more beautiful than ever in the cool light of the lamp, stood a step from him, immobile and silent, with her large lustrous eyes moving slowly and sensuously from the machine to Peter, from Peter to the machine.

Minutes went by, and for some unaccountable reason Peter, who considered himself a man of the world and as such equipped to handle with consummate facility any situation resembling the one now confronting him, felt fear expanding within him: and while he spoke, he glanced at the couch. The woman's silence, when earlier that day she had chattered away to him and had been gay and restless and full of laughter, now seemed sinister to him. He felt he had to assure himself, to convince himself that his imagination was playing tricks with him.

"Where are your husband and child?" he asked with sudden vehemence.

She did not reply immediately, but gave him a long, lingering look.

"They are not here," she said at last. "We don't live here. We live in a house down the road. I come here to meet you."

"I don't . . . I don't understand," he said. But he did understand. Beautiful or not, this was not his dish of tea. Now that he was aware of the nature of the danger facing him, his fear dissolved and left him collected and calculating. He disregarded all the evidence before his eyes. He was again himself, in full control of a situation with which he could deal without batting an eye.

Shutting down the machine, he put his arms about it to lift it out of the hut.

"I came to sell you a machine," he remarked, before straining to lift. Her manner too changed in an instant.

"What you doing?" she said in a voice without a trace of the purpose of her assignation. At that moment she was the Béti he had talked with that morning.

"I'm going," he said. "What did you bring me here for? I'm a salesman, not a . . ."

She interrupted him with a merry peal of laughter. "But I want the machine," she said when the laughter had died away in the yellow light of the room.

"I know you want it," he said, "because you need it. When can we do business?"

"Tomorrow night at our house down the road," she said.

And on the following night, in the presence of a sullen, silent Ram and a bright-eyed little girl, he sold Béti the machine for cash.

Colour

"Good gracious me!" Milly gasped at last. "They're coming here to Grenada!"

"Coming! Why, who's coming to Grenada?" Cora, her sister, asked.

Milly held the letter in her trembling hands and began to read it all over once more.

"But who is coming?" Cora asked again, a little impatiently.

But Milly, wishing to prolong the joy she felt in the sole knowledge of the piece of news, continued to read the letter without taking any notice of her sister's curiosity.

"Good gracious me!" she blurted out again, and took her pince-nez off, the better to see her sister's impatience.

Cora was now looking out of the window at the blue sea, calm and lovely in the Carenage.

"Well, I never!" Milly exclaimed, disappointed in her sister's nonchalance, and at the same time fluttering inwardly with excitement. "Mother, Mother!" she called out, whereupon Cora turned to her sister and snapped:

"You might say what all the fuss is about!"

"Mother, Mother!" Milly called out and ran to the back with the letter gripped in her brown hand. Cora followed her.

Mrs Harriman, brown and withered from age, stood in her kitchen, counting over the cook's morning marketing. Her back was bent and she wore an expression on her face as if she carried the world on her shoulders.

"What's wrong, child?" she said to her forty year old daughter. Then, seeing the letter, she placed her wrinkled brown hand over her heart and added: "If it's bad news, don't, don't, child!"

"Bad news, Ma?" and Milly laughed, a little hysterically.

"Since you won't," said Cora, and snatched the letter from her sister's trembling hand. Milly's glasses fell to the floor.

"Oh my!" said the mother, covering her face with her hands, "Don't tell me they're broken! That would mean bad news."

"They're not, Ma, and Frank and Freida are leaving New York on the seventeenth." She was determined to be before Cora with the extraordinary piece of news.

"Frank and Freida?" said Cora, incredulously, raising her eyes from the letter for a moment.

"Leaving New York?" the mother said, her intensely blue eyes brightening. "Where for, child?"

"Here Ma, Grenada, here!" Milly said.

"Oh, you do give me the creeps, you children. Among you, *do* be calm and let me hear what you all are saying!"

"But today is the sixteenth," Cora said. "That means they are leaving tomorrow."

"But what do you mean?" Mrs Harriman said weakly. "Frank, our Frank, is coming here?"

"Frank, our Frank, Ma," Milly said. "Freida writes to say so. She and Frank are coming down to spend a month or so with us."

"Oh my!" the mother exclaimed, the cares of this world passing away from the corners of her mouth. Even her back straightened in her effort to grasp the significance of what Milly had said.

"And it takes only eight days to get here," Cora said.

"Do be quiet, child." Mrs Harriman said.

"That means that they'll be here in a week's time: let me see, the twenty-fifth," and Cora gave her attention to the letter once again. "And oh! Ma, listen to this . . ."

"This is *my* letter," Milly said, snatching the letter from her sister's hand. "*I* must read it to Ma, not you."

"Well, the idea! You two children squabbling over a letter. Give it to me."

"But you can't read it, Ma. You never could read Freida's handwriting," Milly said. The letter trembled so in her hands that it was with difficulty she opened it.

"What does the letter say?" Mrs Harriman asked. "Among you will be the death of me!"

"That part about the baby," Cora prompted her sister, leaning towards her in her excitement.

"The baby?" Mrs Harriman said weakly.

"Do be still, Ma!" Milly adjusted her pince-nez and pored over the letter.

"But what baby?" Mrs Harriman said in a stronger voice, her weak legs beginning to give way under her. "Among you will be the death of me!"

"Not the baby, Ma. It isn't a baby at all, and that's the trouble. Freida says . . ."

"That's not fair," Milly pleaded. "I received the letter, not . . ."

"You can't find the passage, Milly. Here, let me help you," and rudely she took the letter. At last she found the passage, and began to read: "But what a pity . . ."

"Oh yes," Milly chimed in. "I remember. 'What a pity we haven't a little one to bring down with us so that our dear old mother's heart might be glad-dened a little.' "

"Not 'a little one', 'a little baby'," Cora corrected.

"It's the same thing," Milly said.

"Oh you children! Do be quiet: what's it all about the baby?"

"No, no, Ma," Cora explained. "She's saying how sorry she is that there isn't a little baby to bring down to gladden you and all of us."

"How sweet of her!" Mrs Harriman said, her blue eyes dimmed with tears.

"But that's what she's always saying in almost every letter," Cora said. "She's always saying how sorry she is that she and Frank haven't a baby. But perhaps that's not *so* surprising when we remember the times in which we live."

"What *do* you mean, Cora?" Milly's tone was slightly indignant.

"Well, with all this new idea of birth-control."

"What *is* the child saying?"

"Cora, I'm surprised at you!" Milly's tone was now shocked. "She's always said how much she would just love to have a baby."

"We're not white, you know, only brown coloured people," Cora said sardonically.

"Oh dear, oh dear, among you will be the death of me!" Mrs Harriman wailed.

"Oh, disgusting!" said Milly. "I never can understand you for that!"

"What on earth's wrong with it, I should like to know! And isn't Freida white, and an American at that? And isn't it true that we are coloured? It's true Frank's married her. It's true, if we are to believe their letters, they've been happy together all these years, but what's to prevent her, in these times, from not having a child if she does not want one?"

"But she says she wants one. She's always saying she wants one. And why should she not want one, I should like to know! What's wrong with our Frank? . . ."

"Coloured, that's all."

"Please don't use that word, Cora. It's callous of you." Cora made a juicy noise with her tongue in the roof of her mouth. "You may stupes as much as you like! Freida must have known Frank was a brown man. He was there for her to see him."

"Oh Cora, Milly, please!" the mother wailed. "Don't quarrel, please!"

"But Ma, Cora is . . . is horrid, just horrid. And fancy her saying things like that when we get such good news! She's always putting a damper on things when they're brightest."

"Have it your own way," Cora said, shrugging her shoulders and making a little petulant gesture with her short, brown, well-shaped arms. "Freida is a white woman, Frank, our brother, is a co . . . sorry, brown man. Freida and Frank are coming down to spend a month with us. It's years since we've seen Frank, and Freida we've never seen. I suppose we should know something of her from her letters. Please don't interrupt me, Milly. I suppose we know what she's like from her photographs: tall and blonde and, we think, beautiful. To be frank, I like her. I like her even before I have seen her. Her letters tell me she's a nice, intelligent, well-educated young lady. Very well. Now what are we going to do about it?"

"Why, what a pity Jack isn't here now!" Mrs Harriman complained.

"Well, we are here, Ma, and Jack will be in on Sunday morning. And in any case, he's got his wife and child to see after, so we can't expect him to help us very much. Then there's Alice, but she's got her husband and children to attend to."

"Wait, among you, wait," Mrs Harriman said, the old expression of weighty sorrow once again on her face. "I'm tired, very tired. My back's breaking. Let's go into the hall and talk it over. Cook, I'll attend to you later, or Miss Milly or Miss Cora."

As they walked in, Mrs Harriman, shuffling along, kept murmuring "Well, well, who would have thought it? Who would ever have thought it?" She was past sixty. Although her husband, long since dead, had been comfortably off, his drinking had burdened her life with sorrow and shame. And then her favourite child, Frank, soon after the father's death, had gone off to the States. That had nearly bowed her down to the grave, and it took her a long time to overcome the grief of his absence. Her other two sons, Jack and Jim, had gone to sea; and one night the news of Jim's drowning somewhere in the South Seas had renewed the ache in her heart.

After long years of vagabonding about the world, Jack had returned, one blue and sunny morning, to the island where he had been born, and, to everyone's surprise, had married and settled down. Now he owned and captained a small schooner, trading between his island and Trinidad. Every fortnight he made the to-and-fro trip; and although he was so much nearer to her, old Mrs Harriman still troubled her soul about him when he was at sea. In the hurricane season she went to mass every morning, when she knew his ship was out, to pray for his safety.

Alice, her eldest daughter, had married and reared a large family. Milly, when young, was scornful of men and had kept on being scornful of them until now. Cora had, on the other hand, long ago brought disgrace to the family by carrying on with a white bank-clerk and bearing him a still-born child. Of course, as everyone had foretold, he had never married her, and the whole island knew why. That had happened fifteen years before, and the gossiping tongues of the little place no longer wagged over Cora's scandalous behaviour. Now she was thirty-five. How often, with the sea-breezes rushing in on her in the quiet of the night, she had lain on her bed and longed for escape from the island! Lack of money had kept her where she was.

The Harrimans lived in a quaint, pink-washed house facing the quiet blue water of the Carenage. On the opposite side of the bay, not a mile away, curved the green hills of the island, making of the Carenage a perfect landlocked harbour. From their windows they could see in the bright distance the white beach of Grand Anse where, as children and young women, they had many a time picnicked to their hearts' content. What glorious days they had spent there, running along the firm white sand of the beach bordered by coconut trees, diving and swimming and splashing about in the blue pellucid sea!

Sometimes a large steamer would come into the Carenage and cast anchor just a stone's throw from their house. Then the little, sleepy old town of St George's would suddenly waken up, for all its brown and black population would come crowding down on the water-front, some to go off in row-boats to barter their wares, others to see whom they might recognize leaning over the ship's rail or landing, and yet others to stand idly about looking on at the hustle and bustle for want of something better to do. Always there were sailing ships sitting on the water like proud swans, and in the evening two or three pleasure yachts, the property of the more well-to-do folk, tacked and careened around the bay to the swift, clean breezes.

On the right of their house, some two or three hundred yards down the water-front, the old fort rose steeply to three hundred feet. On Sunday afternoons the Police Band played up there. Then all the town would be dressed up in its finery to sit on the benches and listen to the music and inhale the fresh air of the height, and watch the island's neck stretching out to Point Saline.

The Harrimans' house was made of bricks and concrete. It boasted no pretence to architecture: it was simply a two-storeyed box with windows back and front. All the houses flanking the street were like it, the only difference being the colour of the wash used for the fronts. Some were green, some yellow, others pink, and yet others a bright red. This array of colours was one of the town's attractions; an artist might find there in houses, sea, land and sky all the colours he would wish for making his canvas come to burning tropical life.

The Harrimans had lived in their present house almost all their lives. It was, one might say, part and parcel of them. I'm sure old Mrs Harriman could never have moved from the house and survived the parting. Milly and Cora would have suffered deep spiritual pain from such an experience. They loved the old-fashioned place with its four large bedrooms, its large drawing-room and its back gallery. The ground-floor was used as a place of business, and this gave Mrs Harriman something every month upon which she could depend.

But now the news that Frank and Freida were coming to Grenada put them all in a flutter and flurry. The everyday monotony of their lives, for the first time in many years, was broken. Old Mrs Harriman and Milly skipped mass the next morning and were perturbed by such a sin of omission. It was seldom that Cora went to church. She preferred, she said, to stay at home and gaze at the beautiful sea or read a book. But she too had caught the fever of excitement and sacrificed her book and her sea-dreams to the matter at hand. That very day the news spread throughout the circle of the Harrimans' friends and acquaintances; and finally everybody who was anybody at all knew that Frank was coming to Grenada for a holiday with his American wife. There was much speculation: did Mrs Frank Harriman know that her husband was a coloured man? Some said that although Frank's skin was a deep, rich brown, his features could pass for white; others did not think so. All recalled the surprise with which the news of Frank's marriage to a white woman had been received so many years ago. How would the American wife get on with Mrs Harriman and Milly and Cora? And especially Milly, who was, even in such a small community, considered to be so narrow-minded and fussy? Indeed, the topic of conversation that evening over almost every respectable dining table in the town was this extraordinarily exciting bit of news.

On Sunday morning, as soon as Jack's schooner was seen sailing into the Carenage, Milly and old Mrs Harriman went down to the water-front to meet Jack. So bubbling over with joy and excitement were they, that they could hardly wait until Jack came ashore. He received the news with characteristic imperturbability.

"All right," he said, his rich brown skin shining in the sun, his curly hair tousled, his blue eyes holding in them a suspicion of fatigue. He was a tall man, burly and strong. His great horny hands bore evidence of his struggles with the seas of the world. "All right," he said. "I'm tired now. I'm going home for a rest. You'll see me later."

"But Jack," the mother ventured, for she was always timid in the presence of her son and gave him the respect that his dour temperament and magnificent physique demanded, "isn't it great to know that we shall all be seeing Frank once again?"

"Have you told Jane as yet?" he asked, disregarding his mother's emotional question. He disliked, intensely, emotion of any kind. Jane was his wife.

"Yes," Milly said, "and she's been giving us a hand with the house." Both women, although they knew Jack's manner so well, were chagrined by his indifferent response. They left him with his mate on the wharf and walked home to a busy, fussy day.

Two days before the arrival of the homecomers, Milly discovered that there was no framed photograph of Freida in the drawing-room. Almost every member of the family was in the house that day, helping to make it spick and span. Voices filled every room with incessant chatter; and when Milly, in the midst of the confusion of contradictory suggestions, voiced her discovery, all flocked around to exclaim how fortunate it was that Milly had seen, just in the nick of time, what everybody else had failed to see. Milly felt quite proud and elated. Then a long argument followed over the choice of photograph; and at last Mrs Harriman, because she was old and said least of all, had her way. The picture was framed in an opulent gold moulding and hung in the most conspicuous place in the drawing-room. Everybody said how beautiful Freida was, how beautiful and how *good* she looked. In everybody's mind, however, rang this frantic thought: how will she feel with Frank's mother and Frank's sisters? What will she think of them, with their complexions darker than Frank's and their hair curly and showing the negroid blood?

The great day arrived in a cloudless sky. Sunlight scintillated on a blue, shivery sea. A cool breeze slid down the hills from the north and rippled the water as it passed out from the Carenage into the open, to join the broad-bosomed winds that swing grandly between Grenada and Trinidad. Birds put songs into the throat of the morning and the multicoloured house-fronts caught the sunlight in blue and green and pink splashes.

Countless inquiries as to the arrival of the steamer were made the day before by the Harriman family. Old Mrs Harriman, exhausted unto death by the commotion around her during the past few days, sat in a corner mumbling: "Among you will be the death of me, among you will be the death of me!" And yet her withered bosom held a timorous joy. Now and again she looked at the framed photograph of her so-long-absent son and wondered if it were really true that she would once more see him before she died. How would she touch him again without crumpling at his feet and bursting into tears? She did not know, for even now, with the mere mental picture of that meeting, her intensely blue eyes were clouded with rheum and her spirit quailed with a mixture of joy and sadness.

She did not sleep that night. Indeed, neither did Milly nor Cora. All night long they kept starting up from brief snatches of unconsciousness to peer at the clock in the darkness and look through the window to see if there were any signs of the eastern light. They rose bright and early, sustained by a sense of nervous expectancy. To the accompaniment of desultory chatter and with cold and trembling fingers, they dressed. Milly, in her plain, simple frock of white, looked as well as it was possible for her to look. She was tall and thin, painfully thin, and her bosom was flat and her feet large. The brown skin of her face was tightly drawn; indeed, she was anything but pretty. Cora, on the other hand, was not only pretty but attractive. Her brown skin had not the pallor of her sister's, but was rich and alive. Unlike her sister again, she was short and lithely figured, and she looked charming in the flowered dress she wore. She walked with a quick step. Every movement she made was quick. You could see, in a short time, how much vitality she had in her. She looked much younger than she was.

The whole family foregathered on the wharf to watch the steamer thread her way through the narrow passage leading into the Carenage. Every now and again, Alice's children, all clad in their Sunday-best, ran through the tunnel and on to the esplanade where they could see the open sea and return with news of the steamer's advance. The agents, the day before, had said that the steamer would anchor inside the Carenage. There was great consternation, therefore, when the little group on the jetty heard the siren lifting up its heavy, sonorous note outside. The children, the colour warm in their faces with running and excitement, trotted up to say that the "big boat" had anchored already: and then they all knew that she would not come into the Carenage.

They all looked at each other, no one knowing what to do in this emergency.

"Among you will be the death of me!" Mrs Harriman wailed, wringing her hands.

"Where's Jack?" Milly asked. "His brother, his own flesh and blood is arriving this morning and he's not even here to welcome him!"

"Jack's at home," Jane, his wife, said. "You know what he is, my dear."

"Ah, but this is the very limit, past it! Here, Harry, run off and tell your father to come quickly. Quick, quick."

Harry ran off, followed by two of his little cousins.

"Damn fussy old maids!" Jack muttered when he was given the message.

Without any haste and quite calmly, Jack put on his jacket. Only stormweather at sea could disturb his equanimity and drive him to impetuous action. He sauntered down to the little group.

"For heavens sake, Jack, why weren't you here before?" Milly said, a little hysterically. "Don't you know your brother, your own flesh and blood, is coming this morning?"

"What do you want?"

Jane stood in the background, looking at her husband. She didn't want him to think that she'd had anything to do with the message.

"The steamer's anchored outside," Milly ejaculated.

"Is that my fault?"

"For God's sake, Jack, don't annoy me. Don't you know that we want to go off to meet them on board now?"

"All right; keep your hair on, fuss-pot!" And he walked off to bargain with a boatman.

During this altercation, Cora had observed Mr Perrin, the customs officer, making ready to go off to the steamer in his launch. Without a word to the members of her party, she approached him and, with a winning smile, explained their predicament.

"Certainly, come along with me and I'll bring you all back," he said.

Jack did not go on board; he preferred, he said, to wait on the jetty for them. As soon as the launch was a little way out, he went home, took off his jacket and sat in his verandah. He was anxious to see his brother, perhaps as anxious as anybody else; but to show his anxiety was, in his view, vulgar and unnecessary.

Mrs Harriman, fearing sea-sickness and the ways of the sea, stayed behind on the wharf with the children. Hither and thither they romped among the crowds of people, every now and again coming to their grandmother with questions and cross-questions which she did not hear. She stood in the sunlight and her heart palpitated and her blue eyes searched the blue sea for signs of the returning launch.

At last they came ashore and Freida, taking the cigarette from her mouth, went up to her mother-in-law and said:

"Well, well, Mother, I'm *so* pleased to see you," and kissed her on both cheeks.

In Frank's arms, Mrs Harriman wept and laughed alternately. The crowd around gazed on the scene and exchanged critical remarks in whispers and silent eye-words.

Freida was very flashily dressed, rouged and lipsticked, and she was wearing a pair of white gloves and looked the grand lady. Mrs Harriman felt a strange sensation when the gloved hands touched her. All the family said afterwards that it would have been more discreet of Freida to have landed without gloves.

And Freida was indeed beautiful: tall and fair, with eyes that were even a clearer blue than old Mrs Harriman's. She carried herself statelily and there was about her a certain *hauteur* which put everybody out and created a coldness in the atmosphere for which no one was prepared. She spoke in a slightly nasal fashion, imperceptible at first, drawling her words; and her voice was low and musical. Milly was awed by her, and very proud and very nervous: she had not so far said a word, simply because she was too nervous to speak to Freida, who appeared to be so grand a lady. Cora's first impression was a disappointing one, which developed during the course of the day, without her deliberately acknowledging it to herself, into a subtle antagonism. That did not prevent her, however, from chatting away. The children gazed at Freida with open mouths and believed her to be a princess from a fairy-land, a princess remote and alien. She kissed them one after the other; and Cora, watching her closely, thought that she kissed them in a remote and alien fashion.

Old Mrs Harriman would have felt completely out of the picture were it not for Frank. She could scarcely believe that he was standing once again before her, that she could touch him and hear again the voice she loved and knew so well. The speech had changed, true, but the voice was still the same. He looked fine and big in his fashionably cut clothes. His skin had cleared up considerably, and only the suspicious widening of the nostrils told the practised eye that he was not of pure European descent. Boisterously he greeted many of his old friends who had come on the wharf to see him land: and even the carter-men and sailors who were young men when he was a boy, he had a word for. He spoke with a marked American accent.

Old Mrs Harriman, so engrossed in her son was she, had no time to be upset by Freida's smoking, but all the others thought that it would have been more discreet of Freida had she landed without a cigarette in her mouth. Only Cora said that she could see nothing wrong in it.

"Lack of respect for Ma," Milly said sternly.

"Oh, rot," Cora muttered between her teeth.

"You always have had strange and loose ideas," Milly flashed at her sister.

"Prig, hypocrite!" Cora hissed, losing her temper for the moment and as quickly recovering it.

"Well, my dears, and you must both be very tired and very hungry," old Mrs Harriman said when they were in the house. "Milly, is the coffee and eggs ready?"

"Oh, Mother," Freida, standing at the window, said, "just wait a minute, if you don't mind. Isn't this marvellous, Frank? Blue sea and green, beautiful hills and oh! just look at that white beach, over there!" and Freida pointed out the Grand Anse beach.

"Ah, my dear," Frank said, "I guess that all this hasn't for you what it has for me." He stood at the window with her, with his arm about her shoulders. He was taller than she. They made a lovely pair. "In the old days – they seem so long ago – we used to picnic on that beach. Do you remember, Mother?"

Old Mrs Harriman was too overcome with emotion to reply. She smiled at her son through her tears.

"Where are my binoculars?" Freida asked. "Fetch them, Frank."

"Can't you wait until you see it for yourself, until you walk on it and dry yourself on it in the sun?" he asked teasingly.

"I'm the typical woman, you see," she drawled to the company standing about the room. She had taken off her hat and her fair, bobbed hair was golden in the sunlight streaming through the window. Frank searched around the room for the glasses, but could not find them.

"Perhaps they're in my bag," Freida drawled.

They were not there.

"Damn, I've left them on board then. Yes, I remember now. I left them in the smoking-room this morning."

"Just like you," Frank said, irritably. "Always leaving your things about."

For a fraction of a second, a hard light came into Freida's eyes. However, she smiled to say:

"Sorry, darling, but you must fetch them for me. They cost a great deal of money, you know."

"All the more reason why you should have been more careful with them," Frank said.

Jack came in at this moment. The brothers shook hands, Frank slapping Jack affectionately on the back. Then awkwardly he bowed to Freida. Freida showed her teeth in a small smile.

"So this is my brother-in-law?" she said, and went up to him and shook his hand.

"I say, Jack," Frank said, "Freida's forgotten her glasses on board. Do you mind fetching them for me?"

"I should much prefer if *you* fetched them, Frank," Freida said.

Frank frowned to say: "But I'm hungry, my dear."

"After that large breakfast you had on board this morning? I should prefer *you* to fetch them for me." Her voice was musical.

"Come along, you people," Milly called out from the dining room door. "Your coffee is ready."

In the end it was Jack who went on board for the pair of glasses. He didn't know why, but he felt sorry for his brother. The manner in which Freida had repeated: "I should much prefer *you* to fetch them for me," convinced him that she had something of the virago in her. He was annoyed, very annoyed, to think that any man should allow a woman to boss him about. That had never happened, would never happen to him: it was the last indignity he could be made to suffer. And he had put himself out in this way because he wanted to rob Freida of a triumph his brother was only too willing to award her. "That's the worst," he said to himself, "of a coloured man marrying a white woman."

During the day they talked incessantly. Freida talked a great deal. She spoke of the trip down and her friends of ship-board, and the islands they had passed. Her manner was affable and familiar. She told them of the great city she had left behind and all the wonders of it. The children sat around with open mouths and wide eyes. More and more they thought of Freida as a princess from a far-off fairy-land. They gazed at her pink and white skin with awe and admiration; and her hair, like gossamer, was a glory to them. Freida, however, took no notice of them, and the mothers noticed this and silently resented it. For most of the time, Milly acted the part of maid. To and fro she went doing little services for her grand sister-in-law. Cora sat near to Freida, chatting away. She told Freida of all the beauty spots of the island: the Grand Etang, Glover's Island, Fontenoy Beach, and the wonderful time there was to be had in bathing in the clear blue Grand Anse waters.

"You have nothing like it in the States, I bet," she said.

Freida, looking through the window, did not think so.

"The coconut trees are unique," she added.

Frank related some of his early struggles in New York. Now, he said, he was quite comfortably off. "Aren't we, dear?" he said to his wife.

"So, so," she replied, unenthusiastically.

His mother's heart expanded, and in her love for him she quivered with joy.

"And I hope," she said weakly, "you've not forgotten your church and your God, my boy?"

Freida made as if to speak, but Frank interrupted by saying:

"Oh no, no, Mother!" Then he gave his wife a searching look.

Old Mrs Harriman loved Freida because she was Frank's wife; but she did not as yet feel comfortable with her. Her grand airs and white beauty disconcerted her, but she did not admit that to herself. She was trying her best to look upon Frank and Freida as one, the child of her womb.

"Have you no social life here, no dances or clubs?" Freida asked.

"Oh yes," Cora said. "There's a dance at Government House some time very soon. I expect we shall all go. And we have the Marine Club at Grand Anse, of course. Everybody belongs to it."

"Everybody?" Freida asked.

"Well, everybody who is anybody," Cora replied, catching the banter in her sister-in-law's voice.

"Oh," Freida said, showing her teeth in a small smile.

Jane and Alice did not know whether or not to like the newcomer. They resented her coldness to the children, but gave her the excuse of thinking that perhaps she was a little excited in her new surroundings, and forgetful. They sat in their corners listening, without adding anything to the conversation.

In the evening friends and relatives came in. By that time, the morning incident of the binoculars was forgotten by all. Frank held forth to the company on the land of glorious opportunities, on the country of limitless wealth. Perhaps he spoke in a braggadocio manner; at any rate, you could see that he believed in what he was saying. He made exaggerated statements with a force of conviction that completely disarmed his listeners, and all admired his fine American accent.

Jack said very little, his voice was heard only when he was spoken to. He hated the land and all its artificial contacts. Always when he was ashore, his mood was irascible, the least thing would make him angry. At sea he was a completely different person. He laughed and talked with his sailors, and sometimes sang with them when the weather was fine and his ship sailing merrily along. For one thing, there were seldom women at sea; and even when there were, sea sickness silenced them into docility. For another, the sea had no cramping rooms about it; it was open and wide and free, and the winds were real, and the song of the waves natural. Now, sitting in a stiff-backed chair, he wished he were in his schooner, rocking and tossing, instead of in this smoke-infested, stuffy room. And he did not like Freida. If only because she was white he did not like her. He looked upon all white people with suspicion; they seemed always to be trying to lord it over coloured people. He could never feel comfortable in their presence, and here was his brother's wife, a white woman. He put a meaning into almost everything she said that Freida did not intend. The truth is that Jack suffered from a colour complex.

The kerosene street-lamps of the little town were little pools of suspended light spaced far apart along the streets. The narrow streets held the darkness as if it were a liquid thing. Here and there on the town's hillside flickered house-lamps, and higher up a single house glowed with electric bulbs; that was where the priests lived. No one was about, for in these small West Indian towns the people, having little or nothing to do at nights, retire early. Along the esplanade was silence save for the rhythmic wash of the waves upon the beach. Starlight was on the sea. The sea was a great, expanding sheet of bright darkness under the stars. The smell of it, mingled with the warm odour of the earth, was in the air, caressing and restful. The to-and-fro sound of the waves on the beach was like the little town's breathing. Even in the darkness, there was something of the sky's day-blueness above.

That night everybody slept soundly at the Harrimans. Only old Mrs Harriman could not sleep. The presence of Frank filled her mind and her spirit, and it was like a miracle to her that she had been given the joy of seeing him after all these years of absence. She thanked the Holy Mother, telling her beads in the darkness.

Early the next morning, Frank went into his mother's room. In the press of greeting all his old friends the day before, he had not found the time to talk alone with her. He found her still in bed, her brown face browner than ever against the dead whiteness of the pillow. He noticed for the first time how much she had aged. He loved his mother very much. Bending over, he kissed her smiling cheeks.

"It's like old times," he said, recalling the days when he had been a boy. He had always been her most affectionate child. He sat on the bed beside her.

"Like old times, my boy," she said, "only I've grown older and weaker."

"So have I," he said.

"But not weaker," she reminded him.

He laughed. "Isn't this fine?" he said, bending over again and kissing her. She was too filled with emotion to say anything.

"Well, Ma, and what d'you think of her?"

"I think she's grand, my boy, grand."

"Really?"

"Really, my boy."

"You know, Ma," he said, a little frown clouding his handsome face, "she's not happy."

"Oh, my boy!" she said, immediately concerned.

He was silent. She watched him, full of increasing distress.

"And you, my boy?" she said, sitting up.

He gave a short laugh before saying: "As happy as I can be. Life isn't *always* a bed of roses, you know, Ma."

"I know, my boy."

"But I'm very, very fond of her, Ma."

"I know."

"She's very kind to me."

"I'm *so* glad to hear you say that."

"And yet . . . and yet . . ."

"Well, Frank?"

"She's not as happy as she might be."

"You mean . . . ?" She didn't know how to frame the thought that now stabbed her.

"Yes, Mother? I don't know what you mean."

She laughed awkwardly, weakly. She wasn't so sure of what she was thinking and she did not want to pain him.

"You see, Ma," he said, his brows wrinkling and his large grey-green eyes narrowing, "she has no children."

"Oh," she sighed, infinitely relieved. "I didn't think it was that."

He glanced quickly at her. "Then what . . ."

"No, no, my boy," and she laughed uncomfortably. A great happiness shone in her face when she was silent.

"You see, Ma, it's like this. She's always wanted a baby and I think she blames me for her barrenness. And she holds that against me. Things would be so different if she had a child!"

"But why, my boy, why does she hold that against you?" Distress again invaded her heart.

"You see, Mother," he said after a hurtful silence, "as a young man I was rather wild. Sowed my wild oats, like a fool!"

"And you . . . ?"

"Yes, I told her all about it, and she's never forgotten it."

"And never forgiven it?"

He was silent. Then she said: "Doesn't that show how much she loves you, my boy?"

"That's it, Ma," he said gratefully. "You know, she's not like the ordinary New York girl. She's never been accustomed to the comforts that money can give. She'd always worked for her living, up to the time I married her. And worked hard, I can tell you. She's not the giddy, pleasure-seeking American girl."

Mrs Harriman saw with the quiet, piercing perception that old age alone can give, that her son was talking against his convictions. But she said nothing.

"I think you'll like her more and more as time goes on. I'm sure you will. And we'll have such a jolly time, Ma, won't we?"

"I'm sure we shall," his mother said as brightly as she could. And then they talked of old times like two children until Frank heard Freida calling him. Mrs Harriman also heard the call and it grieved her, for it was a symbol to her that her son was no longer entirely her own. She watched him leave the room, anxiously, and then rose to the day's duties.

Later that day Frank felt very proud walking around the town with his beautiful wife. Cora accompanied them. Everybody stared at them as they passed by, and sometimes Frank met people who spoke to him, but whom he did not recognize. Cora was not in her best mood; she felt shabby and insignificant beside Freida and would have turned back were it not for Frank. They went into all the stores and Freida was amused by them, and did not hesitate to show her amusement. The dark and frizzly-haired clerks and clerkesses gaped at her from behind the counters. They nudged each other and whispered to each other: "There's Frank Harriman's tourist-wife." And Freida heard them, and smiled at first. Then they took her into the market, a little shed in the centre of an open square, where a few *marchands*, all Negresses, sat around before their trays of fruit and vegetables, jabbering away at each other in the indigenous *patois*. Freida asked questions like a child. It was the first time Cora found herself liking her sister-in-law, for now she seemed to have put aside her airs, and was natural in her curiosity tinged with excitement. Freida laughed quite a lot at almost everything she saw, because it was all so quaint, she declared in her musical, drawling voice. And Frank, overjoyed to see his wife happy, said:

"Not like New York, eh darling?" and she laughed again at his joke.

"But are there any white people in the island?" she asked suddenly; and added quickly: "besides ourselves, of course."

Cora heard Frank say, quite composedly:

"Yes, of course. But there aren't many, just a few families scattered about the island."

"Any in the town?"

"Two or three families."

Cora was puzzled. Could it be possible that Freida, after all, did not know that they were coloured? Was it possible that Frank had, all these years, kept it a secret from her? Or had Freida, by her: "besides ourselves, of course", thought to avoid hurting anyone's feelings? And with this last self-put question, Cora, for some unaccountable reason, found herself hating her sister-in-law. A strange rage boiled within her and the blood rushed through her body in a hot, angry flow. What right had Freida to be playing the hypocrite, she at last asked herself. And what earthly right had she for being so frightfully insulting as to suggest that colour was something to be ashamed of? Priggish, sycophantic fools like Milly, Cora reflected, were surely the ones who should be held responsible for this patronizing manner white people adopted towards coloured people. And she said not another word for the rest of the walk. She was afraid to speak, but Freida and Frank were so wrapped up in each other and what was happening around them, that they failed to observe Cora's stubborn silence. They bought some sapodillas and pumpkins, and in triumph, their cheeks glowing from the tropic heat, walked home with them.

Old Mrs Harriman, as soon as they entered, saw that Cora was upset; but, fearing to know what the matter was, did not inquire what was wrong. And she was reassured by Frank and Freida's high spirits.

The tops of the green hills across the bay were golden with evening. Lower down, deep purple shadows lingered, in which evening was drawing her first quiet breath. Golden wisps of cloud hung high up in the sky, unmoving, and the rippleless sea already held in its bosom the purple shades of oncoming night. A few boats, trailing wakes behind them, skimmed over the water, and at the mouth of the Carenage a three-master slept, becalmed. There was just the faintest suspicion of a breeze. Freida and Frank, strolling around the water-front with Mrs Harriman, the old lady hanging on an arm of each, gazed on the sea and on the hills, and on the houses across the water, and felt the beauty that was in the darkening world.

"It's a beautiful island," Freida said.

"Oh, but you haven't seen it as yet, has she, Mother?"

"No, my boy. But she will see it all, she will see it all. I do wish I was younger."

"Oh no, Mother!" Freida exclaimed. "You're just lovely as you are, as lovely as your island."

"It's sweet of you to say that, my child."

They were passing by Jack's home. Jack was in the verandah, smoking his pipe and reading. They called out to him. He looked up, and Jane came running from the back. They asked Jack to join them, but Jane came instead, Jack saying he was tired. Little Harry suddenly toddled up from nowhere. Freida behaved as if she did not see him, and Jane, timid creature that she was, felt uncomfortable, and wanted to turn Harry back. She regretted her precipitancy in coming out.

"There's only one thing to complete my happiness," Freida said.

"Oh come, my dear, why fret yourself?" Frank said.

"And it's a child," Freida went on stubbornly. A hard look came into her blue eyes.

"It's God's will, my dear," Mrs Harriman said.

"I do not believe in God's will," Freida said.

"Please don't listen to her, Mother. She's talking nonsense."

"My child," the mother said in pained tones, "you shouldn't . . . you shouldn't say that."

"But I'm not talking nonsense!" Freida said to her husband. She was angry. "And you know it, and you know why we haven't had a child," she added bitterly.

This little dispute destroyed the beauty of the evening for all and chased away the peace from old Mrs Harriman's soul. She felt very tired and very old and her hands rested limply in the crook of her supporters' arms. And Jane suddenly remembered the incident of the binoculars, and said to herself that Frank could not be so happy with Freida after all, and found consolation in this thought.

That night there was a strained atmosphere in the house. Freida spoke little and Frank appeared to be irritable; he kept asking if everybody did not find the night hot and stifling.

Mrs Harriman related to Cora and Milly what had happened during the walk. They were in Cora's room and they spoke in whispers.

"She's a bit of a cat," Cora said venomously. She was very pretty and alluring in her night dress, her breasts upstanding. Milly looked old and tired, like her mother.

"Don't say that," Milly said. "It's unkind."

"Oh, only because she's white you're taking up for her."

"Rubbish! It's because I'm a Christian, which you're not."

"Among you, don't quarrel," the mother said.

"Christian!" Cora exclaimed contemptuously.

"You're always ill-speaking people."

"Any more than you?"

"Ma, have you ever heard me ill-speak anyone?"

"Oh my, among you will be the death of me!"

"The less we say to each other about this affair, the better," Cora said. "And have it your own way. She's a grand lady, a very grand lady, but you'll see what's going to happen."

"Happen? But listen to her!" Milly exclaimed.

"Sh, sh!" Mrs Harriman warned.

"We were all right before she came. She's upset the whole house," Cora said.

"That's only in *your* imagination. You've got a mischievous mind, that's what."

"All right, *all right* . . ."

"Please, *please* be quiet! Among you will be the death of me!"

The following day dawned rosily and a burning sun climbed over the hill-tops and filled the Carenage with warm light. The whole Harriman family, with a few intimate friends, went down to the Grand Anse beach on a picnic. Instead of going by taxi overland, they hired rowboats and went across by sea. Freida was very excited, bubbling over with high spirits. She admired, with little exclamations of delight, everything she saw: the hills around and the blue sea. And she listened raptly to the lash of the water against the sides of the boat. And when they were skimming over the reefs, she looked down and saw the quaint and beautiful coral formations. Everybody talked and laughed. Frank started to sing, and the others, with the exception of Jack, joined in. The boats shot along in tandem-fashion. The sky was blue, flecked with lovely cloud-forms, plump and white-hot.

Arriving on the beach, the children got into their bathing suits and romped about the firm white sand, leaving their little foot-prints winding and twisting. The pendulous arms of the coconut trees made sibilant slapping noises in the breeze. The waves came up and receded in a regular splashing antiphon.

"How beautiful!" Freida exclaimed, her fair hair ruffled and golden in the sunlight. Her dress clung to her with the wind, revealing a perfect figure.

Under the coconut trees was cool and green and the sandy soil was stippled with sunlight. Freida walked under them and looked up at the green fruit clustering about the hearts of the trees. Her arched neck was white like pearl. Then they drank coconut water, and afterwards the white, soft jelly slipped down their throats. And then they all changed into their bathing suits and went into the clear, shining water.

Old Mrs Harriman stood on the beach and wished she was young again. The shouts and the laughter brought back to her ancient mind, memories of her young days. But she was happy. The white-green-pink morning obliterated all the unpleasantnesses for her. It was still good to be alive, though old and weak. Her children were all once more foregathered around her, and she watched them with shining eyes. Now they were all grown-up, and her grandchildren had come to give youth again to the family. She was perfectly happy, perfectly content in the knowledge that she had fulfilled her purpose in life.

Until the afternoon, everything went swimmingly. And then one of Freida's rings slipped from her fingers and sank to the bottom of the sea. The water was shallow, and all joined in the search.

"What a nuisance!" Freida exclaimed.

"You're always losing things, or leaving them behind as if they cost nothing!" Frank said pettishly.

"You didn't give me *that* one!" Freida flung back.

"That's beside the point. It cost money, a lot of money . . ."

"Damn it all, but that's *my* business!"

"You needn't swear! This isn't New York, you know!"

"But it's I; and I do wish you'd shut up and not show yourself to be what you are!"

"What am I?" Frank asked angrily.

"*You* know. I don't want to shame you, I don't want to . . ."

"Oh, shut up!"

"Hypocrite!" Freida hissed.

Frank glared daggers-drawn at his wife, but said nothing. He was afraid to continue.

"Never mind, Freida," Milly said placatingly.

"Oh, you're all a set of . . ." But she did not complete her accusation. Instead, she ran out of the water, sat on the beach, and began to cry.

Jack, a little apart from the others, boiled with anger. What a fool his brother was to allow a woman to talk to him like that! *He* would have slapped her.

And Cora wondered what the unspoken word was. A flame was in her head, but she controlled herself by flinging herself in the water and swimming out. She swam out far enough to alarm her mother.

Everybody was dreadfully upset by what had happened. Poor Milly, to hide her confusion, searched for the ring more diligently than anyone else. Jane glanced at her husband and saw the wrath in his face. The children stood at a little distance, wondering why their princess was weeping. And little Harry, remembering a fairy-story told him by his mother, whispered softly to his cousins:

"Her prince has gone 'way."

"Oh, here it is, here it is!" Milly cried, running from the water with the ring in her hand. She felt, oh, *so* relieved! Had she not recovered the talisman of peace?

Freida smiled, and at once her dark mood was gone and she was pleasant with her husband and everybody again. She behaved for the rest of the afternoon just as if nothing had happened.

And then the excitement grew apace over the approaching Government House dance. All the Harrimans received invitations. Everybody who was anybody at all in St George's was invited. The stores sold more dresses in that week than they did in a twelvemonth. "Are you going to the dance?" was the stock greeting, and the women discussed the frocks, and the men looked forward to what they called a good time.

The weather continued sunny and the Harrimans went down to Grand Anse again, but nothing untoward happened. The house was divided against itself. Cora was sulky and sharp-tempered now because she had grown intensely to dislike her sister-in-law. But Milly defended Freida, and heavy words passed between the two sisters frequently. Poor Mrs Harriman wavered and did not know what to think. She only knew that she loved Frank, and supposed that she should love anyone connected with him, and especially his wife. Fervently she prayed for his happiness. And time was passing, and she dreaded the approach of the day when he must leave her.

Milly and Cora were busy with their dresses. Never had they given out anything of theirs to a seamstress. From the time they had been girls, they had made their own clothes. Freida's dress was out. And one day Frank, observing his sisters plying needle and thread, said to his wife, who lolled on a sofa reading a book:

"You should have learnt to sew. D'you see now what you are losing?"

"I was occupied with other things," Freida said curtly.

"With *other* things! Say you were out in an office, working, and be done with it. You're too fond of putting on airs!"

Freida rose from her chair and rushed across like a tragic actress to her husband, and slapped him on the face.

"Take that!" she cried, and flounced out of the room.

The thing happened so quickly that Milly and Cora were left wondering if what they had seen had really happened. Frank stood, irresolute, biting his under lip, his fist clenched.

"You shouldn't have spoken to her like that," Milly said.

"Is that any reason why she should have slapped him? Damn piece of cheek! She wants Jack for a husband to put her in her place!" Cora's face was flushed in anger.

And then Frank's wrath gave place to shame.

"You know, I love her very much," he said. Milly understood, and her heart was flooded with pity for her brother.

"Coward!" Cora hissed at him in an undertone.

But Frank was bowed down with shame and said nothing. How he had begged Freida, during the week on the ship down, always to try and control her temper and save him the humiliation of her slaps! That was the last thing he wanted his mother or his sisters to know about her. And Freida had promised, and failed him.

"Please don't tell Mother," he pleaded.

"And why shouldn't Mother know?" asked Cora.

"Girl, you ought to be ashamed to ask such a question!" Milly exclaimed. "At her age, you would pain Ma?"

Cora's grey-green eyes shone with anger. "But why not, why not?" and she stamped her foot on the floor.

"I know I'm not like Jack," Frank told his younger sister. "I guess I'm weak, and . . . well, never mind. She's very fond of me, you know, and please forgive her for this little display, Cora! I was wrong to insult her, and in front of both of you, too."

"Is she any better than we?" Cora flashed back.

"I didn't say so. I only . . ."

"I'll bet you she wouldn't have slapped you if you were white!" Her voice was raised.

"Cora!" Frank pleaded.

"What a horrid, uncalled for thing to say! You ought to be ashamed of yourself! You ought . . ."

"You're both fools, fools!" she screamed, completely beside herself with rage now. "You'd let any white person do what the devil he likes with you!" and she strode out of the room as Mrs Harriman came in.

"Children, among you, what's the matter? What's wrong with Cora? Why is she crying? What have you done to . . ."

"Nothing, Ma, nothing," Milly said. "Cora's impossible."

"And where's Freida?" They were both silent. "Among you will be the death of me!"

And Frank changed the subject, simulating a bright manner.

The day of the dance dawned with heavy dark clouds. Rain fell in the morning and the sea was green and rough. But in its fury the rain soon spent itself, and the sky was blue and shining by midday. Jack was in Trinidad with his sloop.

"Isn't Jane going with among you tonight?" Mrs Harriman asked.

"You should know better than that, Ma." Cora said, and laughed.

"But why not?" Freida asked. She and Frank had already forgotten the slapping incident and were the essence of sweetness to each other.

"She would not *dare* go without Jack!" Cora said.

"Well, I'm damned!" Freida exclaimed.

Both Milly and the mother were terribly shocked by the cool use of the word. They had been trained to believe that only men could be loose in the choice of their language. They had never become accustomed to Cora's swearing propensity, and always remonstrated with her about it.

"So am I!" Cora said blithely.

"You see, Mother," Freida explained, "in New York the women have won their complete emancipation. No wife would dream of paying such obeisance to her husband."

"Times have changed since I was a girl," Mrs Harriman said in sorrow. "We always obeyed our husbands."

"And used proper language," Milly thought.

Government House was a blaze of light that night. When the Harrimans arrived, there was already a large number of guests present. Freida and Frank were presented to the governor by Cora. Freida, taught earlier in the day to do what she had never before done in her democratic country, curtseyed and smiled. The governor smiled and shook her hand.

"I've heard of you, Mrs Harriman," he said.

"That's nice," Freida drawled.

"The island is so small, you know."

"Everybody knows everybody else, I suppose."

"Quite," the governor said. "I'll see you later."

And they strolled into the ballroom.

"You've made a hit with his Excellency," Milly whispered to Freida.

And Freida, glancing around the bright, crowded room, said, "I wonder how much of that can be taken as a compliment?"

"Oh, you mustn't forget me!" Cora chimed in, looking very charming and pretty in her pink frock, and forgetting for once in her excitement, to resent her sister-in-law's remark. Freida smiled admission of the truth of the retort.

Milly was subdued and felt out of the picture. If the truth be told, she had never enjoyed herself at dances; she was always a wallflower. Cora, on the other hand, experienced great difficulty in allotting the dances to the men who, on seeing her, flocked clamorously round her. Now they came and demanded her programme. She introduced then all to Freida and Freida's programme, like Cora's, was booked up in a short while.

"And what have you left for me?" Frank said.

"Oh never mind, ducky," she said playfully. "You should long ago have got tired of dancing with me."

"But I haven't, dear, and you know it."

"Frank, you're not going to spoil my evening?" she asked testily.

And Frank said nothing. Instead, he danced the first with Milly, the second with Milly, and the third with Milly. Then he went off and she saw him no more.

People of every complexion under the sun were there. Freida, looking around while dancing, was intrigued to see black men, some of them quite handsome, in full evening clothes. Her partner remarked:

"There are very few white people in Grenada, you know, and in any case the majority of the black men you see here are all officials in the Government Services."

All she saw and heard was so intensely new to her; and for some strange reason she blamed her husband for keeping her in the dark about things that he should have told her.

A little later the governor came up to Freida and asked her for a dance. Her programme was completely booked, but looking at the tall, handsome figure before her, she could not resist the request. She crossed out a name and handed the little card to Sir Howard.

"I hope you do not regret letting your partner down," Sir Howard said.

For answer, Freida gave him her sweetest smile. She was all affability and vivacity. There was nothing affected about her; she was natural in her gaiety and enjoyment of him. He was the essence of courtesy, an English gentleman. He danced beautifully and Freida's step never faltered. They talked as they danced. He asked her from what part of the States did she come? She told him.

"I've always been told that the Bostonians speak very much like educated English people."

"Thank you," she said, and looked up into his eyes and smiled. And after a moment she asked: "But where is your wife?"

Sir Howard laughed. And then he grew serious to say: "My wife and I are divorced."

"How exciting!" she exclaimed.

Sir Howard laughed again. "The women in Grenada don't take it that way," he said. "I don't think they like me for that reason."

"Does that surprise you?" and she told him of Milly and her mother-in-law. "I guess they are typical Grenada ladies."

"It isn't a bad island," he said, ruminating.

"You mean . . . ?"

"Now, by Jove, be careful! You're on the point of slandering me!"

"Or paying you a compliment, which?" she asked, looking up into his eyes.

"Perhaps, perhaps. I hadn't looked at it in that way. And, by Jove, some of the Grenada girls are most fascinating, what?"

She pouted her objection.

"Why, Mrs Harriman . . ."

"Call me Freida, please."

"Well, Freida," he paused. "Would you believe it? You've completely disarmed me. I've forgotten what I was going to say –"

"That I'm not a Grenadian?" Her eyes held a touch of mischief in them. She was enjoying this banter immensely.

"You're clever," he said, tightening his grip of her hand.

"Only a woman," she said, "which comes to the same thing, of course!"

He laughed, and they danced on in silence for a while.

"But tell me, your Excellency . . ."

179

"Sir Howard," he quickly interrupted, and his blue eyes twinkled.

"All right, Sir Howard, but you haven't disarmed *me*, you know! I notice you've got some black men as officials in your service."

"It may seem quaint and even queer to you . . ."

"Very, to say the least of it!" she broke in.

"Nevertheless, they're all right," he said. "Unlike the white Creole and the colonial Englishman, they have charm and little guile. And we English have not the same prejudice towards coloured folk which you Americans have."

"Hence your far-flung Empire!" she teased.

He looked down at her, holding her away from him. "Not only that, my dear lady," he said. "And yet the French have been more successful at colonizing coloured countries than we English have been."

"And why not a larger Empire than yours? Shall I tell you?" He waited. "Your fleet."

He laughed out loudly as the music ceased. In the eyes of everybody he led her across the hall and into the garden. He led her away from the spooning couples until they came to a bench in a quiet corner. Starlight trickled down through the bougainvillea above them. The melancholy croaking of distant frogs troubled the silence of the night. There was no wind and every upstanding shadow-tree stood still in its own breathing. She was a little excited and a little timorous. She wondered if Frank had seen her come out into the garden. Her fair beauty was aglow in the starlit darkness. She did not know what to say, so she waited, hoping and yet fearing that he would make the first advance. She liked him: she liked his tall, vigorous body, his refined, unfamiliar English manner. At last he said:

"The night is as beautiful as you."

"Can the night be said to be beautiful?" she asked in mock-*naiveté*.

"When there are stars in it, like the two stars in your eyes."

His words and his voice stirred her; and when he took her hand in his, she could not resist. And so, glancing about him, he kissed her lightly on the lips. In the starlit darkness her eyes shone, but she controlled the stirrings within her. The frogs croaked and a tender breath of wind wakened the sleeping shadows of trees. The awakening of life about her brought her to a sense of her surroundings, and she stood up quickly, and walked a little way from him. She was trembling, excited, afraid now, for she realized how imprudent she had been; was the island not small and filled with the murmurings of gossip?

A form emerged from the obscurity. It was Cora.

"Why, here you are!" she said; and in an undertone to Freida: "Frank's looking all about for you, and I suspected. Let me come in with you – Ah, your Excellency, do you know that this is our dance?"

As they walked up the gravelled path, they met Frank.

"Why, where *have* you been, Freida?"

"We were having a chat with his Excellency," Cora put in blithely. She loved the little part she was playing; and although she had that very day decided that she disliked Freida intensely, her sense of adventure was roused by her knowledge of Freida's flirtation and she gloried in it. Freida, for the moment, became a symbol for her, a symbol of everything she ached for, of everything that was significant and rousing in life.

And Freida regained her composure, but did not know how to interpret Cora's behaviour.

Frank was a little drunk. She did not like him when he was drunk, for then his features became coarse and vulgar and his complexion tawny-dark.

She avoided Sir Howard for the rest of the night. And in driving home she again wondered, as sleepy and tired as she was, about Cora's behaviour. It had been strange and perplexing.

Later that day, old Mrs Harriman wanted to know how they had all enjoyed themselves.

"Fine!" Freida said.

"We had a great time," Cora said, glancing mischievously at Freida through the corner of her eye.

Only Milly was silent, and the mother understood.

The topic of conversation throughout the island that evening was the dance of the night before. Gossip was rife about all the young women who had been seen dancing too often with any one man: were they in love, or were they just flirting, or were they secretly engaged? It was fun in the garden: so-and-so had been caught kissing so-and-so; "And can you believe it, my dear? That American wife of Frank Harriman's was going it strong with his Excellency."

"Yes, I noticed that. I wonder how *far* they went?"

"The governor is not slow, by any means."

"Did you see her husband chasing all around for her? – in the ballroom, if you please, when she was hidden away somewhere in the back of the garden!"

"Ah, the wives these days!"

"She's an American, don't forget."

"And Sir Howard is very handsome."

"Still, there's a limit, that's what I always say."

And so the talk buzzed with innuendoes.

. . . . .

Milly was strolling about the fort one afternoon with Freida. Two yachts, looking like two toys from the height, were tacking and careening inside the Carenage. The reefs were brown in the bright water and took on the fantastic shapes of gargantuan crabs and prehistoric dinosaurs. The rays of the westering sun tipped the hills opposite with gold. A faint scent of frangipani was in the air and a few white wisps of cloud sailed serenely in the sky like lovely yachts. Away to the south the blue sea stretched and blended with the misty blueness of the heavens. Little puffs of wind came and went.

Freida was already burnt by the sun into freckles. There was health bursting in her cheeks. Her holiday was nearly ended, and she thought of the day when she must leave her husband's beautiful island: with regret now and joy the next moment. She had enjoyed, up to a point, the peace and quiet of her holiday, but now she longed for the noise and movement of New York. She wanted again the obliterating artificialities of a large city. There, there was little enough to bring you face to face with your inward self; here, there was pain in the beauty of the world.

"I'm sorry to be leaving you so soon," she said. "I shall always think of your lovely island."

"It *is* lovely, isn't it?" Milly exclaimed enthusiastically.

"It is, and all good things must come to an end."

"I'm glad you've enjoyed yourself, Freida."

"Yes, you folk have been very kind to me; you and mother and Cora, particularly Cora."

And Milly thought: "If only she knew how Cora dislikes her!"

"We shall miss you a lot," she said aloud. "We shall miss our Grand Anse baths with you."

"Let's hope you'll always find lost rings," Freida said, showing her teeth in a small smile.

Milly had grown quite accustomed to her sister-in-law now and no longer regarded her as a grand lady from some fairy place in the cold North. She had seen too much of the warmth of her human nature and she liked her. It was really impossible for Milly to dislike anyone.

"I love finding lost things," she said simply. "They always come back to us with renewed affection."

For the first time, Freida looked at the frail, unprepossessing creature beside her with interest.

They sat in silence for a long time. The hills opposite were no longer golden-tipped and already could be felt the first nip of dusk. Milly felt sad and forlorn in the darkening world. Now the scent of frangipani was stronger in the embrace of dusk. Freida took in a deep breath of it and it filled her soul with a sentimental sensation, and she thought that, perhaps, she would always remember the island for its scent of frangipani. And then she looked across at Grand Anse and knew that she could never forget its white beach and its blue, clear sea, and its coconut trees standing like rows and rows of sentinels all along its curving sweep.

"I should like to live here for ever!" she said in an excess of emotion.

"I love the island," Milly said.

"And wouldn't you like ever to go away?"

"I don't think so, Freida. It frightens me to think of going away. Life is frightening enough here, in this small place, to go searching for its larger frights abroad. Life frightens me, it is so dark and so unknown!"

Again Freida looked at her sister-in-law. She was seeing a side of her that she had never dreamt was there.

"But what is there to be afraid of?"

"I know I sound silly," Milly said, and laughed a little nervously. "You are different from me. You were born in the big wide world, grew up in it. I was born here, and only once have I ever left the island, and that was to go to Trinidad. There I was very frightened and came back to Grenada gladly."

"There's only one thing I cannot understand in life," Freida said, meditatively. Milly waited, excited by what she had been saying. "And that is," Freida continued, "that I have not had a child. Otherwise, Frank and I have been as happy as it was possible for us to be."

"That's God's will," Milly murmured.

"I don't believe that, I don't believe in God's will. I think it's wicked."

"But Freida . . . but . . . what then do you believe in?"

"Nothing supernatural, nothing extra-human. I believe I haven't a child simply because there's something wrong with me or Frank."

"But, what *do* you believe in?" Milly asked again.

"Nothing."

"You don't believe in God?"

"No, I don't believe in God. I tell you, I don't believe in anything."

Milly was amazed; she had never before heard anyone deny God.

"Oh Freida, how . . . how utterly sad! I don't know what I should do if I did not have God to fall back upon now and again."

"You should fall back upon yourself."

"But look at the lovely world around you; who made it all?"

"I have heard that before. It's old-school, Milly. And in any case, we're talking like two old philosophers! Life's short and I'm here to have a good time. You know, I think I am a hedonist." She gave a little snort of laughter, and rose, and stretched out her arms like a tragic actress.

And they walked home in silence. Milly was thinking: "I must pray for her, I must pray for her!"

The day arrived when Freida and Frank must sail. Old Mrs Harriman had been weeping from the day before, and Frank tried his best to console her by telling her, amongst other things, that they would come to see her soon again. Old Mrs Harriman knew that that would never be, and she was inconsolable.

Once again there was a general hubbub in the old house. All the family was there and friends and acquaintances came in to have a last look at, and a last word with, Freida and Frank.

Cora was alone with Freida, helping her with the packing. They exchanged only necessary remarks. Then when Freida had left the room to fetch something which she had suddenly remembered, Cora's nervous fingers came upon a queer little secret drawer in Freida's private grip. Mechanically she pulled it out, and immediately her attention was attracted by its contents. She took the small box into her nervous fingers and opened it. It contained a rubber contraption. At first she failed to recognize it for what it was. When she did, she held it up, suspended between her fingers, while angry suspicions raced through her mind. Freida re-entered and found her like that, her angry eyes fixed on the rubber contraption. Quickly she snatched the thing from Cora's hand and blurted out:

"Why don't you mind your own business!"

"But . . . but I thought you always said that you wanted a baby," Cora stammered, taken aback for the moment.

"A baby?" There was a world of scorn in her voice. But then a strange change came over Freida. She seemed to be panic-stricken, scared, and she wrung her hands. "Please, please Cora," she pleaded, "you've been good to me before. You've kept a secret of mine and even helped me out of a quandary. Please, please Cora, I beg you, don't tell anyone of this!"

Cora remained rigid. The blood was in her cheeks. "Does Frank know?" she asked in a cold, hard tone.

"Please, Cora please . . ."

"Does Frank know?"

"How can he? How could I have told him? Don't you understand?"

Without another word, Cora rose and walked out of the room. She understood.

Glossary

agouti Forest-dwelling rodent, rabbit-like and fleet of foot; hunted for its meat

alpagarta(s) Cheap sandal of Venezuelan origin, made of cloth, with a leather sole

among you You all, all of you

axe Ask

bandanna A head-tie, scarf

barrack-yard Tenement consisting of two rows of wooden buildings facing each other across a communal yard space used for cooking and washing clothes

Bajan From Barbados; Barbadian

behind God's back Somewhere remote, far from towns and people

Boca Mouth (Spanish); Trinidad is separated from the mainland of South America by channels, the Bocas del Dragón (Dragon's Mouths) in the north, and the Bocas de la Sierpe (Serpent's Mouths) in the south

bourgeois Middle-class (French); a term of respect for a person considered important by the speaker

buh But

canaille The rabble; the populace (French)

cascadura A type of fish; legend has it that those who eat the cascadura are fated to end their days in Trinidad and Tobago

confrère A fellow-member of a profession or scientific body (French)

coralita Flowering vine with tightly packed pink inflorescences

court side At the court, over at the court

dancing the cocoa While the fermented cocoa beans dry in the sun, female labourers tread and trample them rhythmically so as to remove the outer coverings and "polish" the beans

Demerara window A wooden window of angled slats, with hinges at the top and propped open with a stick at the base

dey's They are

dong Down; "We goin' dong Carenage" = "We're going down to the harbour"

enh ben *Eh bien* (French), well

enh, enh! "Look at that!"; may express surprise or derision

entr'acte An interval between two acts of a play (French)

fanega A measure of weight for cocoa or coffee beans, the equivalent of 110 pounds

flambeau A flaming torch composed of several thick waxed wicks (French)

foo For

frangipani Tree with fragrant star-shaped flowers of white, pink or red

fus First

gie Give; "I go gie she" = "I am going to give it to her"

haen Phonetic rendering of "um", used as assent; mimics the accent of the East Indian cocoa grower

I go be ready jes' now I'll be ready shortly

immortelle A tall shade tree with a thorny trunk and bright red blooms, used in Trinidad to shade the cocoa

jalousie A blind or shutter made of a row of angled slats to keep out rain and control the influx of light

jumby Ghost, evil spirit

keeper Companion with whom one lives in a sexual relationship; applies to both men and women

keskidee Bird of the family of Tyrant Flycatchers, named for its cry of "Qu'est-ce-qu'il dit?" (French: "What is he saying?")

lappe Large, forest-dwelling rodent resembling a guinea-pig in appearance, brownish with white spots on its sides; hunted for its meat

maljo Evil eye; misfortune

manicou Nocturnal, marsupial rodent, brown with pointed snout, big ears, and long prehensile tail; hunted for its meat

marchand Vendor (French)

merino A man's sleeveless white cotton undershirt or vest

mooma Mother

nennen Godmother

never-see-come-see Overdone; ostentatious through lack of exposure or *savoir-faire*

obeah Of African origin, a belief in the power of supernatural forces to intervene in human affairs; practices associated with this belief

oder Other

orhani Head-covering which hangs down to drape the shoulders, worn by East Indian women

pélau Traditional Trinidadian dish made with chicken, pigeon peas and rice, and cooked with coconut milk and seasonings

pip A disease of poultry causing thick mucus in the throat and white scale on the tongue

poopa Father

poor-me-one Nocturnal bird of the nightjar family with a mournful cry, hence nickname; potoo

Po'tegee Portuguese

poui A decorative shade tree, flowering annually with yellow or pink blooms

run a binge To go on a drinking spree

saman A large shade tree with pale pink blooms and edible sweet, pulpy seed pods; also known as guango or cow-tamarind

sans humanité Without mercy or restraint (French); a calypso refrain meaning "no quarter will be given", "expect no mercy"

sapodilla Brown-skinned tropical fruit with sweet, sometimes gritty, pulp and shiny black seeds; naseberry

The Savannah The Queen's Park Savannah in Port of Spain, Trinidad, a large park of about 232 acres known as "the lungs of Port of Spain"

semp Bird noted for its sweet song; the violaceous euphonia

Shango A Yoruba deity, god of thunder and lightening; the worship of the god, celebrated with drumming, dancing and chanting, and animal sacrifice

sou-sou money Cooperative saving scheme in which the participants draw a "pot" in turn

stink Stinking, crude, angry (of behaviour)

stupes To suck one's teeth in derision

Sweet Drunk

tong Town

toute suite At once (French: *tout de suite*)

whey What, where

whey's Where is

wuking Working

wut'less Worthless

you Your

you like ef Would you like

Works by Alfred H. Mendes

The Autobiography of Alfred H. Mendes. Edited by Michèle Levy. Kingston: University of the West Indies Press, 2002.

Black Fauns. London: Gerald Duckworth, 1935. Reprint, Millwood, NY: Kraus Reprints, 1970; London and Port of Spain: New Beacon Books, 1984.

Pablo's Fandango and Other Stories. Edited by Michèle Levy. London: Addison, Wesley and Longman, 1997.

Pitch Lake. London: Gerald Duckworth, 1934. Reprint, Millwood, NY: Kraus Reprints, 1970; London and Port of Spain: New Beacon Books, 1980.

The Poet's Quest. London. Heath Cranton, 1927.

Spare Moments. Port of Spain: Spack Printing Office, 1924.

Three Poems. Port of Spain: N.p., 1924.

The Wages of Sin and Other Poems. Port of Spain: Yuille's Printerie, 1925.